FÜR VOLK AND FÜHRER

THE MEMOIR OF A VETERAN OF THE 1ST SS PANZER DIVISION *LEIBSTANDARTE SS ADOLF HITLER*

Erwin Bartmann

Translated and edited by Derik Hammond

Helion & Company

Helion & Company Limited
26 Willow Road
Solihull
West Midlands
B91 1UE
England
Tel. 0121 705 3393
Fax 0121 711 4075
Email: info@helion.co.uk
Website: www.helion.co.uk
Twitter: @helionbooks
Visit our blog http://blog.helion.co.uk/

Published by Helion & Company 2013

Designed and typeset by Farr out Publications, Wokingham, Berkshire
Cover designed by Paul Hewitt, Battlefield Design (www.battlefield-design.co.uk)
Printed by Gutenberg Press Limited, Tarxien, Malta

ISBN 978 1 909384 53 8

British Library Cataloguing-in-Publication Data.
A catalogue record for this book is available from the British Library.

For details of other military history titles published by Helion & Company Limited
contact the above address, or visit our website: http://www.helion.co.uk.

We always welcome receiving book proposals from prospective authors.

Contents

List of photographs

A girlfriend posing outside the Radio Station in Berlin at the last of
 their annual floral displays, 1943. I didn't meet her until about
 a year after this was taken.

My new cap with the wire removed, as was the fashion, taken autumn 1943.

Sharing a smile with a fellow machine-gun instructor while
 stationed in Alt Hartmannsdorf, March 1945.

Horst and me, taken shortly after the birth of his first child.

POW camp near Aldershot. I'm fourth from the left, top row. It
 seems I was fated to be a baker.

Paperwork issued on 27 November 1948, the day I was released
 from captivity in Scotland. It entitled me to claim a German
 military pension for more than seven years' service.

I took my Oath of Allegiance to the Queen on 5 November 1955
 and became a British citizen.

List of maps

Acknowledgements

My thanks must go to Mr. Derik Hammond of Broughty Ferry, without whom this memoir would never have been written. I first encountered him on the *Forum der Wehrmacht*, a meeting place on the internet for those interested in the history of the Second World War. When I discovered he lived just over an hour's drive away, I invited him to visit my home in Mid Calder, near Edinburgh. After chatting with him at length about what it was like for me growing up in Berlin under Hitler, and my experiences as a *Leibstandarte* soldier, he suggested it might be worthwhile assembling the many episodes I had already written down in German, into a publishable memoir in English. During monthly visits lasting six hours at a time and stretching over two years, he probed every corner of my memory to reveal details hidden by the passage of time. Also, a recent minor stroke had left me unable to use a keyboard, so the task of preparing the manuscript was left entirely to him. The end result is an account that follows the major events in my early life, from the day I witnessed Horst Wessel's funeral until my release from a POW camp in Scotland in 1948.

Introduction

My name is Erwin Walter Bartmann. My parents married on 14 February 1914, a romance that produced four sons. Tragedy visited their young lives when their first born, Hubert, died of a lung infection. My brother Horst was born in the summer of 1920 and little Heinz soon followed but, at the age of just eighteen months, he too died and was buried beside Hubert, in Schlochau's *Waldfriedhof.* As the youngest of the four boys, I only know Heinz and Hubert through photographs and the wistful reminiscences of my mother.

We left Schlochau in 1927 and moved to Berlin where my parents rented a room from a Jewish family. Then my father, who had retired from the Post Office on medical grounds, came up with the idea of opening a fruit and vegetable business and we moved to a tiny flat in Liebig Strasse where he set up shop. Every morning with his squeaking handcart, he brought produce from the market hall on Alexanderplatz for Mother to sell from a stall at the roadside. The business failed, compelling my father to abandon his dream of self-employment. To make ends meet, he took a job in a grocer's shop on Lichtenberger Strasse and, just as he had done when he had his own business, set off early each morning for the same market hall on Alexanderplatz to load up a cart with fruit and vegetables. Eventually, he saved enough money to enable us to rent a two-roomed flat at 38 Strausberger Strasse, in the Friedrichshain district and a little closer to the city centre. An iron stairway, its handrails worn thin and brown, led to our new flat, which shared a toilet in the stairwell with three other families, including a Jewish family who lived next door on the same landing. There were two girls in this family, one about my age, the other a little older. By the end of 1929 my father lost his job. To supplement our meagre family income my mother, a seamstress by profession, made blouses for well-to-do ladies and scrubbed the stairs of the apartment block to earn a reduction in rent.

I attended the local *Volksschule*, which lay almost directly across the street from our flat. From the outset Herr Werth, the headmaster, was my class teacher. A small man with a great love of music, he told us of his boyhood ambition of becoming a musician and encouraged us not to repeat his mistake. 'Always follow your dream,' he advised. He was eternally cheerful and helpful to his pupils, characteristics that made it impossible for me not to hold him in high regard. During his frequent departures to attend to official duties in his office, the presence of volunteers – aunts or mothers of fellow pupils, and the promise of corporal punishment for any boy who overstepped the bounds of acceptable behaviour – maintained class discipline.

Hitler came to power shortly after my ninth birthday. As I grew into my teenage years I watched with admiration Hitler's personal guard, the *Leibstandarte*, parade the streets of Berlin. Immaculate in their black uniforms and shining helmets, their ranks marched in precise step – a sight that made my boyish heart race with pride.

In the streets, in the media, the voice of the German people rang with optimism. Everyone around me was happy. A rising mood of confidence overwhelmed my world and I felt secure, valued. As a young Berliner – too young to have an interest in politics – what could be more honourable than aspiring to join the elite, the *Leibstandarte SS Adolf Hitler*? That the situation was not as idyllic as it appeared was something I had yet to learn.

This is neither a tale of the mechanisms of war nor of great strategic manoeuvres. This is my story – memories from my youth and the time I served as a soldier of the *Leibstandarte*. The events I describe are those experienced from my own perspective as an ordinary soldier. With pride, naïve pride perhaps, I took my oath to Hitler and swore, '*gehorsam bis in den Tod*' (obedience unto death).

Most of those I write about are now long dead; *Kameraden* upon whom my life once depended, officers who won the devotion of their men and townspeople and farmers of the lands we occupied in our fight against Bolshevism. In a very few instances I have taken the liberty of changing a name to protect the identity of an individual. The reader should also bear in mind that the dates I give for particular episodes in my life at the *Ostfront*, unless they relate to some personally significant event like a birthday or anniversary, or a highpoint in the calendar, are either approximate or taken from reliable published works such as Rudolf Lehmann's series *The Leibstandarte*. An ordinary soldier of the *Leibstandarte* was not permitted keep a diary that an enemy might use to gain useful intelligence. Furthermore, keeping a record might well have brought accusations of spying.

At the age of 88 years, I am, in the words of the song of our *Pionierkorps*, '*zur Himmelstür*' (at heaven's door). I have nothing to gain by misrepresenting the truth. My aim is simple: to give the reader an insight into the life of a boy who grew up to become a soldier in Hitler's elite division, the *Leibstandarte SS Adolf Hitler*.

1

A Diary of Indoctrination

Saturday 1 March 1930

A chill mist saturated the air over Berlin but even the worst weather could not dampen my father's passion for walking. 'Are we going to the park *Vati*?' I asked, breaking into little runs to keep pace.

'Not today Erwin – there's something I want to show you.'

Two left turns took us into Lichtenberger Strasse, where we stopped close to the open door of a public house. 'In there,' said Father, crouching by my side, his lips close to my ear, 'that's where Horst Wessel held his political meetings, his *Sturmlokal*.'

'Who was Horst Wessel?'

'A hero of the German *Volk*, Erwin, a National Socialist, a young man who gave everything for his beliefs, just like Jesus, until a communist swine knocked on his door and shot off his jaw.'

We continued towards the centre of Berlin, adding to the steady stream of humanity making its way towards Bülowplatz and voices singing the communist anthem, *Die Internationale*.

'That's a nice tune *Vati*.'

'There's nothing nice about communism, son.'

As we emerged onto Bülowplatz – overlooked by slogans written in enormous letters hanging on the walls of the on the Communist Party building – the singing gave way to a contest of poisonous shouts and jeers between opposing factions.

'What's happening *Vati*?'

Father raised his voice to make himself heard above the clamour. 'It's the day of Wessel's funeral. I didn't expect things to be so rowdy – there was supposed to be a ban on crowds and flags. These communist thugs are here to cause trouble.'

Across the street, police wearing shiny black leather helmets struggled to keep opposing factions at bay as the cortege, led by a troop of bandsmen playing funereal music, approached.

'*Vati,* who are the men in brown shirts?'

'A guard of honour Erwin, Hitler's *Sturmabteilung* men, the *SA* – I wish these communist idiots would shut up so we could hear the music.'

A hearse pulled by horses draped with black mantles and black plumes on their heads followed the ranks of *SA* men. Suddenly, stones ripped up from the pavements showered the cortege. Women screamed in horror as demonstrators burst through the police cordon to grapple with the *SA* men in an attempt to seize the coffin. Police cavalry, batons flailing, launched into the mob. Tyres screeched as armoured cars sped up and down the street. I cowered in a doorway behind Father until the police restored order.

'Now son, you see just what sort of people these communists are – traitors and hooligans bringing endless disruption to our streets. They won't be content until they ruin everyone's life.'

Although I was only six years old at the time of Horst Wessel's funeral, I can recall the events of that day with absolute clarity – fear had burned the images of chaos on the streets of Berlin deep into my memory.

Summer 1930

On our way home from Friedrichshain, a park close to our flat, we took a little detour to join the crowds lining the pavements on Palisaden Strasse. Onlookers craned their necks or stood on tiptoes to get a better view as a detachment of *SA* singing *Die Fahne Hoch* (Raise up the Flag) approached. Horst Wessel had written the words of this song which, set to a traditional folk tune, was now a Nazi anthem.

'We'll hang on a bit,' said Father, 'but make sure you don't drop your ball – we don't want it to spoil the parade.'

Across the road, a woman who lived in the flat above ours stood at the edge of the pavement. As the *SA* parade drew near, I waved to attract her attention. She returned my greeting then to my astonishment, turned her back and pulled up her skirt. Shrieks of laughter spilled from the spectators as she dropped her knickers and bent over to expose her bottom, and everything else a woman should keep private. This was a bad mistake. The woman struggled hopelessly as two well-built *SA* men grabbed her arms while their colleagues took turns at delivering hard slaps to the exposed flesh, which rapidly turned fiery red.

'She was asking for that,' said Father.

A few days after this incident the woman, an avowed communist, dropped into our flat to show my mother the purple imprints left by *SA* hands.

Monday 30 January 1933

Hitler, appointed *Reichskanzler* by President Paul von Hindenburg, took control of Germany. That evening I stood with my parents and brother Horst on Unter den Linden, at the corner of Wilhelm Strasse, to witness the torchlight procession pass through the Brandenburg Gate on its way from the *Tiergarten* to the *Reichskanzlei*, now Hitler's official residence. The whole thing started late in the evening and went on until the early hours of the next day. Though it was still deep in wintertime, I cannot recall feeling cold as the *SA* and war veterans – members of the right-wing *Stahlhelm* organisation – paraded their colourful standards. Behind them marched a column of massed torchbearers and bands playing military marches. Every onlooker wore a broad smile. Police lining the pavements laughed as they joined hands to push with their backs against an enthusiastic surge of the crowd. Waves of sound rose up, waves that swelled in my ears until I could hear nothing else.

'Heil...Heil...Heil...'

Her grey-blue eyes glistening in the light from the torches, my mother turned her gaze from the parade to look at me. She smiled as she squeezed my hand. I returned her squeeze, her smile, to tell her that I too had felt the power of the moment. Together, we held our right arms aloft and added our voices to the chant, 'Heil...Heil...'

After the parade, we joined the jubilant onlookers gathered in Wilhelmplatz, directly in front of the *Reichskanzlei*, to shout ourselves hoarse with the chant: *Wir wollen unseren Führer sehen* (we want to see our Leader).

Hitler appeared at a floodlit window on the first floor – there was no balcony on the *Reichskanzelei* at that time – to acknowledge the adulation of his *Volk* with his right hand flung back in the salute that was to become his hallmark.

It seemed the mood of the city had changed for the better. For the first time, it was safe to play in the streets without the threat of violence throwing the whole district into disorder. Everyday life settled into an orderly, industrious routine. I was of course oblivious to the news that Himmler had announced the need for concentration camps throughout the *Reich* for the '*Beruhigung der nationalen Bevölkerung*' (reassurance of the people). What did I care if the prisoners were Marxists, common criminals, or homosexuals? Who could have foreseen, let alone a nine-year-old boy, that this was the first stepping-stone to the horrors of the extermination camps?

Spring 1934

As Hitler's fortunes blossomed, there appeared on the streets boys smartly dressed in shorts and shirts. Some rode bicycles carrying hand-written notices on cardboard tied to the handlebars urging others to join them: *Hinein ins Jungvolk*. Word soon spread that these boys, members of the *Deutsche Jungvolk* (*DJ*), enjoyed trips to the cinema and weekend camps. Before long, most of the boys over ten in my class had joined, some of whom were former members of the *Socialistische Arbeiterjugend* (*SAJ*), the left wing equivalent of the *DJ*. In many ways, these two organisations offered similar pursuits but the *DJ* was better organised and, unlike the *SAJ* which was predominantly a working-class organization, included boys from all strata of society, from *Volksschule* and *Gymnasium*. Social class was no longer a barrier to *Kameradschaft*, a manifestation of the chant that had now become familiar to me: *Ein Volk, ein Reich, ein Führer* (one people, one nation, one leader).

My parents whole-heartedly approved of my enlistment in the *DJ*. 'It's better for the youth to be well organised than hang around street corners,' they said.

One of the first things that struck me when I joined – at that time membership was voluntary – was that I was granted a degree of freedom and trust that made me feel grown up and responsible for my own actions. In general, it was older boys in the organisation who acted as instructors. Youth itself was valued, a thing of beauty.

Summer weekends were great adventures spent camping in the forests around Berlin. Fluttering above the camp was always the flag of the *DJ* which carried, like a bolt of lightning in startling white against a black ground, the angular *Sigrun*, the runic 'S' symbol of victory.

I always looked forward to the 'Battle of the Flags', my favourite activity at the *DJ* camps. This was a competition between rival *DJ* groups, often from different parts of Berlin. The object of this contest was quite simple – to capture the rival's flag. But to carry out such a seemingly simple objective required considerable strategic planning. Was it better to leave the biggest and strongest boys to guard the banner, should they lead the raid on our rivals, and who among us were emerging as leaders? I'm sure the instructors looked out for such things but as far as I was concerned, the fun was in the sheer physical activity of the game which could, and usually did, get quite rough. Often, I arrived home on a Sunday evening with bruises, marks of honour proudly displayed to my parents as proof that I had 'done my bit' for my *Kameraden*. Through my adolescent eyes, such events appeared to be nothing more than vigorous sporting activity. There

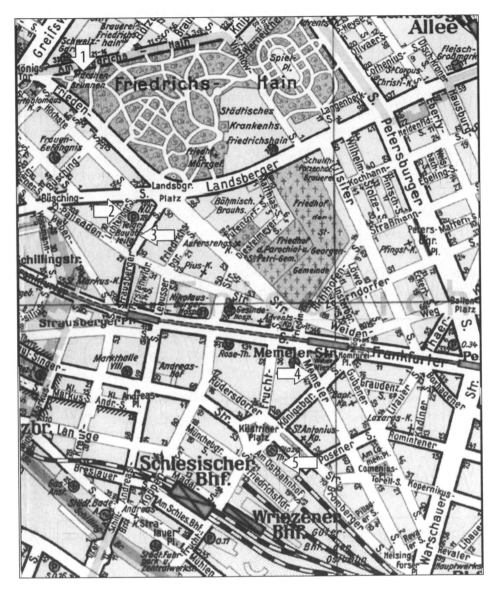

1. Maerchen Brunnen

2. Horst Wessel Sturmlokal

3. 38 Strausberger Strasse

4. Glaser bakery

5. Plaza Theatre

Locations connected with Erwin's home and youth in Berlin.

(Reproduced by kind permission of Westermann Verlag).

was never any training with weapons so it never occurred to me that this was preparation for life in the military.

Drums, flags and marching were our constant companions in the *DJ* but my head knew nothing of my legs as we trooped tirelessly along sunlit country lanes and through villages where admiring onlookers watched us pass. We sang with happy voices *Die Fahne flattert uns voran* (the flag leads us forward). That the path I marched so joyously could lead to the destruction of all that I held dear was a concept too distant for my imagination.

One can read nowadays that the youth of Germany was brutalised by their membership of the *DJ*. It is true that the activities in the *DJ* helped develop strength, discipline, loyalty and obedience; that we learned respect for women and to be prepared to die for our country. But these were exactly the same attributes and attitudes described by Baden Powell in his book *Scouting for Boys*, published in 1909, which placed the ordinary boy at the centre of Britain's Empire – a sign of the times in which we lived.

Everything we did as members of the *DJ* was approved by our parents and by the *Reich*, the *Reich* that Germans had yearned for, the *Reich* that found a place for every 'true' German. Our parents were members of Hitler's Party, the *Nationalsozialistische Deutsche Arbeiterpartei* (*NSDAP*/Nazis), or the Nazi trade organization, the *Deutsche Arbeitsfront* (*DAF*), or both. Encouraged by the authorities, our mothers performed good social deeds for the benefit of the community. My own mother stitched the flags that decorated the bugles of my *DJ* unit as she hummed traditional folk melodies. Once a month, on a Sunday, my father collected the *Eintopf* contributions (money saved by each family by preparing a stew from leftovers and donated to the Nazi Party) from the residents of the flats at 38 Strausberger Strasse. We, the youth of the *DJ*, were simply another piece of the jigsaw.

Summer 1936

In Berlin's streets and parks, the brash English of rich Americans mingled with the rise and fall of animated Italian. In shops, the delectable scent of beautiful French women lingered long after they had left. Flamboyant colour spilled from flower baskets hanging from every lamp standard and balcony in the sunny streets of central Berlin. Long scarlet banners, with black swastikas inside white circles, adorned public buildings. Berlin was exciting, pulsating with life as my brother

Horst and I made our way to the *Neue Wache*, the classically styled building dedicated to the memory of German soldiers who had made the ultimate sacrifice during the Great War.

'Hey you kids, what do you think you're playing at?'

Ignoring the complaints, Horst pushed me through the crowd of tourists gathered to watch the changing of the guard. With my brother's hands resting protectively on my shoulders, I gazed in wonder at the three approaching *Leibstandarte* men. Dressed in immaculate black uniforms and wearing belts and gloves of purest white, they were an awe-inspiring sight. A tourist next to me looked at his pocket watch, nodded in approval, and declared, 'Exactly on time.'

Stopping only a few metres from our vantage point, the *Leibstandarte* men turned smartly and marched up to the two guards waiting to be relieved of their watch. With perfect precision, a seamless – and to my young eyes fascinatingly complex – interchange of personnel took place.

'Horst, do you think I could join the *Leibstandarte* one day?'

'They only take you if you are *very* tall *and* you need to pass a strict medical examination.'

'Do you think I would pass the medical?'

'I doubt it Erwi, the scars from your appendix operation still haven't healed completely. You even missed school swimming lessons.' He patted my shoulder. 'The *Leibstandarte* accepts only the tallest and fittest men.'

❧·☙

On the day of the Olympic Games Opening Ceremony, as I travelled across Berlin with other pupils from my class – part of the massed choir of 3000 drawn from Berlin's schools – I was looking forward to making my contribution to the important historical event.

We took our places in the magnificent new stadium, on the opposite side of the arena from which Hitler would declare the opening of the Games from a private balcony. At key points, camera crews prepared to transmit the world's first live television pictures of a major sporting event. As 4 pm drew near, trumpeters on the great stone pedestals either side of the Marathon Gate played a fanfare. The excited clamour of a 100,000 voices faded to a diffuse murmur. At precisely 4 pm, Hitler entered the stadium to tumultuous applause. Everyone stood to get a better view of the *Führer*. Even foreign visitors, as if compelled by the same invisible force that governed us Germans, raised their right arms in the Nazi salute.

A girl, six or seven years of age and wearing a white summer dress, stood on the running track, her sun-browned arm held high in salute as Hitler approached. In her left hand, she grasped a bunch of flowers. As Hitler bent to accept the bouquet, the girl made a nervous courtesy. Then, to the rousing melodies of the *Deutschland Leid* and *Die Fahne Hoch* – just one stanza from each – Hitler and his guests settled into their places on the private balcony. A brief stillness fell across the stadium before a voice on the PA system called out, '*Hisst Flaggge*' and on the high rim of the stadium, the flags of the gathered nations were hoisted to the majestic peal of the specially cast Olympic Bell. Like a call to prayer, it seemed to demand submission to the cause of a greater Will. In reaffirmation of our loyalty, we responded devoutly: *Sieg Heil ...Sieg Heil ...* until, resonating within the confines of the stadium, the words merged into a chorus of adulation for our *Führer*.

One after the other, in a gloriously colourful procession, the national teams paraded on the running track to the sound of stirring Prussian march music. A standard-bearer led the sportsmen and women of each participating nation, dipping his flag as he drew opposite the balcony where Hitler stood – except for the Americans, whose flag remained held high and whose team members, instead of saluting, took off their straw hats and held them over their hearts. This apparent act of defiance displeased the crowd whose cheers abruptly turned to disapproving mumbles.

After a speech by the President of the Olympic Committee, Hitler duly declared the Games open. A gun salute fired by an artillery unit of the *Wehrmacht* signalled the release of thousands of doves that circled above the Marathon Gate before disappearing into the summer-blue sky, a symbol of peace that belied the tumult soon to shatter much of Europe and change my life forever. The massed choirs sang Richard Strauss' Olympic Anthem and I too sang, sang with all my heart, proud to be a young German.

An air of expectation fell upon the crowd with every eye fastened on the steps at the main entrance to witness what would become an Olympic tradition. Fritz Schilgen, a popular German athlete, a model of Aryan manhood, appeared holding aloft the Olympic Torch. Saluted by officials dressed in white, Schilgen descended the steps to the running track. His elegant stride carried him past the *Führer's* balcony, onwards to the steps that led to the receptacle of fire above the Marathon Gate at the western end of the elliptical stadium.

On reaching the cauldron, Schilgen presented the white magnesium flame of the Olympic Torch to the crowd. Overcome by the spectacular nature of the ceremony, we sat open mouthed and silent. As Schilgen lowered the torch to ignite the flame that would burn for the duration of the Games, the expectant hush gave way to the ecstatic applause of the onlookers.

Silence once more descended on the stadium as German weightlifting champion, Rudolf Ismayr, grasped the corner of the Olympic Flag to take the Olympic Oath – an act that brought to mind the Oath of the Teutonic Knights that I had learned about at school. Then, to the glorious refrain of Handel's Hallelujah, the teams left through the Marathon Tunnel – the conclusion to an Olympic Games Opening Ceremony so perfect it would form the prototype for those that followed. That day will remain in my memory until I die. As I left the stadium, it was easy to believe I was living in the best country in the world. Without realising it, I had surrendered to the *Zeitgeist* cultivated by the *Führer*.

❧ ❦

At the cost of around two to five *Reichsmarks*, tickets were too expensive for our family to attend the Olympic Games in person but television parlours – Germany had the world's first public television broadcasting service – had been prepared in various locations throughout Berlin with entry by free ticket. As soon as he heard that tickets were available, my father set off for the Post Office in Palisaden Strasse where the viewing parlour closest to our flat had been set up.

'There's a problem,' Father said with a concerned look on his face when he returned to our flat. 'I only managed to get three tickets and they're only allowing viewers over the age of fourteen.'

'I'll look after Erwi,' offered Mother, 'you can go with Horst.'

'No, wait here Papa.' I had an idea and disappeared into my parents' bedroom. When I returned I was wearing a pair of my brother's long trousers.

Mother laughed. 'Erwi, you'll never get in dressed like that.'

'It's worth a try,' offered Horst. 'He's tall for his age.'

When we reached the door of the Post Office, an official with a silver beard and moustache took the ticket from my hand and bent forward to look me in the eye. Then, with a wry smile, he nodded his head and tousled my hair with a big rough hand that smelled of fresh tobacco.

Led by the flow of the crowd, we came to a darkened room where a television receiver perched on a shelf, high up on the wall. We waited in silence as a technician stood on a stool to adjust the control knobs. A collective gasp rose up as images from the Olympic Stadium formed. And my father declared, 'What wonders Hitler has given the German People!'

2
The Apprentice

During my last year at school, twice a week, the first lesson took place in the Parish Hall of the Evangelical Church of the Resurrection where we studied the Bible in preparation for our confirmation ceremony in March 1938. With about twenty other students, I became a registered member of the congregation that my father served as an elder. At the end of the month, I left school to take my place in the world of work.

'It was good enough for your grandfather,' declared *Mutti* as she bent over the kitchen sink, 'so it's good enough for you.'

'But I liked working with wood when I was at school – I was good at it,' I protested. 'Horst's a carpenter and if *that's* good enough for him...'

Mutti turned from her dishes, her chapped, wet knuckles on her hips in the manner of a Russian folk dancer. 'That's enough backchat Erwi. Look at your grandfather – he was a baker for over forty years and he's still fit and healthy.' She wagged a finger earnestly. 'I'll have none of this nonsense. Baking is a good trade – you'll never be cold in winter again if you take that job with the bakery – and Memeler Strasse isn't too far away. You can be there in ten minutes on your bike. Think of the money you'll save in *S-Bahn* fares. Oh, I almost forgot. That nice Polish gentleman from upstairs, he offered to fix up your bike for you, paint it so it looks like new.'

Friday 1 April 1938

Cajoled into submission, I reported to the front shop of the Glaser bakery at 6 am. *Frau* Glaser, a short fat woman with ruddy cheeks, looked me up and down.

'The new lad's arrived,' she called over her shoulder.

Herr Glaser, a big wide-shouldered man with a broad face, appeared from a doorway behind the counter.

'Ah Erwin – good, you're on time – come, I'll take you into the back shop to meet Fritz – you'll be working with him – final year apprentice, nice chap.'

I followed Herr Glaser into the corridor behind the front shop.

'That's my living-room door, next to the entrance to the bakery – and don't forget what I am about to tell you – the door to the bakery is on the right and the toilet is at the far end of the corridor. Now, remember which door is which,' said Herr Glaser earnestly, 'and don't get them mixed up.'

In the workshop, military music blared from a radio on a shelf as Herr Glaser led me to a pile of 50kg flour sacks. 'Just arrived from the mill,' he said sending a cloud of fine white dust into the air with a smack of his broad hand on the topmost sack. 'Go on,' he coaxed, 'pick it up.'

I grabbed the sack with both hands and pulled, but it refused to shift more than a few centimetres.

'Don't worry – you'll soon get stronger Erwin,' Herr Glaser said with a chuckle. 'Can't carry the bloody things myself – something wrong with the old feet.'

After meeting Fritz, I found myself cleaning bread tins while he mixed the next batch of dough. 'Is there really something wrong with the boss's feet?'

'It's hard to say but he never does any of the heavy work,' replied Fritz.

'And why did he keep telling me about the doors?'

'Ah, it's spring – the birds and bees Erwin – when the weather gets warmer he likes to have a daily shag in his living room – his daughter shares their bedroom so where else could he do it? I just wish he wouldn't leave his used condoms in the toilet.'

Thursday 10 November 1938

After nearly eight months as an apprentice baker, I resented every turn of the pedals as I cycled under a nearly full moon towards the start of another day of tedium in the bakery. Herr Grünfeld, the Jewish butcher, was as reliable as a chronometer but he was nowhere to be seen on Palisaden Strasse. Was I late? There were certainly more people than usual on the streets. Fearing I had overslept, I pushed harder on the pedals.

As I sped into Frankfurter Allee, I saw a crowd gathered outside Leiser's shoe shop. I slowed to get a better look at what was going on. Onlookers watched in silence as a handful of individuals sat on the kerb trying on shiny new shoes from boxes piled at their sides.

'Watch your tyres, son,' warned a woman at the edge of the pavement, 'they smashed the shop window – there's glass all over the place.'

I pulled on the brakes, bringing my bicycle to a standstill. 'What happened?'

'It's the worst kind of theft son,' said the woman within earshot of a man trying on a pair of stolen shoes, 'looting.'

'They asked for it,' snapped the man. 'These Jews – murderers the lot of them – they think they can kill German diplomats anywhere in the world – first it was Gustloff in Davos and now its vom Raft in Paris – well, it's high time we showed them who's in charge here in Germany.'

'That's idiotic,' said the woman, 'the murder of a few diplomats by madmen who happened to be Jewish doesn't make the whole Jewish race guilty.'

Although news bulletins reported many other examples of *Volkszorn* (anger of the people against the Jews) in both Germany and Austria, I witnessed only one other incident. Later that day, as I was travelling home after attending the Trades College in Friedrich Strasse, I passed the Neue Synagogue in Oranienburger Strasse. The main door was scorched, witness to an attempt to set fire to the building, which was otherwise unmarked.

Farewell to childhood

By my fifteenth birthday – 12 December 1938 – I was strong enough to lift the heavy bags of flour without cringing at the thought. To mark the occasion, Herr Glaser informed me that my working day had been extended to include a daily – except for Saturday – spell of duty from 6 pm to 9 pm during which I would clean the baking tins in preparation for the following morning. Cleaning, I had discovered, was a very important part of the work in a German bakery.

As a fifteen-year-old, I officially transferred from the *Jungvolk* to the *Hitlerjungen* (*HJ*/Hitler Youth) but was exempt from having to attend the frequent meetings because of my long working hours at the bakery. I was nevertheless, charged the same fees as other members and was therefore a sort of honorary member. I must add that I rather resented the fact that my job as a baker prevented me from becoming an active member of the *Hitlerjungen*. As a member of the *Jungvolk,* I had enjoyed the communal singing and sports competitions at the weekend camps with squads from other parts of Germany. I was however, obliged by law to report to the offices of the *Deutsche Arbeitsfront* (*DAF*), our trade union. As I shivered in a long queue waiting to register with the *DAF*, it happened that I got into conversation with Robert Ley, the Minister for Work, and complained bitterly about the seemingly endless hours I spent in the bakery.

After muttering something about the value of every worker, he said in a slurred, stuttering voice, 'Everyone must w-work harder. Germany needs b-bread. You should b-be happy in your w-work.'

Unable to face the world sober Ley was, as ever, somewhat the worse for wear.

It was rumoured that his stammer was the result of injuries sustained when his plane was shot down in the First World War but my own belief is that his heavy drinking was to blame. I watched bemused as, in the back seat of his official car, he took a hip flask from his pocket and swigged the contents. This chance encounter left me with a badly dented impression of one of our political elite.

The following April, Herr Glaser celebrated the completion of my first year as an apprentice by extending my working hours. 'Saturdays will still be free,' he said with a grin, 'but on Sundays, you are to report for duty at 10 am, to heat the ovens.'

Like a donkey on a beach, I plodded through the week with only the brief freedom of Saturday dangling before me like a carrot. Work dominated my days, leaving little time to dream about the things that should occupy the mind of a boy on the verge of manhood.

Friday 1 September 1939
After a humid night that offered little sleep, I pedalled to work with my shirt clinging to my back. The dark sky threatened thunder. Reluctantly I stepped across the threshold of the door to the bakery, wedged open to allow a non-existent breeze to clear the heat generated by the ovens. In the yellow light of the electric lamps, a mist of flour dust hung in the air. As usual, my day began with a sack full of *Brotchen* (German rolls) on my shoulder, and a long list of deliveries to the bags hanging on the door handles of our customers – a welcome respite from the stifling heat of the ovens. It was only when I noticed the absence of the routine bickering pouring from the open window of the flat at 52 Memeler Strasse, home of the Binders, that I became fully aware of the ominous stillness haunting the area.

I arrived back at the bakery to hear the radio playing the usual background music. Following Fritz' example, I stripped to my vest and helped him mix a fresh batch of dough. A fanfare interrupted the programme, the signal that an important announcement was about to follow. We stopped work to listen to the broadcast of a speech given by Hitler to the German Parliament earlier that morning, a speech in which he said our troops were in action in Poland. He ended with the declaration: 'Our Will and German steel will see us through'.

Fritz shook his head. 'I knew this was coming,' he sighed.

That weekend Britain and France declared war on Germany.

On Monday morning, I waved to the Jewish butcher in Palisaden Strasse. As ever, he walked in his knee-high boots with one foot on the pavement, the other on the road. '*Guten morgen* Herr Grünfeld,' I called.

Herr Grünfeld grunted through his long, frizzled grey beard, 'Hmmph – not for us Jews.'

December 1939–Spring 1940

Just after my sixteenth birthday, the temperature plummeted, signalling the start of a colder than usual winter with day after day of sub-zero temperatures. For once, the prospect of working in the heat of the bakery seemed almost inviting. I pedalled more vigorously than usual, keeping close to the ghostly white lines painted on the kerbs to make driving safer in the absence of street lighting.

I arrived at the bakery to find Fritz, now a journeyman baker, working alone. As usual, we shook hands in greeting. 'Where's the Chief,' I asked.

Fritz laughed. 'He's the first to be drafted – *Wehrmacht. Frau* Glaser told me he was posted to a military bakery just outside the city.'

'I wonder when our turn will come,' I mused.

'Who knows? But the loss of old man Glaser is bad news for us – one less pair of hands. As I see it, this war is getting far too serious. Mark my words Erwin, those bombs that fell in Landsberger Strasse were just the first. Did you see the damage?'

'*Naja*, I went with my parents at the weekend – big crowds but not much to see – a few roof tiles blown off. The police were gathering up the leaflets the plane dropped.'

❦ ❦

With Christmas approaching, the bakery was busier than ever and by the time it came to sweeping up at the end of the day, the smell of freshly baked bread turned my stomach.

'You did well kid,' said Fritz in a fake American accent. Until recently, he had frequented the cinema in Potsdamerplatz to watch American movies but *Reichsminister* Göbbels put an end to that when he declared them too foreign for Aryan eyes.

'See you tomorrow,' I said, turning at last for the door.

As my hand clasped the doorknob, Fritz called, 'Erwin.'

I stopped with the door opened just a little, eager to make the best of what remained of the furtive December daylight.

'Erwin,' he repeated, 'you haven't heard the important news yet.' His tone was almost musical, but full of irony.

'What news?'

'We start at three o'clock tomorrow.'

Poor Fritz was so busy he never even had time to go home. For a while, I too slept in the bakery but I soon became too drained to keep this up. In order to arrive at work on time I now had to coax my weary body from bed at quarter-past two until one spring morning, when I reported for work, I was surprised to find Herr Glaser already busy mixing the dough for the *Brotchen*.

'*Guten Morgen* Erwin,' said Herr Glaser pointing to his feet, 'it seems they were not made for army boots after all.'

My doubts about the truth of Herr Glaser's claim to have some undefined medical condition affecting his feet dispelled, the prospect of shorter working hours immediately lifted my spirits. Sure enough, at the end of that day, Herr Glaser announced, 'Work starts at 4 am tomorrow – we keep going until all the orders are finished.'

A few weeks later, as if to make up for their loss of Herr Glaser, the *Wehrmacht* drafted Fritz into its ranks. When I arrived home that evening, there must have been a glum look on my face.

'What's troubling you Erwi?' asked *Mutti*.

'Fritz was drafted – its back to a 3 am start tomorrow.' I flopped into my father's armchair, already pulled close to the heat of the *Kachelofen*. 'Mama, I'm sick of the baking trade.'

'But it's a good trade Erwi – you'll get used to the long hours.'

I consoled myself with the thought that, on Saturday evenings, I was still able to meet up with my best friends Horst Musch and Gunter Schmidt. Together we were the 'Three Musketeers', classmates who became inseparable from our first days at school. Muschi had always been good at drawing and had taken up an apprenticeship as a graphic artist. Schmidti had a job with the *Reichsbahn*, the German National Railway. Most Saturdays we visited the Plaza Theatre where variety shows played. Sometimes we tried our luck with the local girls but our advances invariably met with little success.

3

The Applicant

The *Leibstandarte* held a summer recruitment drive in 1940. Disillusioned and frustrated by the long working-hours as a baker, I picked up an application form from the office of the *Wehrmacht* High Command in Bendler Strasse. In it was provision for the nomination of alternative units in case the applicant failed to match up to the entry requirements of Hitler's elite military force. My brother Horst, who was now serving as a *Luftwaffe* telephonist at the Air Ministry, advised me to name the *Flieger Abwehr Kanonen* (*Flak*) unit of the *Luftwaffe* as second choice. I filled in the form in my neatest handwriting and within a week, received an order to attend a hall in Alexanderplatz for a medical examination.

On a gloriously sunny June day, I made my way to the hall where I had previously taken a few ballroom dancing lessons in the hope of one day impressing a future girl friend. Inside the hall, a hundred other young men stood around wondering what would happen next. Mostly they were between the ages of sixteen and seventeen although there were a few who were a bit older. An *Unterscharführer* (sergeant) of the *Leibstandarte* pushed among us, arranging us into neat rows. A hush fell on the waiting hopefuls when a high-ranking officer in an immaculate uniform appeared on the stage.

'Remove your clothes and set them in a neat bundle at your feet,' announced the officer.

Stripping naked in public was a new experience for me. I felt the blood rush to my cheeks as I glanced at the other would-be recruits, several of whom still wore underpants.

'Remove all clothing – strip – everything, everything.' roared the *Unterscharführer*. 'Never mind looking at each other – it's not a bloody beauty parade. You were given an order, get on with it.'

The officer left the stage and began his inspection. I swear I could sense his eyes scrutinising every inch of my naked flesh as he passed behind me. The applicant standing next to me jerked forward a little.

Having completed his inspection, the officer made an announcement. 'Those of you who were tapped on the shoulder are dismissed. Have your hair cut before you try again.'

A wave of hope, of relief, swelled my spirits – I had passed the first stage of the selection process and dared to think that the tedium of the bakery would soon end. Then the real inspection got underway. A doctor measured my chest and asked questions about my past illnesses and operation scars with every answer fastidiously recorded in his file. Then, still naked, I was required to pull back my foreskin to allow the doctor to examine my penis – not the sort of weapons inspection I had anticipated. Endless questions by an officer probed every part of my life to make sure there were no Jewish connections. 'Why do you want to join the *Leibstandarte*?' he asked.

'Because I am a Berliner, and tall,' I answered with the simple innocence of youth.

On a snowy day in January 1941, a letter arrived from the *Wehrmacht* High Command. My mother looked on as my trembling fingers opened the brown envelope. The blood drained from my face in disappointment as I read.

'What does it say Erwi?'

'The *Luftwaffe* Mama – the *Flak* unit.'

'That's good Erwi. Your father will be happy. He was worried about you getting into the *Leibstandarte* – they're always in the thick of the fighting.'

Straight away, I shook off my disappointment and headed for the door.

'Where are you going Erwi?'

'To the recruiting office Mama – there must have been some mistake.'

I arrived at the recruiting office to find the reception area already packed and took my place in a slowly moving queue. The officer in charge asked why I had come and I told him the whole story about receiving my call up papers from the *Luftwaffe*. Then something quite out of the ordinary happened. *Reichsführer* Heinrich Himmler, chief of the SS and the second most famous man in Germany, strode into the office and stopped to exchange a few words with the men in the queue. To my astonishment, he asked where I lived and if I was looking forward to life as a *Leibstandarte* recruit. Full of hope, I spilled my story about how I thought the recruiting office had made a mistake by assigning me to the *Flak* unit.

'I'll see what I can do about it,' he said before disappearing into a back office.

I had almost resigned myself to wearing the blue uniform of the *Luftwaffe* when Himmler reappeared and made straight for me.

'You will hear from us soon,' said the bespectacled *Reichsführer*.

In February 1941, my call up papers from the *Leibstandarte* arrived. I was overjoyed that the whole business with the bakery would soon be over and that, from now on, life would take a more exciting turn. Special radio announcements, one after the other, proclaimed our military successes. What did I have to lose? I was desperate to play my part before the *Endsieg*, our ultimate and inevitable victory.

❦·❦

Feeling like a student who had just won a coveted place at an elite university, there was – despite the sunless sky – a spring in my step as I made my way along Finkenstein Alle on Mayday morning, 1941. I stopped for a moment in front of the closed main gate to the barracks, to admire the *Ewigen Rottenführer* (Eternal Corporals). At about four metres tall, these statues formed an imposing welcome. I took a long deep breath before making my way to the sentry at the side gate who looked at my pass and, with a sharp nod, welcomed me to my new world. Walking briskly across the assembly area, I joined the crowd of recruits gathered in front of the four central pillars of the main building. A parapet above the pillars carried the words: *LEIBSTANDARTE SS ADOLF HITLER*. Perched above the parapet an enormous statue of an eagle, wings half-outstretched as if testing the wind, surveyed its domain. At last, I could believe that my days as a baker were over, that my metamorphosis into a soldier of Germany's most elite regiment was about to begin.

As I waited impatiently with my fellow recruits, a soldier wearing riding breeches materialised mysteriously, as if from thin air. The single silver pip on the dark 'mirror' of his tunic collar identified his rank as that of *Unterscharführer*. 'I am the Laughing Devil,' he cackled as his eerily long fingers moved near his pointed face, making slow movements as if conducting an invisible orchestra, 'your *Unteroffizier vom Dienst* for today. Follow me.'

Our *Unteroffizier vom Dienst* (*UvD*/duty NCO) led us to a large sports hall smelling of beeswax polish laced with sweat. In the centre of the hall was a boxing ring and against the walls, sports apparatus of many different kinds was stored. For the best part of an hour, we hung around self-consciously looking at each other until the Laughing Devil returned to escort us to the dining hall for a meal of sandwiches and sausage meat. After we had eaten, we returned to the sports hall where an officer explained the regulations that governed our stay in the barracks. Blankets were distributed and suddenly it was 'lights out'. With 200 other restless young men sharing the hard floor of the hall, I hardly got a wink of sleep.

❀⸱❀

At 7 am, the Laughing Devil appeared to direct us to the washrooms. 'Shave – and make sure your fingernails are clean. When you have finished washing you will be allocated to your platoons before proceeding to your dormitories.'

The tallest men, giants measuring upwards of 190 cm, made up the first platoon. With my 186cm, I joined the second of the four platoons billeted in the Hermann Göring block, one of four named after prominent figures in the *Reich*. Three stairways served our sleeping quarters on the top floor. Upward traffic used the left and middle stairwells while the third stairwell served only as an exit. This, explained the Laughing Devil, would avoid confusion if the need arose to empty the barracks quickly. Each room had six sets of double bunks. Between each set of bunks was a metal locker.

'The lockers are to be left open – a *Leibstandarte* man is trustworthy,' said the Laughing Devil. 'He will *never* steal from his *Kameraden*. Loyalty and honour – from now on these are your guiding principles – at *all* times. You will store your uniforms in a particular order – long coat, first uniform, second uniform then drill suit. The drill suit will be your daily wear while training. The space in the lower part of the locker is where you will store your boots – one pair to be worn while on watch and a second pair used in training – and one pair of dress shoes which are to be kept clean at *all* times.

'In the uppermost section of the locker you will hang your shirts and underwear. Steel helmets and backpacks are stored on top of the lockers. Belts and ties must be hung on the hooks on the back of the door. Finally, there is a small but adequate space at the left hand side for bread and fillings such as butter and jam. In this part of the locker you will also store plates, cutlery and cups. And remember – I check daily to see that everything is kept clean and in the correct place.'

Later that day we collected our uniforms from the quartermaster's store and between us, somehow managed to remember the list of instructions issued by the Laughing Devil. Like a child, I marvelled at the name 'Adolf Hitler' sewn in silver thread onto the cuff band on the left arm of my tunic.

The following morning we reported for a medical examination that would establish our blood groups. My blood group proved to be type 'O'. A doctor inscribed this letter by means of small cuts made with a scalpel on the inside of my left arm, near the armpit, a mark that is still discernable after more than seventy years.

I received my *Soldbuch* (passbook) and aluminium dog tag; both carried the identification code '*17.Kompanie Nummer 15 O SS Verfügungs Truppe*'. The elliptical dog tag had three slits down the middle, on the long axis. This made it quick and easy to break off half the tag while still leaving the other half on the chain around the neck of a dead soldier whose identity might otherwise be difficult to establish. Of course, my young mind did not dwell on such grisly matters.

Training began in earnest. At first roll call, our *Kompanie* commander, *Obersturmführer* Hans Becker, welcomed us recruits. Even though it was not quite midway through 1941, Becker was already an experienced combat commander having served in France, Poland and Greece. Our instructors then examined our fingernails for cleanliness, boots for shine, faces for signs of forbidden stubble, hair for length and handkerchiefs for neatness. They opened up our backpacks to check the cleaning kit, toothbrush and the other items we would need when on active duty. Finally, an officer announced the password for the day.

Endless drills formed the core of our activities during the following weeks until our *Kompanie* merged with another to form the *5.Wachbataillon Berlin*, a unit that performed guard duties in and around the city. Life as a recruit suited me and I have to admit that the months that followed were some of the happiest times of my life though by the time 'lights out' came around, I was often thoroughly exhausted and perhaps closer to tears than to laughter.

On four occasions, I stood sentry at the southern end of the Lichterfelde compound close to the vehicle workshops and a cage in which lived a brown bear. The animal was a gift, presented to the *Leibstandarte* during the recent campaign in Greece and its antics provided amusement for a weary sentry. On another occasion, I was on guard duty at the lobby of offices occupied by *SS Gruppenfürher* Leo von Jena, a high-ranking and highly-decorated officer, a typical officer type of the old style from the First World War. When the doorbell rang, I would open the door and examine the documents of every visitor, noting their name in a logbook even if it was von Jena himself. These were the regulations and I carried them out without exception. Only twice did my duty rota take me to the gardens of the *Reichskanzlei*.

A 500-metre stretch of asphalt at the rear of the barracks, known among us recruits as *Plattfuss Allee* (Flatfoot Alley), provided the scene for marching practice with sessions often lasting several hours. Usually, we warmed up with the basic infantry commands and rifle drill.

'Eyes straight. Shoulder arms. March.'

Up and down we marched until the commands sank in. Then, the *UvD* would roar *'Achtung!'* the signal for us to throw our legs high in the air, in the *Parademarsch* (commonly referred to as the 'goosestep'). Accompanying our instructors were regimental bandsmen who played the *Badenweiler Marsch*, chosen by the *Führer* himself as the signature tune of the *Leibstandarte* and only played publicly when he was in residence in Berlin.

If anyone failed to perform well, he received extra 'lessons'. I recall that one of the recruits had difficulty in holding his head at the correct angle. The *UvD* tied a brick to the poor man's ear with a shoelace and it stayed there until he overcame his deficiency.

In the evenings, if we were free, we could go to one of two canteens in the barracks where we could buy things for our personal use such as toothpaste, razor blades and biscuits. Like many of my fellow recruits, I bought a peaked cap and immediately removed the wire bracing to give it a more casual appearance. Beer was also available and if we had visitors, we could take them to the canteen for a drink. My brother Horst, who was an *Unteroffizier* in the *Luftwaffe* at the time, usually accompanied me to the dormitory when he visited. There was also a cinema, located in a long narrow room on the first floor of the main building. Capable of accommodating an audience of several hundred, it showed all the latest films including *Stukas*, a film in which Wagner's *Götterdämmerung* fills a jaded young pilot with the spirit to continue to risk his life for the future of the Fatherland. Although there were exciting scenes of aerial combat, the message conveyed by the film was clear: we too should show the same spirit of sacrifice as the young hero.

I was among the first of the recruits granted leave. This was thanks to my brother who, one Sunday, dropped by the barracks with his new fiancé. At the orderly's office, he asked the *Unteroffizier vom Dienst* to issue a pass for me so that I could spend a few hours outside the barracks with them. Permission granted, he signed a paper saying that he would be responsible for my return by a specified time. We went to a local bar in Lichterfelde and had coffee and cakes and a just a single glass of beer since it was frowned upon for *Leibstandarte* men, the elite soldiers of Germany, to been seen drinking too much alcohol outside the barracks. Inside the canteen, this rule was cast aside and I spent several enjoyable evenings drinking beer and singing soldiers' songs with my new *Kameraden*.

We passed between the larger-than-life stone reliefs of a naked man and woman either side of the double wooden doors leading to the Lichterfelde barracks swimming pool. Inside, an instructor issued swimming shorts. 'Get into these – diving area in five minutes,' he said. As a schoolboy, the hours I had spent shivering at the poolside because of my appendix operation while my classmates enjoyed swimming lessons had finally caught up with me – I couldn't swim.

At the deep end of the pool, an enormous *Oberscharführer*, his face as hard and bright as the finest *Kruppstahl*, waited with a clipboard in hand.

'Watch the instructor,' ordered the *Oberscharführer*. 'Nothing complicated – just do as he does.'

The instructor trotted up the stairs of the ten-metre diving tower. He stopped for a moment at the edge of the uppermost platform before stepping into the void and, feet first, plummeted into the water only a few metres from where I stood. After what seemed to me an eternity, he surfaced and swam to the ladder at the side of the pool.

'Form a line at the bottom of the tower. Don't worry if you can't swim,' said the *Oberscharführer*, 'the instructor will pull you out if you get into trouble.'

My heart raced. I was not fond of water and even less fond of heights. The presence of the instructor offered little comfort.

The *Oberscharführer* glanced at his clipboard. 'Bartmann, you're first.'

I grabbed the handrail and began climbing the steps, convinced that the tower was swaying under my feet. At the top of the tower, I reluctantly let go the handrail and stepped up to the edge of the precipice. Far below, the reflected light from the tall windows at the far end of the hall waltzed woozily on the surface of the water. To falter, even for a second, would have meant instant dismissal from the *Waffen SS*. I took a deep breath, sealing the air in my lungs with lips pressed hard against each other, and stepped into the unknown.

The rush of air gave way to the crash of water against my eardrums. Tiny bubbles fizzed over my skin. When I opened my eyes, everything appeared blurred, bathed in milky blue light, silent. My arms flailed instinctively, propelling me upwards with agonising slowness. At last, with lungs clamouring for new air, I let go a gasp of triumph as my head broke the surface.

The side arm issued to the *Leibstandarte* during training was the Pistole 08, the Lüger. It hung comfortably in its holster and, for a handgun, was highly accurate though it was prone to jam if mud or sand got into the mechanism. In a break from the usual routine, an instructor introduced the weapon to us in our dormitory.

'Now listen carefully,' he said. 'At the firing range, I will issue each man with five cartridges at a time. Load them into the magazine and count them as you fire,' warned the instructor in a serious tone.

After lunch, we took our 08s to the indoor range in the barracks, firing at targets just 25 metres away. At first, my shots missed the target completely but my aim soon improved.

When shooting practice was finished, the instructor gathered us together. 'Before you return to your dormitory to clean you weapons, I must warn you that the Pistole 08 is a little bit different from other pistols. When the barrel is removed from the handgrip, a little spring is exposed which, if pressed, releases the firing bolt. If there is a cartridge in the firing chamber – this can happen if you didn't bother to count the number of rounds fired – the bolt will strike the cartridge.'

Back in the dormitory, as we cleaned our 08s, a loud crack echoed through the room. In stunned silence, everyone looked around to see what had happened. The reek of cordite filled the air. Sitting on the bunk directly opposite my own, Max, a blond-haired recruit from around Kiel, clasped his knee with both hands. Blood oozed between his fingers.

Attracted by the sound of the shot, the Laughing Devil rushed into the dormitory. 'What in the name of God happened here?' he screamed. '*Always* make sure you count the shots fired.' His mood softened as he examined Max's wound and said, 'Remember – pain is in the brain.'

The rifles issued to us were the *Gewehr 98* model from the First World War but since all the recruits in the *Leibstandarte* were tall, the large size of these old weapons suited us just fine. The particular weapon that came to me had the most beautiful grain pattern on the butt which, polished to perfection over the years, was much admired by my *Kameraden*.

At a firing range just outside Berlin we practised shooting at targets from prone, kneeling and standing positions. After every shot we reported to the officer in charge, who observed the target through binoculars, telling him where we thought the bullet had struck. After a few days, I became something of a marksman.

With the basic shooting skills mastered, we began combat training. In a mock assault on an enemy trench, I threw myself to the ground and began firing from the prone position. A bolt of pain coursed through my legs.

'Heels must lie flat on the ground,' roared the instructor standing on my ankles, 'unless you want to lose them to bullets or shrapnel.'

Hardly able to walk, I reported to the medical room the following morning. The doctor examined my badly swollen ankles and asked how I came by them. I described the circumstances leading to my injuries and received two days bed rest during which I learned that *Kompanieführer* Becker had summoned the instructor to discuss the incident. A few days later, I chanced across the instructor in a corridor.

'Ah, Bartmann,' he said with a malicious gleam in his eye, 'report to my dormitory in ten minutes in full parade uniform.'

The instructor greeted my arrival with a quizzical look. 'Did I not say to you to come in sports kit? Get changed – back here in five minutes.'

When I returned he smiled sadistically. 'Fifty knee bends.'

I knew what was coming; sports kit, knee bends, parade uniform; sports kit…a cycle that soon had sweat streaming from every pore in my body. How long I would have to endure this punishment would depend on the mood of my tormentor. In the event, he lost interest after about an hour. *Maskenball*, as we soldiers called this ordeal, was over but my respite was short lived.

'Now,' said the instructor, 'I want *every* pair of boots in this dormitory cleaned till they are spotless.'

⚜⚜

After a hard day on *Plattfuss Alle*, my *Kameraden* were already fast asleep by the time I finished my turn to clean the dormitory. Only after the *UvD* had inspected my work, and was satisfied with what he found, would he allow me to go to bed. Fighting to keep my eyes open, I heard footsteps approach in the stairwell. The door opened to reveal the Laughing Devil. Theatrically, he took a pair of white cotton gloves from his pocket.

'Now, let's see what sort of job you've made,' he said sliding his long fingers into the gloves.

With a peculiar grin on his face, he opened the door of every locker to scrutinise the contents and found no grounds for complaint. Even the coffeepot on the table was spotless. I had taken every precaution to avoid presenting him with an excuse to keep me from collapsing into my bed and had just let go the faintest sigh of relief when he pointed to an iron bracket supporting the roof joists, high in the corner of the room.

'I'll have a look up there,' he announced looking around the room, 'bring that table over.'

Even if he stands on the table, I thought, the bracket would still be out of his reach. Nevertheless, I dragged the table to the desired spot.

The Laughing Devil clambered onto the table and peered up towards the bracket. 'I'll need something else to stand on. Fetch me something so I can get higher.'

I brought a little table, the one we used while playing cards or chess, and placed it on top of the large table, directly under the bracket.

He looked up at the bracket once more. 'I'll need something else – a stool.'

As the Laughing Devil stood on the stool perched on top of two tables, he ran his gloved hand along the top of the bracket, a daring act considering the height. When he clambered down, he stood close to me and moved his gloved hands in front of my nose, like a mime artist pressing against an invisible wall.

'What,' he asked, head tilted slightly to one side, 'do you call that?'

'Dust, *Unterscharführer*,' I replied shamefacedly. In the *Leibstandarte*, we never addressed anyone of higher rank as 'Herr', as was necessary in the *Wehrmacht*.

Like a flash of lightning, the gloved hands clapped together. A cloud of dust swirled around my face. I coughed and sneezed.

'I want the whole place washed. I'll be back later to check that everything is in order.'

I shook my head in disbelief as the Laughing Devil's cackle echoed in the stairwell and with a weary sigh, steeled myself for the irksome task. I wiped every one of the high brackets, emptied every locker and washed them inside and out. I scrubbed the floor. My roommates complained about the noise so I hurried to finish so they could get back to sleep. Exhausted, I finally sat down and listened above the snores of my *Kameraden* for the approach of the Laughing Devil's footsteps. At about 3 am, *Kompanieführer* Becker appeared and asked why I was still awake. I told him what had happened.

'Get to bed,' he said. 'I'll see to all this.'

Because of 'all this', Becker gave the Laughing Devil another 24 hours *UvD* duty and I did my best to avoid him for a while.

On the assembly area, under the ever-vigilant statue of the eagle on the parapet, we formed into ranks to make up three sides of a square, in front of *Obersturmführer* Hans Becker and a platoon leader carrying the regimental standard. At a signal from Becker, the platoon leader lowered the standard, its gold-braided borders glinting in the sunlight, until the flagpole was horizontal. Representatives from each platoon marched up to place their left hand on the pole, the signal for everyone present to raise their right hand.

Obersturmführer Hans Becker read the *Fahneneid*, an oath that echoed that of the Medieval Teutonic Knights, which my schoolteacher Herr Werth had described to my class some years earlier: 'I swear to you, Adolf Hitler, *Führer* and Chancellor of the German Nation, loyalty and bravery. I vow to you, and to my superiors appointed by you, obedience unto death. So help me God'.

Shoulders thrown back in pride, I repeated the oath to pledge my life to the *Führer*.

4

Auf Wiedersehen Lichterfelde

Every man polished his boots until they shone, brushed his uniform until not a single speck of dust remained. What a glorious sight we were. I was looking forward to my first official leave. We had breakfast in the dormitory. The Laughing Devil popped in to make sure we lived up to the high expectations of the *Leibstandarte* and, satisfied with our appearance, nodded in approval before retreating down the stairwell. Elated chatter, reminiscent of the sound of a school playground, filled the room as we waited for dismissal. Half an hour later, the Laughing Devil's head appeared round the door.

'*Kompanieführer* Becker wishes to give you a little talk – assembly area in five minutes.'

We straightened our caps and uniforms and rushed for the stairs. The Laughing Devil and *Kompanieführer* Becker were already waiting for us on the assembly area.

'*Achtung*. Right dress...eyes front.'

There was a shuffling of feet as we formed smartly into precise rows under a faultless, shimmering blue sky.

'*Kameraden*,' said *Kompanieführer* Becker solemnly, 'I have some unwelcome news for you. I regret to inform you that the barrack gates are now closed. Leave is cancelled until further notice.' After a long pause, he continued his address. 'This morning, the *Führer* made a special radio announcement. I have a transcript of that announcement which I will now read to you.' Stern faced, Becker reached the final sentence, 'The fate of Europe and the future of the *Reich* are in your hands, and may God help us in this struggle.'

We stood in silence, drinking in the enormity of the announcement – we were at war with Russia.

'Soldiers of the *Leibstandarte*,' said the Laughing Devil, eyes wide and piercing, voice quivering with pride, 'you know what to do when you return to your dormitories. You must be prepared to be underway at a blink of an eye. *Kompanie* dismiss.'

Fuelled by the realization that training, marching practice and guard duty were at an end, an excited murmur rose up as we made our way back to our dormitories. Operation Barbarossa, the attack on the Bolsheviks, was underway. Our leaders had anticipated that the Russians, despite their treaty with us, would take the opportunity to attack our rear just as we seemed on the verge of invading England. To ward off this danger, our troops were advancing on a front that stretched from the Baltic to the Black Sea.

We packed our rucksacks and waited. The sound of trucks manoeuvring in the assembly area at first drew everyone to the windows but still there was no call to action. The excited babble faded to resigned silence. Evening mealtime passed without any further news. It grew dark as we lay on our bunks, dressed in full uniform apart from our boots.

After morning roll call, we resumed our usual routine. The day passed without further event and after a spell on sentry duty, I bumped into Max.

'Did you hear about Becker?'

'I was on guard duty – haven't spoken to anyone,' I replied.

'He's been shot – carted off to the SS hospital on Unter den Eichen.'

It was astonishing news. 'Who did it?'

'A sentry at the *Reichskanzelei* – that's the rumour,' replied Max.

No one knew any of the details of the shooting but some wild rumours were already spinning round the barracks. Later we discovered that Becker had been checking out the guard at the *Reichskanzelei* by creeping amongst the bushes. Unfortunately, he failed to answer when asked for the password and the sentry fired a single shot. The bullet entered the front of Becker's right leg near the groin and passed out at the rear.

For his outstanding obedience to orders, the guard was immediately promoted to the rank of *Oberschützen* (rifleman first class). Things could have turned out a lot worse for the guard and for Becker.

❦

At the start of August 1941, we received news of our imminent posting to a field unit. Things went wrong for me a short time later. An infection developed in my right index finger after a minor injury and the tip required lancing to allow the puss to drain. The day before we were due to leave Lichterfelde, I reported to the *Kompanie* doctor.

'*Schütze* Bartmann, I see that your finger has not yet completely healed,' he said glancing at the notes on his desk.

'*Obersturmführer*, it doesn't stop me using a weapon – pain is in the brain,' I replied with the maxim drilled into every recruit.

The doctor made a brief, irritated smile. 'Nevertheless I must offer you the chance to remain in Berlin until your injury is completely healed.'

'I would prefer to be with my *Kameraden*,' I answered with an involuntary hint of pleading in my voice.

The doctor nodded as he took a pen from the holder on his desk and added a few lines to the documents on the table. 'Don't worry,' he said, 'you will be leaving tomorrow, on the same train as your *Kameraden*.'

❦·❦

After morning roll call, every man received a large salami sausage, a tin of meat and some butter and bread. We stuffed them into our backpacks and lined up to march the short distance to the rail station in Lichterfelde where the platform was already crowded with civilians and soldiers. A military band played strident march music, reinforcing the illusion of invulnerability in us, its willing victims. *Obergruppenführer* von Jena gave a speech designed to make us feel like heroes, heroes that would slay the red bear of Bolshevism and rescue European Culture. When von Jena's pep talk was finished, we crammed enthusiastically into the carriages of the waiting train.

Everyone tried to jostle his way to a window, to look out onto the colourful scene on the platform. Sixteen or seventeen-year-old girls from the *Bund deutscher Mädeln* (League of German Girls) waved little red flags with swastikas while a *Kompanie* of *HJ* cheered. A shrill whistle pierced the incongruous holiday-like atmosphere and the military band played *Preussens Gloria* as the locomotive snorted like some black mechanical dragon impatient to be underway. Those inside the carriage jerked back in unison as the train lurched into motion. An athletic looking girl on the platform, pigtails and breasts swinging, ran alongside blowing kisses to a favoured soldier.

Gathered in a loose crowd, mothers dabbed their faces with handkerchiefs. As our train gathered speed, I pushed my way to an open window and waved, catching my mother's eye at the last possible instant. She forced a smile onto her pale face and, raising her limp handkerchief aloft, returned my farewell.

❦·❦

Blood red, the sun hovered over the spires of a large city. The train slowed. Life returned to the bored faces of my *Kameraden*. A sign drifted past the window: Kraków. Even before the train juddered to a halt, the carriage doors crashed open. We poured onto the platform and lined up in our platoons to await further instructions.

'There is no transport available. We must march to our destination,' explained an officer.

The evening air was pleasantly mild and I looked forward to stretching my legs after the long journey. Singing our soldiers' songs, our hob-nailed boots struck the cobbled road in perfect synchrony – a thousand feet, a single entity, a single will – the realisation of my boyhood dream of joining the *Leibstandarte*.

In the fading light, a double set of tram rails led us over a bridge spanning the River Vistula. After a short distance, they disappeared under two massive timber gates, each surmounted by a curving archway carrying an inscription written in Hebrew. On top of the central pillar separating the gates was the *Judenstern* (Star of David).

As if by its own will, the gate on the right creaked open at our approach, the entrance to a dark and sinister world. Our mouths fell silent as we marched through the dingy streets. From the open windows of apartment blocks, gaunt faces stared at us with haunted eyes. Jeers of hatred rose up from behind the open doors of the dilapidated buildings. Hands with piss pots in them darted from upstairs windows to fling their contents over us.

'Do not react,' ordered an officer, 'they have their own customs and laws here.'

After leaving the ghetto, we followed the rise in the road until we reached the barracks where units of the *Waffen SS Division Totenkopf* were billeted. We slung our backpacks onto the bunks. Those who had fallen victim to the cascades of urine cleaned themselves up as best they could. Fortunately, most of those in my platoon escaped the soaking. As I waited for sleep, the squalor of the ghetto played on my mind. Suddenly, war seemed less than heroic.

In the morning, it was back to the usual routine – roll call, more instructions, more training. This carried on for four or five days then it was back to the railway station, this time to cattle trucks with straw covered floors. With our glorious . departure from Lichterfelde just a few days earlier already seeming a million miles away, we set off on a journey made tedious by intricate detours designed to confuse enemy spies.

⚜ ⚜

After a few sweltering days, we came to a remote railway halt. I looked in wonder at the vast landscape – a sea of shimmering yellow sunflowers that stretched as far the eye could see. We disembarked and boarded trucks that took us along a winding lane, to a barn where we would spend the night. Already, I had cast my misgivings about the Jewish Ghetto to the back of my mind, it was after all 'none of my business' – ah, the eternal naïvety of youth!

As nightfall approached, we gathered timber from a nearby copse and lit a blazing fire, which we sat around singing the songs we had sung a thousand times. An elderly farmer appeared and stood, holding his distance, listening to our music. The *Unterscharführer* (*Uscha*) in charge of our troop waved for him to approach. Tentatively, the man made his way towards the welcoming glow of our fire. We smiled. One of our comrades, who knew a few words of Russian, spoke to the man.

The old farmer answered in perfect German. 'Do you mind if I listen?'

He was an Ukranian *Volksdeutsche*, an ethnic German whose ancestors had settled in the Ukraine many years earlier. Everyone laughed and looked at the *Uscha* expectantly. He nodded and beckoned to the Ukrainian. 'Come – sit with us by the fire.'

As we chatted, more Ukrainians joined us, among them a woman around twenty-five years old. 'Just a few months ago,' she said, 'I had three brothers – all of them gone – carted off by the communists – and they have long memories these swine. Five years ago my brothers complained about the organisation of the collective system,' she explained. 'Immediately, they were condemned as *Kulaks* – enemies of the people. I have no idea where they are now. My letters to the authorities go unanswered. Now they've arrested almost every man under sixty as a spy. God alone knows where they all are.'

'We here are all lucky to survive,' the old man said, stretching his arm out to include his companions. 'It's not ten years since they nearly starved all of us to death. It was bad – there was cannibalism – people kidnapping children to eat. Sometimes, they say, this was done by the children's own relatives because they were driven mad by hunger.'

I could hardly believe that starvation could get hold amidst such fertile countryside. 'Did you see any of this happen, the cannibalism?'

'I didn't see any of it myself. It's not the sort of thing you would do in front of your neighbours,' said the old man as he lowered his gaze. He picked up a twig lying by the fire and with a sad, vulnerable look on his hard weather-beaten face, held the twig in the flames until it began to smoke. 'I lost four grandchildren to starvation, to the *Golodomor* as we call these evil times.' In his moist eyes, the reflected flames flickered brightly. 'Communist Party lackeys nailed posters to the walls and telegraph poles saying it was barbaric to eat children.'

'What caused the famine?'

'Oh, it was no famine,' said the old farmer, his voice rasping with disgust. 'It was deliberate. We resisted the collectivization of our farms even when they made us dig our own graves and shot us for it. They stole our farming tools and crops. It was truly heartbreaking to see our people starve like that – mothers with faces black through hunger, children with bones thin as drumsticks. God hear my words, I hate Stalin.'

Now, feeling more like a liberator than conqueror, I was convinced that our presence in this beautiful part of the world was entirely justified. With my own ears, I had heard the victims of Stalin's cruelty confirm that Hitler's depiction of Bolshevism was no exaggeration – or so it seemed at the time.

The *Uscha* interrupted the gloom with a cheerful voice.

'My friend, we are here now so you don't have to worry about Stalin any more.' With a strong voice, he broke into song, '*Auf der Heidi blüht ein kleines Blümelein...*' (On the meadow grows a little flower)

By the power of music, the atmosphere of despondency evaporated. One song followed the other, German and Ukrainian. Everyone was enjoying the companionship until an *Untersturmführer* arrived to remind us that it was time for 'lights out'. We pleaded for permission to continue our little party. '*Untersturmführer*, it can't do any harm to get to know the locals,' argued our *Uscha*.

The *Untersturmführer* raised his voice. 'When I give a command I expect to be obeyed *without* hesitation and *without* question. Do you understand? You are a soldier of the *Leibstandarte*.'

'*Untersturmführer...*' another of our companions ventured but the officer immediately cut him short.

'One more protest and every single one of you will be in front of an *SS* Court-Martial.' He turned on his heels and disappeared into shadows of the surrounding trees.

Our *Uscha* – a ruddy-faced farmer's son – muttered loud enough for everyone to hear, 'He's a stickler for regulations, a real 100 percenter – hasn't a clue how to handle men.'

I should perhaps point out that the *Untersturmführer's* poor leadership qualities were somewhat unusual – the other leaders we served under were, without exception, fine men. Despite the order to wind-up the party from the *Untersturmführer*, our *Uscha* decided to allow it to continue until well past midnight.

Refreshed by a good night's rest, we continued our journey towards the frontline, gazing like tourists at the passing landscape with the sun shining in a sky of perfect azure, high above our heads. In the fields, sunflowers bloomed on stalks higher than a man.

'They're beautiful,' I said to the *Uscha*.

'Beautiful yes – but a death trap for infantry.'

A few days later it rained hard. The dirt-track roads quickly churned into to soft mud under the wheels of our vehicles. Time after time, we had to jump from our trucks to push. Once, when it seemed impossible to shift our truck from a sump of mud that filled a dip in the road, a column of prisoners – the first Russian soldiers I had seen – was enlisted to pull on ropes like a tug of war team to free our vehicles. The following day the sun returned to harden the mud.

As one of 674 replacements for the heavy losses suffered by the *Leibstandarte* during the recent battle of Uman and the capture of Kiev, I stood in a field close to the picket fence of a fine country house that served as our Regimental HQ. Sepp Dietrich, commander of the *Leibstandarte*, moved among us, exchanging handshakes and a few friendly words with the recruits while his officers selected men for their units. Gradually the numbers dwindled until I was one of a dozen newcomers left standing in front of Sepp Dietrich, an *Untersturmführer* and a *Rottenführer*.

'4.Kompanie is a heavy assault group equipped with 12 mortars and 12 heavy machine guns divided amongst three platoons,' explained the *Untersturmführer*. 'Each machine-gun crew has five *Schützen*. *Schütze Eins* carries and fires the weapon. *Schütze Zwei* is in charge of the *lafette*, a tripod stand used to direct the fire from the machine gun into a defined area. Each of the remaining crewmembers carries two ammunition boxes – six hundred rounds in all – and a spare barrel for the machine gun.' Counting along our line, he selected eight of my companions. 'This group will leave with the *Rottenführer* who will escort you to the machine-gun platoons.'

The *Untersturmführer* resumed his address with Sepp Dietrich looking on. 'The remaining group will join the *Kompanietrupp* responsible for maintaining communications. This task is vital to our combat success. Your duties will include laying telephone cables and carrying messages. Our machine-gun and mortar fire is directed just over the heads of the frontline infantry units whose task is to winkle the enemy from their defensive positions into killing zones. It is an effective technique often resulting in the total annihilation of our foes but it depends on communication, *precise* communication between...' With furrowed brows, the *Untersturmfürhrer* looked to the sky.

Instinctively, I turned to see what was happening and gazed like an idiot at a growing dot swooping towards us. A powerful thud sent me tumbling over the picket fence into the shallow ditch on the other side. Sepp Dietrich was lying next to me as bullets kicked up the dust all around. A Russian fighter zoomed low overhead.

'Next time you see one, dive for cover,' said a smiling Sepp Dietrich 'I won't always be there to look after you.'

5
A Lesson in Practical Telephony

We took Cherson where an *Oberscharführer* continued to give orders as a dagger of shrapnel cooled inside his arm. We passed the graves of fallen Soviet soldiers, laughed at our *Kameraden* of the *Gebirgs Division* with their unlikely trains of camels. For a few glorious days, we rested in the sunshine nibbling sunflower seeds as we looked onto the Black Sea, its inky blueness intensified by waves crowned with white foam, before heading northeast to Berislav on the banks of the River Dnjepr.

At first light on 10 September 1941, we reached the edge of a plateau overlooking the Dnjepr. Ahead, the silhouettes of the men seemed to sink into the ground as they began their descent into the valley, towards a long pontoon bridge that stretched hundreds of metres into the misty shadows on the opposite bank. Soon it was the turn of *4.Kompanie* to move. The rustle of clothing, the occasional metallic chink, a nervous laugh in response to an equally nervous witticism: these were the sounds of young men about to risk all in the fight against Bolshevism.

A high-pitched whistle attracted my eyes skywards. A scream went up, '*Volle Deckung!*' I dived for cover, hugged the ground. Shockwaves jarred every bone in my body. Earth and rocks burst into the air as if ejected by an erupting volcano. From somewhere on the opposite riverbank, a Russian spotter was directing an artillery bombardment onto our lines. My hands and legs trembled. Like the other green recruits around me, I had no idea what to do.

A voice came to our rescue. 'Follow me.'

It was *Uscha* Heinz Nowotnik. Although only twenty-one, to us recruits, he was an 'old hare', an experienced soldier who had come unscathed through the Battle of Uman, a man familiar with the art of survival. Throwing our trust in with his experience, we ran forward and flung ourselves to the ground at the lip of the plateau as shells shrieked overhead.

'You see,' roared Nowotnik above the din, 'there are hardly any strikes here – the shells land on the slope or flat ground behind.'

As the bombardment continued, I managed to regain control of my taut nerves, to ignore the screams of the wounded that seemed to rise up on every side.

Uscha Nowotnik rolled onto his back, pointed to the sky. '*Stukas!*'

In the commotion, I had not heard the aircraft approach. *Uscha* Nowotnik's ears, better tuned to the clamour of war than my own, had picked out the note of the *Stuka's* engines. Cheers rose up from hundreds of grateful men as, wing-to-wing, the *Stukas* passed overhead. As specks in the distance, they stooped on their targets with their 'Trumpets of Jericho' screaming their terrifying crescendo. Smoke spiralled up from folds in the landscape on the opposite side of the river. The enemy shellfire ceased abruptly. My fear gave way to the first ecstasy of survival.

As we reached the banks of the river, we passed a neat rectangular plot slightly raised above the general level of the ground. In it, crosses fashioned from weathered wood looked out onto the river like a host of pale, grey ghosts with outstretched arms.

'Romanian Engineers – they built the bridge,' explained Nowotnik.

Nearby, a halftrack with a 2 cm *Flak* unit mounted on the rear lurked under the camouflage of foliage cut from riverside bushes, the eyes of the crew impassively scanning the sky. As we skirted the river, a flock of waterfowl rose up suddenly from the reed beds. My eyes followed their low flight across the wild currents, currents that would certainly sweep me, a non-swimmer, to my death if I fell from the unfenced bridge into the murky currents surging towards the Black Sea.

Survival on the *Ostfront*, I had quickly learned, required the protection of a guardian angel and I did not have long to wait for my first next visitation. A Russian unit sheltering in a shallow ravine blocked our advance. The infantry of *2.Kompanie* took up positions along the far side of a field, about 2 km from our *Kompanie* command post and in contact with the enemy. I reeled out my telephone cables to them, across the dry, stubble-covered field.

There was only the occasional whine of stray bullets, as I ran out the final connection. I was making good progress, pleased that I had carried out my duty effectively. Twenty metres ahead, a handful of infantry reinforcements were moving in the same direction. When we were half-way across the field, the sudden thud of an explosion sent me diving for cover. I looked up to see a column of fine dust hanging in the air like a transparent spectre. As the dust settled, one of the infantrymen called out for a medical orderly, '*Sani, Sani.*'

My blood ran cold. An unlucky soldier had stepped on a mine. Looking around, I noticed a clump of grass, yellower than the rest, a few metres to my right. Amongst it lurked a hastily camouflaged anti-personnel mine. Without communication with our command post, our mortar and machine-gun positions would be unable to support the infantry who would then be vulnerable to counterattack. There was no turning back. I had already crossed the minefield twice without mishap. Entrusting my life to my guardian angel, I sprang to my feet and continued to reel out my telephone cable, dreading every step.

As I passed the wounded soldier, one of his companions was already trying to staunch the flow of blood from the stumps of the shattered legs while another grasped his hand to offer comfort. I tried not to imagine the pain the man would suffer when the shock of the moment had passed.

When I reached the frontline foxholes, an officer beckoned. I slung the Bakelite box containing the telephone onto the ground beside him, and thrust the earthing-spike into the powder-dry earth.

The officer grabbed the telephone and tried to call the command post. 'It's not earthed properly,' he screamed. 'I can't get through.'

I fumbled with the earthing-spike.

'Piss on it man, piss on it. What do they teach recruits these days?'

Having learned an important technique in practical telephony, and not wishing to overburden my guardian angel, I skirted the minefield in a 5 km detour to make my way back to the command post.

6

Onward to Taganrog

Storming along the northern shores of Sea of Azov we took Melitopol despite stubborn Russian resistance then fought back a Soviet breakthrough in the sector of the front line entrusted to our Romanian allies. Continuing eastwards, we took Berdjansk. Although only lightly defended, it was here, while attached to an infantry platoon, that I first experienced the nerve-wracking task of clearing out a Soviet occupied trench system. On reaching the enemy trenches, we divided into two groups and stormed in opposite directions. The uncertainty in the defender's mind – who did not know whether friend or foe would appear around the sharp bends in the trenches – gave us a lethal advantage.

Revelling in the ecstasy of victory – our hair bleached by the hot Ukrainian sun – we sang until our throats turned hoarse as we headed for Taganrog.

❦

A column of refugees brought our trucks to a standstill. They were fleeing, not from us, but from the Soviet Army. They carried their belongings in a large sacks, twisted in the middle and slung over a shoulder so that one half was to the front and the other to the rear of the body, a technique that allowed both hands free to carry additional baggage.

Three officers from the lead truck, just fifty or so metres ahead, jumped to the ground with pistols drawn, and scolded the refugees for slowing our progress. Reluctantly the refugees, mostly women and children, formed a ragged line along the roadside ditch.

As we drove past the upturned faces, a girl of around eighteen lowered her sack to the ground and with a deft flick of her hand passed her shiny dark hair behind an ear. *'Gute Reise,'* she called out, waving her hand. Perhaps that was all the German she knew.

'Danke, danke,' replied a *Kamerad* sitting at the side of the truck, a huge white smile lightening his suntanned face. 'My God, she's beautiful,' he said, craning his neck to hold her in view as for as long as possible as our truck trundled past the officers who stood at the edge of the road to oversee the column's progress.

I had not expected to hear the girl's voice again but her screams pierced easily through the grinding of the trucks' engines. We stood up as a man to look back, to see what was happening.

'What in God's name is he playing at,' a *Kamerad* exclaimed angrily.

Towards the rear of our column, the girl struggled to free herself from under one of our men. The officers, alerted by the commotion and with pistols at the ready, ran up to the girl who, powerless under the weight of her assailant, screamed as he ripped at her clothes, oblivious to the approaching officers.

The three officers yanked the *Leibstandarte* man – a veteran of the campaign in Greece as I later learned – from the girl, flinging him to the ground. Shots rang out from a pistol and the man lay still. With open mouths, we stared at the officers as they hurried back to their vehicle at the head of the column. Left to rot at the side of the road, the dead man was no longer one of us. It was a lesson that required no words of explanation.

❧ ❧

A sizeable town overlooking the Sea of Azov, Taganrog, with its steel pipe and aircraft construction facilities, was an important strategic target. Our attack column, severely depleted by losses sustained in the recent fighting, consisted of around three hundred men and a handful of *Sturmgeschütze* (armoured assault guns that, like tanks, ran on tracks).

With the River Mius behind us, we followed a road that ran alongside the rail line leading south to Taganrog. Where there were dips in the landscape, earthen embankments carried the track high enough to obscure our view of the opposite side. With no interference from the Russians, it was full speed ahead, our *Kompanietrupp* travelling in one of the three trucks donated to the *Leibstandarte* by President von Hinderburg in 1932, somewhere near the middle of our column.

We came to an abrupt halt. Rising to my feet to get a better view I saw *Hauptsturmführer* Krocza, binoculars in hand, climb to the lip of the railway embankment to our left. After scanning the landscape, he ordered the mortar crews to set up their weapons on the flat ground by the roadside. The machine-gun crews took up position at the top of the embankment. Ammunition was distributed. In the distance, a haze of red dust hung above three or four hundred Russian cavalry and accompanying wagons.

In the tone of a man who had come into some great fortune a machine gunner smiled, 'It's a duck shoot if they don't get wind of us.'

The engines of our vehicles fell silent. Each passing minute brought the Russians closer. As if from the very earth of Mother Russia herself, a faint unsuspecting melody, gentle and sweet, rose and fell like a feather on the cool breeze. Completely unaware of our presence, the Russian column was now directly opposite our position.

'Fire!'

Men and horses fell under a cascade of mortar rounds. Wagons disintegrated into matchwood. Panicking, the Russians – civilians amongst them – ran for the safety of the hinterland. The charging handles of our machine guns clicked into place and the air rattled as a scything crossfire sliced through the scattering enemy. A *Kommissar* managed to inspire enough discipline to organise an improvised cavalry charge but we fired from the shelter of the embankment, cutting down the futile attack without mercy.

As the number of targets diminished, the hail of fire from our weapons waned. The order to call off the attack ran through our lines. The burr-burring of our machine guns stopped as suddenly as it had begun. The faint wail of wounded men and horses hung above the field of slaughter. A few stunned Russians staggered to their feet, holding their hands aloft.

An officer yelled, 'Now for Taganrog – the *Wehrmacht* are close behind – we'll leave it to them to deal with the wounded.'

❦‍❦

Two Russian tanks threatened to stall our progress into Taganrog but we were in no mood to be delayed. Four of our machine guns fired on them. The racket inside a tank under machine-gun fire could easily panic an inexperienced crew and there was always the chance that a lucky round would find the space between the turret and the body of the tank, jamming the teeth of the gear on which the turret rotates.

As the tanks snorted and shunted, their guns swinging threateningly in our direction, an anti-tank gun from another battalion fired on them. The first tank exploded from within with a hollow booming sound, throwing the turret to the ground where it clattered to a halt after rolling a few turns. Before the commander of the second tank had time to react, the anti-tank gun fired again. The second tank recoiled slightly before coming to a standstill. Smoke billowed from the wounded vehicle. Despite the continuing hail of machine-gun fire, the hatch opened and a crewmember tried desperately to hoist himself free but he reeled back, arms flung into the air, before slumping into the steel cooker that only moments earlier had been a vehicle of war.

❦

In the heart of the town, armed with my treasured *Gewehr 98*, I made a dash for the security of a shop entrance on the corner of a road leading to the harbour. Sidestepping the rubble to avoid tripping or twisting my ankle, I held my rifle at arms length for balance. Before covering half the distance, there was a vivid purple flash, just to my right. An invisible force grabbed my arm, throwing me off balance. For a moment, I lay absolutely still, listening to the small stones thrown up by the explosion tap against my helmet.

Expecting my arm to be badly injured, I repeated in my head the maxim drilled into me at Lichterfelde: *Pain is in the brain*. In a fog of fine dust I staggered to my feet and was surprised to find that, apart from a few minor grazes to my hands, I was uninjured. I looked around for my prized rifle. At first, I didn't recognise the broken weapon lying amidst the rubble. Shrapnel that could easily have amputated my leg had sliced off the beautiful butt. Once more, my guardian angel had been by my side.

As I caught my breath in the relative safety of the shop doorway, my attention was attracted to the harbour where a Russian warship took hit after hit from one of our *Flak* cannon. Clouds of black smoke rolled into the air above the vessel. Within seconds it sank, blocking the entrance to the harbour.

I soon found a replacement rifle but my work for the day was not yet finished. The *Uscha* called my name, together with five others from my *Kompanietrupp*. He appointed a leader, a *Rottenführer* who had been with *4.Kompanie* since the launch of Operation Barbarossa, a chap who seemed to make a point of keeping to a small circle of friends from which I was excluded.

'These buildings,' said the *Uscha* pointing to the top of a steep hill overlooking the harbour, 'Take your men up there and hold the building next to the lighthouse – it's a radio station.'

We checked we had sufficient ammunition in the leather pouches carried on our belts and without further delay started for the steps that snaked up the hill. Despite the cool October breeze, sweat carved out pink tracks on our dust-encrusted faces as we climbed the steps. On reaching the lip of the plateau where the buildings perched, we threw ourselves to the ground to recover our breath and plan the next move.

Loud popping sounds came from inside the building, each pop followed by the tinkling of broken glass. We looked quizzically at each other for a few moments before deciding the sounds posed no particular threat. Our *Rottenführer* turned to the biggest man in our squad, a 198cm colossus. 'Kick the door in – the rest of us will cover the windows and sides. We'll rush it as soon as you break through.'

The giant launched himself forward without the slightest hesitation, covering the ground quickly with his long strides. The door juddered under a hefty kick. Abruptly, the sound of breaking glass stopped. Russian voices screamed in alarm as our *Kamerad* continued to kick at the door which soon burst free of its hinges.

I was the first to enter, just in time to see the scurrying Russians leave from another door at the end of the long narrow room. Instinctively, I made to rush after them.

'Stop. You don't know what's behind that door,' roared the *Rottenführer*.

I still had much to learn about how to survive.

The other men in our squad edged up to the windows at the rear of the building and tentatively looked out to the scrubby surroundings.

'No sign of them,' reported a *Kamerad*.

With his machine pistol ready to fire, the *Rottenführer* nodded towards the rear door. 'Open it.'

I yanked the door open, allowing the *Rottenführer* to rush out. He looked down the hill on the other side of the building and lowered his weapon.

'It's clear,' he announced. 'Let's see if there's anything left intact – I'll have to make a report for the *Uscha*.'

Among the shards of glass on the wooden floor, a myriad of tiny shining globules glinted – quicksilver from the huge electronic valves the Russians had smashed on the floor.

Before long, a messenger arrived from the command post with news that we had taken Taganrog. Our *Rottenführer* made a verbal report to the messenger and asked for further instructions, which duly arrived: *remove all mercury from the building – leave all doors and windows open – we don't want to lose men to mercury poisoning.* We searched around, found a shovel and brush, and swept the heavy liquid metal towards the back door where it formed a sizable puddle.

❧·❧

We spent most of the following day clearing the town of Russian soldiers hiding in the rubble. As we checked a cemetery, I came across the body of the *Untersturmführer* who had threatened us with court martial as we sang with the bunch of friendly Ukrainians soon after our arrival on the *Ostfront*. Slumped face down against a gravestone in the corner of the cemetery, he had been shot through the head. How this misfortune happened I cannot say; these things happen in war but I have always suspected that the fatal wound was not one inflicted by the enemy.

With the dangerous task of clearing the town complete, and without loss or injury to our little *Kompanietrupp*, we looked forward to settling down for the night with a roof over our heads. No sooner had we found a suitable place to bed down when I received an order to report to the local headquarters of the Russian State Political Directorate (GPU).

It was a beautiful evening with the low sun bathing the streets in a golden light. Under the direction of an officer, I joined a queue of *Kameraden* most of whom I recognised as fellow newcomers. I happened to find myself behind Max, the chap that had accidentally shot himself in the dormitory in Lichterfelde. 'Do you know what all this is about?' I asked.

He pointed to a well that stood close by, in the street. 'They found the bodies of a reconnaissance troop from 3.*Kompanie* in the well – no tags. We're here to identify them.'

I was puzzled – the dead men were from a different *Kompanie* so I was unlikely to be able to assist in their identification.

Inside the GPU offices, the bodies of five *Kameraden* lay on stretchers, under sheets with only their faces exposed. Their expressions were not those of men killed in combat by some sudden catastrophic event but one of utter despair.

As I left the building, I shaded my eyes against the low sunlight to see an old hare cursing angrily as his audience of newcomers listened stern-faced and tight-lipped.

'*Handschuhe*. The bastards – the *fucking* bastards,' the old hare snarled.

A few steps brought me to the edge of the group.

'Saw it with my own eyes,' he went on.

'*Handschuhe* – what's that?' I interrupted.

'Ah,' said the old hare, 'it's a little speciality the Russians amuse themselves with if they capture an *SS* man. They hold your hands in boiling water until they go white.' He held his hands up as if about to pull off a pair of gloves. 'Then they slice around the wrist and pull the skin off. When they're bored with torturing you they shoot you in the back of the head – if you're lucky – but they usually go for the bollocks first. Or they might hang you on a tree by your arms then light a little fire under your feet until they turn to charcoal – *Stalinsocken* they call that!'

An icy shudder ran through every sinew, every nerve in my body. I had seen men who had suffered horrific wounds, injuries inflicted in the storm of battle by bullets or shrapnel, by mines and by fire, but to deliberately torture a prisoner was an act beyond my comprehension.

'Ah, my friend,' continued the soldier, 'haven't you been told yet? Don't let yourself be captured by the Russians. Don't you worry – the bastards will get what's coming to them.'

My stomach churned with hatred for the Russians – my call to the GPU offices had not been without purpose after all.

7

Close Calls

Towards the end of October 1941, we withdrew to defensive positions to consolidate our lines. Reconnaissance units were deployed to keep an eye on the antics of the Russians who, we suspected, were about to throw themselves into a determined counter attack. *4.Kompanie* set up their machine guns on the side of a hill and adjusted the ranging gear on their gun mounts to define the killing zone but, being dangerously far apart, they left large gaps left in our defences.

My own little home for this period, which proved to be about three weeks, was a trench about half a metre wide and a metre-and-half long. It rained heavily and frequently so, to create a little bunker, I went into the nearby town to pick up an old door to cover the hard won slit in the cold earth. To complete the construction, I piled waste soil on top of the door leaving only a tiny opening beside which I placed my telephone and four stick grenades. I spent most of the time alone, sheltering from the rain. Life wasn't exactly comfortable inside my tiny burrow, but I managed.

One afternoon, a prolonged Russian artillery barrage broke the peace in my little nest. It was a strange sensation, crouching alone in a cold hole in the ground so far from home knowing that, if fate saw fit, a shell would rip my body to shreds in a searing flash of light. Worse still was the prospect of some horrific injury, or simply being wounded badly enough to prevent escape if we were overrun by the Russians who, I now knew, had many ingenious ways to kill a member of the *Waffen SS*.

I waited, eyes stretched wide in fearful anticipation until the artillery barrage came to a stuttering end. The approaching battle cry of Russian infantry broke the brief silence and the air buzzed with bullets from rifles and machine guns. Mortar grenades exploded with dull thumps all around. My fingers tightened on my rifle as I prepared to step into the short section of open trench at the entrance of my bunker. Without warning, there was an almighty boom. I came to my senses in total darkness and absolute silence. The thought came to me that I might be dead, doomed to spend eternity in a world of that contained nothing but my lonely soul. Frantically, I clawed at the earth at where I thought the entrance had been. A chink of light showed and soon the hole was large enough to poke my head through. Gradually the zipping sound made by bullets flying low over our trenches came back into focus.

A voice called, 'Erwin, Erwin, are you wounded?'

Half dazed I looked around to see the crew of a nearby machine-gun crew wave their hands. 'No,' I replied. They laughed. I cleared the debris from the entrance of my bunker and found a crater where only seconds before my stick grenades had lain. A bullet or piece of flying shrapnel must have hit them causing the detonation that would have killed me if I had stepped out only a second sooner. There was no sign of my telephone. Once more, my guardian angel had kept me from harm.

'We thought you were a goner Erwin,' called a *Kamerad* from the machine-gun crew.

I waved to show him that I was still in the land of the living.

Now the battle really started. As usual, the Russian infantry threw themselves into the killing fields of our machine guns, their wounded and dead piling on top of each other. It was a senseless way to attack and the Russian soldiers paid a horrifying price for the suicidal tactics of their commanders. Still they pushed across the muddy field, tripping over their dead, standing on their wounded. The attack was petering out. Our guns fell silent. We were ordered to fix bayonets, an order usually only given for the clearing of towns where hand to hand combat was expected, but the Russians put their hands in the air and yelled, 'The war is finished.'

As the prisoners passed, I left the shelter of my foxhole to get a closer look at them. There was panic etched on their faces as they realised they had surrendered to a *Waffen SS* unit. No doubt they had succumbed to their government's propaganda leaflets and feared they would be shot out of hand by their captors. Mostly the prisoners kept their eyes directed to the ground but I caught the eye of one of them and made what I hoped was a friendly gesture, a light wave of my hand. The Russian, a tall sturdy man with high cheekbones, nodded ruefully as he approached. His hands dug into his pockets then he shook his massive head as he showed me his empty palms. I pointed to his cap. Without a word, he took it from his head and ripped off the badge with the Soviet star. He handed it to me with a wry smile that exposed the gaps where his front teeth should have been, then joined his comrades. As he shrank into the distance, he turned to look back. I gave a farewell wave of my hand, which he returned.

I still have that badge. It shares the same cardboard box as my Wound Badge and Iron Cross. On reflection, it was careless of me to accept that gift. If captured with the Russian cap badge in my possession, it may well have provoked my captors to inflict worse than usual tortures. Still, in moments of reminiscence, when I take the badge from its box, my thoughts return to that day and the hope rises in my heart that somehow the Russian managed to rejoin his family.

Black mud slurped on every footstep. Ice-cold arrows of rain drummed on our steel helmets throwing up haloes of spray. We came to the edge of a field overlooking a dismal, dilapidated village with an indecipherable name, waiting for the return of a six-man reconnaissance troop. A veil of drips cascaded from the rim of my helmet.

Our platoon leader was becoming anxious and peered into the gloom with binoculars. *'Verdammt.'* he cursed, 'I can't see clearly in this rain – hold fire,'

His order was unnecessary – none of us would have opened fire without his command. Two hundred metres from our position, figures emerged from a stand of scrubby bushes. One of them waved both arms three times, paused, then waved another twice.

'That's them,' announced the platoon leader lowering his binoculars.

The spy troop reached our lines. As they passed, they cursed the rain. *'Kameraden,'* said one of them, 'we'll have to fight for our beds tonight.'

My *Kompanietrupp* joined an infantry unit to bolster its strength for the attack. With house-to-house combat looming, we snapped our bayonets onto our rifles. As we entered the village, Russian machine-gun fire claimed a few of our *Kameraden*. I took cover in a doorway. Bullets turned the stonework around the entrance to dust. A ricochet whirred like wings of a humming bird before smacking against the wall close to my face. Our MG34s returned fire. There was a muffled explosion. The machine-gun noise from both sides came to an abrupt halt. I risked a quick look around the corner of my refuge and saw smoke coming from a window of a house fifty metres deeper into the village. One of our men had managed to get close enough to toss in a stick grenade. Street by street, we battled in the cold, lashing rain until we captured the village.

Before we had time to set up an effective perimeter, the Russians mounted a vigorous counter attack, forcing us to retreat. We regrouped and pushed forward once more to retake the lost ground with individual houses changing hands several times. By evening, we had driven the Russians out for the final time. Our *Kompanie* had taken only light casualties, fewer than might have been expected in such a situation.

With just four of us occupying the front room of a house on a street corner – the only one occupied by Germans within a hundred metres – we were in a vulnerable position. Nevertheless, after an exhausting day, it was a relief to get out of the rain that still pattered against any windowpane left intact. A chaise longue with tattered red upholstery – the only furniture in the room – stood against the wall opposite the only window. In a fleeting moment of pleasure, we sat on it to enjoy our damp bread and cold sausage – all 100 grams of it – before settling down for the night in uniforms that reeked of mould.

The rain had at last relented when I took the over the watch from Boris, a Romanian of German descent whose fluency in Russian had earned him the task of unofficial *Kompanie* interpreter. Beyond my vantage point at the window, floods of silvery light splashed across the wet street as the moon found gaps in the dashing clouds. Boris slumped into a heap in a corner of the room beside our two sleeping *Kameraden* and immediately began to snore. I leaned my rifle against the wall and tried to ignore the rumbles of complaint from my disappointed stomach.

After struggling to keep my weary eyes open for an hour, the faint rise and fall of voices on the chill night breeze startled me into full wakefulness. I peered around the edge of the window. Were the voices louder? Were they some sort of auditory hallucination brought on by fatigue and hunger? Were they Russian voices? I listened intently. My blood ran as cold as the rods of rain that had plagued the day. Hardly daring to breathe, I grabbed my rifle.

'Erwin,' said Boris in a whisper, 'what is it? I thought I heard voices.'

Without taking my eyes from the glistening moonlit street, I replied, 'Russians – a dozen of them – coming this way.' My finger hovered over the trigger of my rifle as the enemy soldiers stopped directly outside the window. Armed with sub-machine guns, they were certain to storm the house if they spotted me. With only rifles and grenades for protection, we would easily have been over-run. I held my breath and drew back into the deep shadows while keeping the enemy within sight.

An argument in subdued voices broke out amongst the Russians with one soldier vigorously stabbing his finger in the direction from which they had just come. They were lost. Suddenly, they fell silent. Someone was calling from farther up the street. Muted laughter broke out. A comrade slapped the back of the soldier who had led the way as they wandered out of view. I lowered my rifle and took a deep breath – the first for several minutes, though it seemed like an eternity.

The creaking of a window from the back room of the house grabbed my attention.

'*Regenbogen,*'

It was the correct password, in Boris' unmistakable voice. In the excitement, I had not noticed him leave. He came into the front room with a smile on his face. 'Erwin – did you hear their officer call them back?'

'*Ja, ja*, it was lucky for us,' I replied.

Boris chuckled. 'That was no Russian, it was me. Now you owe me an hour's watch.'

Our two sleeping *Kameraden* wakened, unaware of the peril that had stalked the streets just a few metres from our refuge.

8

A Steppe too far

Night frosts hardened the mud. With our vehicles now able to move freely over the undulating countryside, Rostov, gateway to the oilfields of the Caucasus, was within our grasp.

At 0300 hrs on the 17 November, a blanket of chill mist deadened every sound, deepened the darkness. At 0600 hrs, *Hauptsturmführer* von Westerhagen addressed the troops. 'It will be no easy task, expect a hard battle. Refrain from eating in case of stomach wounds.' It was a warning we had heard countless times before.

Shortly after first light, the mist lifted like a curtain to reveal the theatre of combat. The infantry of *1* and *2.Kompanie*, supported by the mortars and machine guns of *4.Kompanie* and a squadron of *Sturmgeschütze*, led the assault. Tanks with the white painted letter 'G' on their armour – they were from *Heeresgruppe* Guderian – took up position some distance behind *4.Kompanie*. They fired off a few rounds but made no effort to advance. Our *Sturmgeschütze* showed no such hesitation and followed the forward infantry units into the thick of the fighting.

We paused in a deep anti-tank ditch to wait for further orders. These ditches, with their steep sloping sides, posed a dangerous obstacle for tanks. With no space to turn, a reversing tank caught in one of these traps would have its gun point harmlessly to the ground. Naturally, every tank crew wished to avoid such a vulnerable predicament and the Guderian tanks pulled back to safety. In the meantime, men from our *Pionierkorps* found mines by the hundred. They quickly cleared the area and built an earthen bridge over the ditch for our *Sturmgeschütze* to cross.

With the roofs of Rostov in sight, we were surprised our tanks did not follow on immediately. Nevertheless, we continued with our plan to push forward for ten kilometres before digging in to await our next orders but the enemy, surprised by the vigour of our advance, retreated at speed. Our plan to dig in abandoned, we chased after them to deny them time to create new defensive positions.

By the time we reached the outskirts of Rostov, we were isolated from our main Army Group with no radio or telephone contact. Sepp Dietrich, our Divisional commander, sent two motorcyclists by separate routes to re-establish contact with our command post and relay the news that we intended to pursue the Russians as far as the River Don where two bridges – a steel rail bridge and a timber bridge carrying the roadway – ran side by side. We soon secured the rail bridge but lacking ammunition, were unable to prevent a large body of Russians making good their escape across the timber bridge in well-organised columns, a matter we would come to regret in the coming days.

When the tanks of *Heeresgruppe* Guderian finally appeared in Rostov, I heard a *Leibstandarte* officer remonstrate with a *Wehrmacht* tank commander. 'Where the hell did you get to?'

'Oh, we don't follow infantry units until the crossings over anti-tank ditches are secure,' he replied.

Shortly after entering Rostov, I was in the company of a few *Kameraden*, among them an *Unterscharführer* by the name of Hahn. We were wandering near a street junction exchanging news of who had survived and who had fallen. As we passed close to a high timber fence skirting one side of the street, a gate – almost indistinguishable from the fence itself – snapped open from the other side.

Unterscharführer Hahn called out, *'Achtung.'*

I caught a glimpse of a Russian officer in a long brown leather coat. He let loose a few rounds from a revolver. Hahn groaned as he doubled up. Before I had time to react, the Russian slammed the gate shut.

Clasping his stomach, Hahn grunted, 'After the bastard.'

Heedless of what might be on the other side, we crashed through the gate to give chase but the Russian managed to make good his escape without us being able to fire off a single shot. We returned to find *Uscha* Hahn face down on the ground.

I rushed over to kneel beside him, ready to apply a field dressing. When I turned him onto his back, it was clear it that it was already too late to save him. Blood drenched the uniform around his abdomen. I stayed there for a moment, helplessly watching the last movements of his lips, thinking how suddenly the end might come for any one of us in that God-forsaken town.

'Here, cover him with this,' said a *Kamerad* holding out his tent tarpaulin.

'We can't just leave him here, in the middle of the road,' I protested.

'We'll drag him over to the fence, someone will find him and bury him later,' was the reply.

Later that day, an *Untersturmführer* caught up with me as I reeled out a telephone cable to a machine-gun crew that had set up shop near the railway station.

'Report to the field hospital and ask to see Hahn's body after you've laid the line to the machine guns. It's just a formality but given the circumstances we need to make sure of the identity of the body,' he explained.

The machine-gun crew was easy to find. They were firing on a Russian train with heavily armoured locomotives front and rear, each belching out clouds of steam that seemed too dense to hang in the cold air. Bullets sparked yellow as they ricocheted without effect from the armour plating on the lead locomotive but the unexpected impact of a shell brought the train to a screeching halt. A second shell hit a goods wagon behind the locomotive, smashing its timber walls to matchsticks. From their vantage point on a hill, the crew of an 8.8 centimetre *Flak* cannon were having fun, tormenting the train as a cat would torment a mouse, pummelling it to scrap with shell after shell. The doors of the two passenger carriages to the rear of the train swung open. Among the figures leaping to the ground were women and children.

'*Scheisse* – it's packed with civilians,' groaned the machine-gunner who instinctively stopped firing.

'Why the fuck didn't they get out the other side,' I hissed as shells continued to whistle down on the scattering civilians, ripping to shreds the fine line that distinguishes honour from barbarity. Nowadays, such incidents are euphemistically reported as 'collateral damage'.

'The *Flak* crew can't see them from that distance, it's a bloody massacre,' snapped the machine gunner.

When the firing stopped, *Kompanie* commander Krocza arrived by car and I helped him search the bodies scattered on the grimy tracks. I learned later that the documents we recovered showed the occupants of the carriages had been *Kommissars* and high-ranking officials hoping to escape with their families.

With my gruesome task complete, I returned to the field hospital to identify *Unterscharführer* Hahn's body. One of our tanks had broken through the fence and run over his head, which was now as flat as a pancake. Curiously, he was still easily recognisable with an almost comical expression on his squashed face.

❦ ❦

I straightened my uniform before stepping into Battalion Commander Fritz Witt's office. Bulli, Witt's German shepherd, lay in a corner, its big brown eyes following my every movement. Four lesser officers listened avidly as Witt pointed out a position on a map spread over a large table.

'*Sturmbannführer*,' I announced with a click of my heels and a smart salute, '*Schütze* Bartmann reporting as ordered.'

Wearing his Knight's Cross, the immaculately uniformed *Sturmbannführer* Witt turned his attention from the map. 'Ah, *Schütze* Bartmann, let me show you something,' he said with a little beckoning motion of his head.

The four lesser officers paid little heed to my presence as I followed the *Sturmbannführer* to a window overlooking the two bridges crossing the River Don.

'*Obersturmführer* Springer's *Kompanie* are engaged in an attempt to form a bridgehead on the opposite bank,' explained the *Sturmbannführer*, 'but as yet we have no means of communicating with them. You, *Schütze* Bartmann, will remedy that failing.'

'*Jawohl Sturmbannführer*,' I replied.

'Since there is no radio contact with *3.Kompanie*, I am entrusting you with the task of laying a telephone line across the bridge.' Returning to the table, he spoke to one of the officers, an *Untersturmführer*. 'Fetch a few bottles of *Sekt* – one each for everyone in the room.' He turned to me briefly and said, '*Schütze* Bartmann, just bear with us a few moments.'

There must have been a good supply of *Sekt* nearby because it didn't take long for the *Untersturmführer* to return clasping five bottles by their necks, three in one hand and two in the other. The thought ran through my mind that the *Untersturmführer* had practiced this before. Not wishing to distract from the celebrations, I quietly took up a position near the corner of the room and stood at attention to await further instructions. Corks popped. Champagne glasses, filled to the brim with sparkling *Sekt*, chinked merrily. A toast celebrated the fall of Rostov, a 1000 kilometres inside enemy territory.

Fritz Witt looked over his shoulder. '*Schütze* Bartmann, where's your bottle?'

'*Sturmbannführer*, I don't have one,' I replied stoically.

Witt turned on the unfortunate *Untersturmführer* and bellowed, 'When I say fetch a bottle for everyone in the room that means *everyone*.'

As the red-faced *Untersturmführer* scuttled out of the office, Fritz Witt waved for me to approach whereupon he gave me his own bottle and glass. 'We'll just wait a moment or two for the *Untersturmführer* to return with an extra bottle so that we can *all* celebrate our success,' he said.

Still grinning from ear to ear, I made the connections at the station-end telephone and began to reel out the cable across the rail bridge. When I was midway across the first of the great steel latticework spans, I heard *Sturmbannführer* Witt shout at the top of his voice from the open window of his office. '*Schütze* Bartmann, do not cross the bridge. Return at once.'

Less than an hour after drinking my glass of *Sekt*, I was with a machine-gun crew guarding the approaches to the station when a handful of survivors from Springer's *3.Kompanie* ran over the bridge towards us. The chief of the machine-gun crew grabbed the first man to make it back to our side. 'Where's *Obersturmführer* Springer?'

'Right behind – we were trapped – in the signals building,' panted the rifleman, his breath instantly condensing into a white cloud around his face. 'Upstairs – six of us – *Oberst* Springer got us out – tossed a couple of grenades down the stairs – we're all that's left of the *Kompanie*.'

I realised then that that Fritz Witt had probably saved my life. From his viewpoint in the station, he had seen the Russian attack on the signals building unfold and had called me back.

Acts of bravery by officers such as *Obersturmführer* Springer inspired the ordinary soldier to give of his best. Springer had stayed in the signals building with a few dedicated *Kameraden* until the last possible moment. There was no place for the *Drückeberger* in the *Leibstandarte*, no place for officers who were shirkers that sent the men under their command into perilous situations while they mused over 'their' military successes in the safety of some comfortable billet. Shortly after this action, *Obersturmführer* Springer was deservedly awarded the Knight's Cross.

Like hungry swine summoned by the rattle of the stick on the swill bucket, the *SS* Security Service, the *Sicherheitsdienst*, arrived the day after we secured Rostov. As far as the locals were concerned there was little to distinguish them from members of the *Leibstandarte* apart from the letters '*SD*' sown onto a lozenge shaped patch on their tunics. With vindictive dynamism, they quickly alienated the civilian population by plundering their livestock and searching out Jews. There was a characteristic manner in these people, a certain air – a subliminal smell that warned they were invulnerable to the natural instincts of man and unassailable by pity. In their hands, they held the power of death over life. Though we had not eaten properly for days, none of us dared barter for even a chicken with the local peasants while the *SD* lurked in the background.

Shortly after the arrival of the *SD* – I had just delivered a message to the command post of another *Kompanie* – I came across a *Leibstandarte Schütze* sitting on the steps at the entrance to a building. When I asked him why he was sitting alone in the cold, he looked up at me with yellowed eyes and with a blank expression on his face, silently shook his head. The reek of stale alcohol caught the back of my nose. I went on my way wondering why the drunkard had not already been arrested. Later that day I discovered that the *SD* had commandeered several men from that *Kompanie* to assist them in tracking down the local Jews. Perhaps the drunken soldier was one of those men – I shall never know for sure – but as far as I am aware, this is the only occasion when the *SD* called upon members of the *Leibstandarte* to help them perform their dirty work.

During the last days of November 1941, the Russian winter set in with a vengeance. The fleeing Russians had cleared out the shops and with our supply lines overstretched, food was in short supply. To keep the fuel in the trucks from freezing, the drivers shunted them back and forth until fuel became precious, then they lit fires beneath them.

By chance, a driver from another platoon told us of a food depot not far from the rail station. At full speed, we drove to the storage facility – miraculously missed by the *SD* – to find metal canisters filled with butter and honey, tins of frozen eggs and some ham and *Schmalz* (a kind of lard made from the fat found around the intestines of cattle – delicious.). With our booty covering the floor of our truck, I sat uncomfortably on a canister of butter, its metal rim digging into the back of my thighs. As we tackled a steep hill on the return journey, a few of the canisters rolled from the rear of the truck and bounced off into the distance but at least this created a little more floor space.

Our over-extended supply lines had left us short of supplies of all kinds but, having secured a good supply of food, our most pressing need was for ammunition. Russian troops now ran across the timber bridge to our side of the river in organised groups without us firing more than a token shot or two to keep them on their toes. With the Sea of Azov at our backs, we were in a vulnerable position.

9

Retreat to the Mius-Sambek Line

Snow was blowing in from the east when word passed round that we were to pull back to a defensive position north of Taganrog. For the first time I sensed an air of subdued panic in the bearing of our commanders. We had no previous failures from which to learn since retreat was a skill we had neither planned for nor contemplated. In effect, it was every man for himself and something of a shambles.

In a flurry of swirling snowflakes, our *Kompanietrupp* piled into the back of our truck, each man finding a place amongst the barrels of food we had picked up earlier. By the time we left Rostov, we had caught up with the rearmost vehicles in the escaping column. Close to Tschaltyr, a town to the west of Rostov, we glimpsed a squadron of fast moving Russian tanks in the distance.

'The bastards are trying to cut us off,' said Boris, our Romanian *Kamerad* who had saved my skin with his impression of a Russian officer a few weeks earlier.

'Who's in charge of the rearguard?' asked a figure sheltering behind the cabinet where our *Kompanie* maps were stored, just behind the driver's cab

'Knittel,' answered Boris. 'If he doesn't do something ....'

The truck juddered as its engine coughed and died. The fresh snow creaked under the wheels as we drifted to a standstill. In abject silence, we looked at each other, none of us daring to speculate on what might happen next. The cab door slammed. A few of us shuffled to the side of the truck, straining our necks like inquisitive monkeys to watch the driver who appeared with a heavy wrench in his hand.

'The fuel must be frozen,' he said, looking up at his staring audience. He bent his body like an arthritic old man and tapped the fuel tank with his wrench. 'Listen to that echo,' he said. 'The diesel in the tank's still liquid. It's the fuel line that's frozen.'

'*Scheisse* – the Russians are chasing our arses and there's no time to light a fire,' someone groaned.

'I have an idea,' offered Boris. 'Do you have a length of hose?'

'*Naja,*' said the driver, 'but it's not long enough to stretch from the fuel tank to the engine'

'And a funnel?'

'Of course.'

Boris turned to us and made gathering gestures. 'Gas mask canisters, water bottles, quickly, anything that will hold fuel.' He passed the containers over the side to the driver. 'Here, siphon fuel into them – and hurry.'

With Boris now at his side, the driver inserted the rubber tube into the fuel tank. He put his mouth to the tube then spat diesel onto the snow. 'My lips are frozen – I can't feel if I'm sucking or blowing.'

Boris grabbed the tube from the driver. 'Get back behind the wheel,'

When he had filled the containers, Boris passed them into the cab and, rubber hose in hand, disappeared round the front of the truck. Moments later, he returned to the driver's door with one end of the tube in his gloved hand and thrust it through the open window of the cab.

'I've attached the other end to the fuel line near the engine – push the funnel into this end. I'll pour in the fuel as we drive.'

The door on the passenger side of the cab slammed – at last Boris was in the cab, beside the driver. We returned to our seats on the barrels of food rescued from Rostov.

'I just hope the battery doesn't let us down,' said a *Kamerad*.

'That's tempting fate *Dummkopf*,' I snapped angrily.

The truck swayed a little on its springs as the starter motor laboriously turned the cold engine. Our eyes, tense and unblinking, stared at each other in hope. The engine grunted and coughed agonisingly before springing into its familiar throaty snarl. Dismay turned to joy and we cheered as we picked up speed.

The inescapable apprehension one feels when death is a constant threat grinds on the nerves, strains them to breaking point. Hours of duty in bitter temperatures drives the life-blood from the limbs. Frigid air hacks relentlessly and without mercy at the face and hands. The chronic lack of sleep saps the body's energy reserves allowing exhaustion to set its pernicious roots into every cell of the body. In such conditions, sleep can overcome the unwary to bring blessed oblivion – or mortal danger – no matter what the circumstances. And so, too cold even to shiver, I tucked the collar of my greatcoat under my helmet to protect my face from the numbingly cold air and slipped into an irresistible slumber.

I wakened with a jolt under the silence of unblinking starlight. My greatcoat was stiff, glittering with frost. I listened. Nothing moved. I was alone in the back of the truck, which stood as if abandoned, close to an isolated house. I tried to push myself from between the barrels of food where I had slumped completely oblivious to the discomfort. Both my legs beneath the knees seemed to have turned to wood – frozen wood. I crawled between the barrels of butter and *Schmalz* to the rear of the truck where I hung my useless legs over the tailgate. With a push from both hands, I launched myself from the rear of the truck but with feet totally without feeling, I was unable to sense their impact with the ground. I lost my balance and fell forward, into the snow. Using my rifle as support, I struggled to my feet and somehow managed to hobble one foot in front of the other until hardly caring what I would find inside, I pushed open the door of the house.

Astonished faces looked up at me. There, sitting in front of a roaring fire with a handful of Russian women, were my *Kameraden*. Stripped to the waist, they nipped lice from the armpits of their shirts, flicking them into the flames much to the unease of their hosts who, for reasons I was never able to fathom, seemed to respect these infernal little pests. Full of apologies, they sat me in front of the fire where I immediately fell once more into a deep sleep.

The sky was already light when I wakened. My legs still had the weight of dense wood, but now the wood was on fire. I groaned in agony. One of the women pulled off my boots and socks. The skin of both legs had turned white with underlying purplish blotching. She looked at them and shook her head.

A pane in the small window at the front of the house rattled in resonance with our truck's revving engine. I shuffled over to the window and rubbed a peephole in the frost fern on the glass. Before the moisture had time to re-freeze, I managed to glimpse my *Kameraden* digging snow from around the truck's wheels. Soon I would have to leave. I returned to a chair close to the still burning fire and, ignoring the throbbing in my legs, pulled on my socks and boots.

Boris called from the open door. 'We remembered you this time Erwin – we leave in a few minutes. The driver says you can sit in the cab to keep warm.'

When the driver, whose name I have long since forgotten, asked about my legs. I described the symptoms.

'Mild frostbite' he scoffed, 'that's nothing – but if your feet had turned black and fallen off you might *just* have got a ticket home.'

He was, I thought, exaggerating though, as I later found out, not by much.

'I've seen it all,' he continued, 'hundreds of cases, some of them terrible.'

I was shocked to learn that so many of our *Kameraden* had been victims of frostbite. 'We should have better winter clothing,' I yelled over the engine noise. 'It was crazy to think the uniforms we wore back home in Berlin would be of any use in the Russian winter.'

'Haven't you heard the rumours?'

I shook my head.

'Well, the story goes that the Chief Quartermaster ordered winter clothing way back in September but when he opened up the crates he found nothing but desert kit.' His voice heavy with irony, he added, 'Now how could *that* happen?'

Instantly I came to the same shocking conclusion that I suspect the driver had already made but had been unwilling to elaborate upon – the arrival of desert kit had not been some kind of incompetent mix up at the supply depots in Germany but an act of traitorous sabotage. Somewhere, back home, high-ranking officials, secret communists, were determined to sell us out to the Russians.

Onwards we pressed until we reached the Mius, a river that flows into a firth that empties into the Sea of Azov. By this time, my legs throbbed agonisingly so I reported immediately to the first-aid post – set up in an unheated house – to await treatment. As I entered, a scene of horror unfolded before my eyes. A soldier wearing thick felt boots – issued to protect feet when on guard duty – screamed in agony as a doctor tried to pull them from his feet.

'These boots are a curse,' the doctor said, 'they suck in water then freeze. It's not the first time I've had to cut them off.' He looked up to the two medical orderlies standing at the end of the table, near the victim's head. 'You'd better hold him down.'

As the doctor cut at the felt boots, their owner suddenly fell silent.

'He's lucky he's fainted,' said the doctor.

I retched as the doctor finally managed to free the first boot. The rotten flesh of the victim's leg ended in a stump of bone, leaving the rest of the foot in the boot.

Feeling a little embarrassed that I had troubled the doctor with my relatively trivial frostbite I rejoined my *Kompanietrupp*. Little did I realise the damage to my legs and feet would continue to cause serious problems more than seventy years later.

Overlooking the banks of the River Mius, we came across a small group of *Wehrmacht* personnel stationed in the open fields, totally without cover. Bone-chilling winds had already carved deep frowns of dejection on their sullen faces.

'Start digging,' said one of the older guys, an *Obergefreiter* who looked fifty but was probably nearer thirty. He flung a spade to a teenager who stood motionless, hands stuffed into the pockets of his coat. The spade clanged as it struck a patch of stone-hard ice.

Eyes streaming with tears brought on by the pitiless icy-cold wind, the teenager looked at the spade and smirked ironically, 'The ground's frozen. How can I dig?'

'You'll change your mind when the shells start raining down on you.'

The teenager sullenly picked up the spade and half-heartedly prodded the ground with it. 'I can't dig this,' he said flinging the spade to the side.

An argument was brewing. The rest of the *Wehrmacht* men looked on, hoping, no doubt, that the excitement might distract their attention from the plummeting temperatures, or better, that some officer would come along to tell them a comfortable billet had been fixed up for the night. What a bunch.

There were never such discipline problems in the *Leibstandarte*. In contrast to the *Wehrmacht*, most of our *Kameraden* were about the same age and our leaders, although often only ten years or so older than the men under their command, displayed excellent leadership abilities. This was a great advantage to us when things got difficult, we pulled together to overcome problems as best we could. Digging a trench was undoubtedly an onerous task in the Russian winter. Ice formed beads on our eyelashes as we dug. Our feet froze in the same boots we had used to march around *Platfuss Allee* the previous summer. Fresh snow filled the trenches as we dug. To add to our troubles, enormous boulders lurked under the surface so that a promising trench – won after hacking through a layer of frozen mud – often had to be abandoned. Intoxicated by the fantasy of our ultimate victory, the *Endsieg*, the men of the *Leibstandarte* shouldered these hardships without complaint.

From our position, we looked across a frozen meadow to the Russians on other side of the river with some envy. They occupied the edge of a forest where they had prepared proper shelters to protect themselves from the penetrating cold. Fortunately, the supply lines to our new position were well established and we had an abundance of ammunition so we fired on Ivan from time to time, just to liven things up a little.

As a respite from our miserable life in the exposed trenches, during which frostbite claimed several victims from our *Kompanie*, we sometimes took to the deep caves found in the area. Although they offered protection from the cutting wind, a heavy immutable chill that gnawed at the bones haunted them.

Somehow, they brought to mind the frightening fairy tales told to me as a child. The Russians must have had the same idea because it was possible on occasion to hear their voices percolating through interlinking voids in the rock, a matter that made it difficult for us to relax completely.

10

Happy Birthday, Merry Christmas

The air was clear, pure, the cold so intense the skin on my face tingled as if pricked by a million tiny needles. My bones seemed to rattle under my shivering muscles and my legs, frostbitten during the retreat from Rostov, were numb. To keep the blood flowing, I danced from foot to foot as I swung my arms across my chest in the entrance ditch to my one-man bunker. Through the cloud of condensing breath hovering around my head, a figure caught my eye. Hobbling from foxhole to foxhole, he spent a few minutes in each. As he came closer, I recognised him as an *Oberscharführer* recently released from the field surgery unit in Taganrog. I put out a hand to help him climb down into my trench. '*Oberscharführer*, you're taking a risk.'

'*Naja*, Ivan's been quiet today,' he replied nonchalantly.

There was a wry smile on his remarkably fresh-looking face – almost everyone else around me seemed to have aged by least ten years since winter took its first hard grip in late November. He pulled back his camouflage jacket to show the collar of his tunic. The 'mirror', where two silver pips had been, was empty. '*Schütze* now,' he said.

Soon we were sharing stories and I ventured to ask him why he had been demoted all the way down to *Schütze*. The smile on his face evaporated.

'You know that girl I was living with?'

I had heard the gossip. It was well known in the *Kompanie* that he had been in private quarters with a very attractive young Ukrainian woman. She had a rose pink complexion and hair so blond it had the sheen of finest gold. Everyone knew what was going on between them. I nodded. 'What happened?'

'Shot herself – used my 08 to do it.'

It was lucky for him that his punishment had been so lenient. As for the girl: it was certain that if we pulled back her 'liberators' would make an example of her. Perhaps it was for that reason she had killed herself. Anyway, I didn't think it appropriate to pursue the matter further.

The *Oberscharführer* – somehow I could not bring myself to think of him as a mere *Schütze* – took his *Soldbuch* from his tunic pocket and opened it. Inside was a picture of the woman. With a sorrowful sigh, he passed it to me. She had beautiful high cheekbones and a wide inviting smile. It was easy to see why he had become infatuated with her. When I handed back the picture he stared at it for a silent moment before ripping it into tiny shreds that he let fall to the snow.

'It's better if I forget her,' he said solemnly. Suddenly his mood brightened. 'Now I can do what I came here for. Happy birthday Erwin,' he beamed as he slapped my back. 'The cook – he told me it was your birthday.'

It had been my turn to collect the large insulated vessel used to carry food from the field kitchen earlier that morning, 12 December 1941, and I recalled having joked with the cook by asking for a little extra goulash because it was my birthday.

'It's my birthday too – today,' said my visitor.

We chatted about how we would spend our time after our inevitable final victory. As he made to leave, a feeling of intense unease gripped me and I hooked a hand over his shoulder to restrain him. 'Watch out, you were a sitting duck when you came over. This still air is perfect for a sniper – no need to allow for wind when he aims.'

'You worry too much,' he said shrugging his shoulders before scrambling out of the trench.

He took a few paces back the way he had come then turned and stood for a moment, lost in some private thought, gazing across the frozen fields before slinging his rifle over his shoulder. There was a metallic clink. His head swayed under the weight of his steel helmet then his arms fell limply to his sides. The rifle slide from his shoulder and he slumped to his knees like a burst sack of flour. He groaned something – it might have been his girlfriend's name – before falling face first into the snow. His helmet rolled away from his head and rocked back and forth a few times before coming to rest on a patch of ice. Bright blood spread under his face, freezing in seconds into a congealed mass, its redness intensified by the purity of the snow. At the front of the helmet, exactly in the centre, was a perfectly round hole. I cursed myself for mentioning my birthday to the cook and kept my head down for the rest of that day.

When the dazzling winter sun had sunk below the horizon, a couple of medics recovered the frozen body of my visitor and took it to Taganrog for burial in a grave marked by the *SS* death rune – a cross with drooping 'arms' – in the soldiers' graveyard. It was in the vindictive nature of the Russians to flatten these graveyards when they reoccupied ground we gave up so it is certain that his grave now lies unmarked, its location forgotten.

A few days later, we moved to Sambek where we constructed strong defensive positions to protect the approach to Taganrog from the east. We, the survivors of *4.Kompanie*, occupied the upper part of the settlement with orders to defend a line of approximately one kilometre in length, a formidable task for about sixty men.

The houses were to become our accommodation and although it was harsh to expel the inhabitants from their homes in such cold weather, they accepted the situation without complaint. It was my hope that they would find accommodation in the undamaged farm buildings scattered across the countryside, away from the village, which was now certain to attract the attention of the enemy's artillery.

A woman with a child holding on to her hand patted my arm as she passed. 'At least we are able to pray in our churches once more,' she said.

With the town cleared of civilians, we began the construction of a deep bunker, partly under the foundations of a house on steeply sloping ground. Thankfully, the earth was not completely frozen and the heavy physical work kept us warm as we heaped the excavated soil at the side of the house. Now and then, we came across buried rocks that required the skill of a *Pioniertrupp* to shift using explosives. Our excavations complete, we gathered a good stock of planks and doors to form the roof. Tree stumps, sawn to an appropriate length, formed the supports necessary to hold the whole thing up when we piled the earth from the excavation on top of the roof timbers. Finally, we installed a fireplace made from a large tin can punctured with air holes made by our bayonets. The smoke from this precious little luxury, which we used only during darkness because of the risk of attracting enemy artillery fire, filtered to the outside through a pipe taken from the oven of an abandoned cottage. Meanwhile, the machine-gun crews were busy building similar constructions. Trenches linked the bunkers. Now, after our retreat from Rostov, there was nothing to do but wait until the Russians made the next move.

Christmas drew near. Sporadic artillery barrages prevented our wagons bringing hot food to the front line. To make myself useful I fetched food from the field kitchens to take to the machine-gun crews in their bunkers where, because the Russian infantry was inactive, I had time to join in a hand or two of Skat – a card game popular amongst the troops – as we chatted about life back in Germany.

'My father brought home an old musical box he found in a junk shop,' recounted a *Schütze* as we played. 'He spent months in secret, taking it apart to clean it until every piece of the mechanism gleamed like new – a Christmas present for Mama. Two ballerinas twirled to the music. Between them were three bells – each chimed a different note. Little bluebirds on wires pecked at two of the bells to make them ring but the third bird was missing. Papa handed her the present as we ate on Christmas Eve. When Mama saw the box, she burst into tears. "What is it?" Papa asked. Poor Mama couldn't speak. Dabbing her eyes with her napkin she left the table and came back with her purse. She opened it and to our astonishment took out the third bluebird. "My father brought that very same musical box from France in 1918, when he was a soldier," said Mama. "I used to play with it for hours on end when I was a little girl but we had to sell it to buy food. I cried my eyes out when I learned it was going so he took off the bluebird and gave it to me to keep. He said it sang a song that only its companions could hear and that one day it would call them back."' The *Schütze* reached into his tunic pocket and took out a small oilskin bag. 'Look,' he said, taking the third bluebird from the bag. 'Mama said it will take me home safely when it returns to its companions.'

'Huh – superstitious nonsense,' snorted another member of the machine-gun crew. 'If a shell has your name on it, you've had it just like any of us,' he said, trumping one superstition with another.

The telephone rang. The *Unterscharführer* in charge of the machine-gun crew answered. '*Ja ja*, he's with us,' he said into the mouthpiece. He thrust the phone towards me.

The line crackled, giving me time to wonder if I was about to hear some bad news from home.

'*Schütze* Bartmann?'

'Here.'

'Krocza here – Bartmann, it seems you were a baker before joining the *Leibstandarte.*'

I sighed in relief. '*Jawohl Hauptsturmführer*, in Berlin – the Glaser bakery in Memeler Strasse.'

'Then I have a special request to ask of you.'

'Of course, I will do anything I can.' I answered without asking any details of the 'request'. After all, a 'request' coming from someone of Leopold Krocza's rank was really a politely disguised order.

'Ah, good, I would like you to prepare a little treat for the men for Christmas – cakes perhaps? You have permission to leave your post to look for ingredients. There is a house close to the field kitchen some way to the rear of your present position – it will be at your disposal when you are ready to start baking – good luck.'

❦ ❦

It was not too difficult to find most of the ingredients for a cake, or pastry for a pie. Most of them, with the exception of baking powder, were available in the truck that brought us from Rostov and, since the local women baked their own bread, every house had a suitable oven and, I hoped, a supply of baking powder. However, after rummaging through several deserted dwellings, I finally had to concede that my search for this essential ingredient of a cake mix was in vain so I settled on the idea of making biscuits instead.

Close to my 'kitchen' was a first-aid post where the lightly wounded were patched up before being sent back to their posts. Its entrance faced towards the Russian lines. In this part of the village, there were also shelters for civilians, chiefly women and young children. Some of them I recognised as those we expelled to make way for our bunkers at the top of the slope overlooking the river at Sambek.

Early on the morning of Christmas Eve, I prepared a biscuit mix with butter, eggs, milk and sugar. I kneaded it thoroughly then rolled it out on a table before cutting it into discs with the open end of an empty tin can. As I put the last batch into the oven, there was the nearby thud of an artillery shell. I rushed outside to see smoke coming from the entrance of a cellar where refugees were sheltering. When I looked inside, I found that only two of them had been injured and took them to the nearby first aid post where our medics treated their injuries, which fortunately were not serious. Returning to my kitchen, I found the batch of biscuits baked to perfection.

The odd burst of Russian shells soon turned into a continual thunderous drum roll – *Trommelfeuer* – a Christmas Day present. The Russians always made a point of mounting an attack on days the German calendar showed a celebration. We of course reciprocated these compliments on days important to the Russians. Nevertheless, I had a pleasant task to execute in my provisional bakery. The aroma wafting from the cast iron oven took my thoughts back to my time as an apprentice baker in Berlin, to Herr Glaser and Fritz, my journeyman. It was my first Christmas away from home and for a moment, an intense sadness threatened to overwhelm me.

With Russian shells still ringing in the celebrations, I set out from my kitchen with a sack filled with biscuits. The shellfire suddenly stopped, the smoke from the detonations evaporating into the brilliant blueness of the sky. Sunlight sparkled on the fresh snow and there was silence, a beautiful peaceful silence.

Like the *Weihnachtsmann*, the German Father Christmas, I visited every bunker to distribute my Christmas treat.

When I reached the bunker where the *Kamerad* with the little bluebird lived, I was surprised to see him lying on his stomach, perched on his elbows and smiling broadly, as he finished writing a letter home.

'Listen to this Erwin,' he said. Then, reading from the letter, 'Have been shot through both cheeks but can still talk. The bluebird is coming home. See you soon.'

'What happened?' I asked.

'Sniper caught me having a shit.'

❦

Shortly after Christmas, a storm of propaganda leaflets fell from the sky. I picked up one with the heading *'Schluss mit Hitler'* (finish with Hitler). It showed our leader in an intoxicated state, depicted by a steel helmet worn at a peculiar angle, drinking the blood of German soldiers from a glass.

'Schütze Bartmann!'

I almost leapt into the air with fright. An officer had crept up on me to bellow in my ear. He picked up one of the leaflets scattered across the ground.

'Filthy lies.' he roared tearing it into tiny pieces, though other leaflets littered the whole area.

Feeling like a naughty schoolboy, I crumpled the leaflet in my hand and tossed it over my shoulder.

In the final days of 1941, the Russians launched several attacks, each floundering on the tangle of barbed wire set up by out *Pioniertrupp* on the banks of the frozen Sambek River. As always, our machine guns cut off the enemy retreat. Unusually, the Russians did not attempt to recover their wounded. They left them to die – sacrifices to the debilitating cold – with wounds that in the summer months would be considered minor. They simply lay where they fell until buried by the next snowfall.

❦

An unusually heavy barrage of artillery fire fell on our positions – the Russians were making every effort to clear us out of Sambek. Shells whistled in from the enormous guns of Russian warships sitting in the Sea of Azov. The shock waves from the detonations rang through the rock-hard ground and through the frozen soles of my boots to jar every bone in my body. When I risked a look from our bunker, it was to see chunks of sharp steel, shrapnel the length of a man's arm, scything through the air with predatory whistling sounds. They travelled at speeds that made their curving trajectory easily visible but impossible to avoid. Anyone caught in the open risked being cut in half.

A deafening salvo exploded close behind. I threw myself into the security of our bunker. Black boulders of ice and rocks the size of a man rumbled across the roof. Not a word passed between us during that bombardment. Bulging eyes and clenched teeth contorted every face into the personification of fear. At last, the pounding of the giant detonations marched towards the centre of the village, downhill from our bunker. Once more, my guardian angel had looked down on me, keeping me safe.

'Thank God that's past – they're aiming for the church now – probably think we have observers in the tower,' a *Kamerad* sighed.

When the pounding of the village at last came to an abrupt end, I poked my head into the remaining daylight. Below, on the slope sweeping down to the river, lay the smoking remains of Sambek's houses.

The *Uscha* in charge of our troop scanned the area through his field glasses. '*Blindgängers*,' he announced looking at the ominous smoking craters with unexploded shells at their centre, 'hundreds of them.' He chuckled. 'Look at them, the crazy bastards – the *Pioniertrupp* is clearing them already.'

11

Spring Smiles on Sambek

Complaints were on everyone's lips. In a futile attempt to gain relief, we made masks from scrap cloth to cover our mouths and noses so that we looked like extras on a Wild West film set.

'How can I eat with that stench in the air? It gets into the food.'

'Never mind the food – it goes straight for my stomach – makes me retch.'

'I can hardly breathe – my lungs can't take it.'

'It can travel against the wind. How can it do that?'

With each passing day, the odious sickly stink thickened as grotesque black mounds of putrefying bodies wrapped in disintegrating Russian uniforms emerged from the retreating snow. Nothing could hold back the revolting stench. Every intake of breath – a subconscious act under normal circumstances – was a nauseating ordeal.

At last, our leaders took heed of our complaints. A *Wehrmacht* unit arrived with a gang of Russian prisoners to clear up the mess. With masks of tattered rags pulled over their noses the prisoners pulled at the heaps of rotting flesh to disentangle one putrid corpse from the next, often finding themselves in possession of a detached arm or leg. In an incident of comic horror, as a prisoner dragged a body by the legs to the nearby pit that was to be its grave, the head came loose. Still holding the legs of his dead comrade, the prisoner instinctively stuck out a leg in an attempt to stop the head escaping but it rolled over his outstretched foot and, gathering speed, bounced erratically over lingering patches of ice towards the river. The Russians on the other side of the river must have seen all this happening but, not wishing to fire on their own men, their weapons remained silent.

Rumours went the rounds that we were to be withdrawn from the Mius-Sambek line but nothing happened until 21 May when the *SS* Police Division arrived. We packed what little personal belongings we had and made ready to leave. It had been an exhausting winter and we looked forward to a period of recuperation as our column of vehicles made its way towards Taganrog.

As evening fell, our trucks turned to head back towards Sambek. There was no need for words; grimaces of disappointment cut across every man's face. Soon we were back at the village repelling an attack that had broken through the lines of the *SS* Police units who were now struggling to hold our old positions. Once more, the *Leibstandarte* showed the enemy our capabilities by vigorously repelling their breakthrough. That evening we were back in the bunker we had constructed just before Christmas.

Every other day, Russian propaganda leaflets urging us to surrender fluttered from the sky. This was a waste of paper not only because the men of the *Leibstandarte* had made an unbreakable oath to Hitler but also because we knew the fate awaiting *Waffen SS* men who fell into Russian captivity. We had not forgotten the *Handschuhe* torture inflicted on the reconnaissance troop in Taganrog.

Their offer of fair treatment to surrendering German troops having met with no success, the enemy continued their propaganda efforts with loudspeakers set on poles. A female voice boomed out over the spring meadows with taunts about the infidelity of our wives and girlfriends but, having never had a girlfriend, this hardly troubled me. The loudspeaker rant finished with, 'We wish the *Leibstandarte* a happy break in France and look forward to seeing you again later.'

We looked at each other quizzically, wondering if it could be true. Given the conditions we had endured over the winter, the prospect of a sojourn in France was appealing though, we thought, too unrealistic for us to take seriously.

A few days of pleasant weather passed and again we received notice that we would be withdrawn. Then, under the cloak of darkness, a Romanian unit took over our positions and we set off once more for Taganrog. We could hardly believe it when once more the order came to turn around. After a day of close-quarter fighting, we again retook our old positions in Sambek. In the end, we left with *both* the SS Police Division *and* the Romanians defending the village. Though severely depleted after our Rostov foray, the *Leibstandarte* had twice retaken a line that required two other full divisions to defend.

❦·❦

After a few days in Taganrog we moved west to Mariupol, a large port on the Sea of Azov, to help keep the coast secure. By this time, it had become warm though there was a refreshing onshore breeze, a welcome change from the white winds of winter. Making good use of our free time, we exposed our startlingly pale bodies to the sunshine and bathed in the sea at the foot of steep cliffs. With the absence of enemy activity, it seemed like heaven to be able to sleep undisturbed through the night until role call at the unusually late hour of 7 am.

At a delousing facility set up near our camp, I was relieved to get rid of the plague of lice and the continual scratching that made my skin raw around the belt line of my trousers. Once more, life was good and the cold that had taken up residence in my bones finally succumbed to the warmth of the sun.

We moved inland to Stalino where the weather was unbearably hot. We slept in tents with the entrance flaps tied wide open at night to allow any cooling breeze to do its work. At this time, a few raw recruits from Lichterfelde joined our *Kompanie* bringing first-hand news of what was happening in Berlin and other parts of the *Reich*. But our stay in Stalino was no holiday, training became the daily routine with morning roll call at 6 am.

On a particularly hot day, an *Oberscharführer* attached to the Divisional Staff Office issued letters to those who had won military awards. Those of us who had participated in the Rostov campaign were presented with the *Sturmabzeichen*, a badge awarded for enduring at least ten days of continuous combat. That evening, after proudly passing my award around newly arrived recruits, I held it between my fingers and, like a child with a new toy, examined every detail of its construction. I had won my first decoration and was beginning to feel like a real veteran.

We were lounging on the grass half-heartedly cleaning our boots when Boris came running with a towel around his neck, shaving lather on half his face. 'We're leaving tomorrow – for France – get packing.'

I was unconvinced. 'Who says?'

'It's official – the *Uscha* got the news straight from Krocza.' He stretched out his arms and bellowed melodically, 'Farewell, farewell to Mother Russ-ia.' Like me, Boris was a great fan of opera.

A spontaneous cheer went up. We sprang to our feet.

'Thank God – I can't stand this heat,' one of the recruits sighed.

'Hey, hold on,' I cautioned. 'Remember that woman on the loudspeaker at Sambek – how did she know we were going to France?'

'Spies,' said Boris, 'spies or some poor bastard of an officer was captured and spilled the beans before the Russians slit open his belly and spilled his guts.'

In early July, our assault guns and trucks were loaded onto long, low-slung transport wagons. The men travelled mostly in goods wagons while the officers had a couple of proper carriages at the head of the train. With jubilant hearts, our *Kompanietrupp* clambered into a goods wagon with a medical orderly for company. As we slid from the station, Boris could talk of nothing but the beautiful girls we would meet and found a willing audience amongst his sex-starved *Kameraden*. 'I was in Toulouse once – on holiday,' he enthused. *'Ach Mensch* – the French girls are so pretty – I can't wait to get there.'

'Are they prettier than the Danish girls?' asked the medic.

'You wait – your eyes will pop out of your head,' countered Boris.

'Well I've still not used *any* of my condoms,' I chipped in. I simply had not had time to think of girls since entering the Lichterfelde barracks the previous summer. Although I was now eighteen-and-a-half years old, I had never 'slept' with a girl but being somewhat shy of discussing such matters I did not intend to disclose this detail to my companions.

'Me neither,' came a call from the corner of the wagon, 'not a single fucking one – never had a girl in my life.'

Everyone laughed. Most of the ordinary soldiers in the *Leibstandarte* had battled unrelentingly for months without a single day's leave, without a single full night's sleep until we left Sambek. The very thought of women had been locked beyond reach in the back of our young minds.

After a few hours, we came to a halt at a small town. Because of the sweltering heat we were allowed leave the wagon and stand around the station. Jokes about returning to rescue the Romanians sprung up although it was by no means beyond the bounds of possibility that we could be called upon to rescue them yet again.

As we lounged in the welcoming shade of a stand of trees, a few locals took pity on our boredom and offered a local alcoholic drink that was taken hot and, out of politeness, we accepted their offer.

A whistle blew and we clambered into our wagons which, still heading to the west, trundled into the vast countryside. Singing broke out the length of the train, different songs from every wagon – a cacophony of joy. Within us, the flame of loyalty to our *Führer* still burned brightly. With body and soul, we were the proud instruments of his Will, a manifestation of the spiritual power he had awakened within the *Deutsche Volk*.

As nightfall approached, I stood at the open door of the wagon watching the high, wispy clouds turn pink, then red, as the Ukrainian countryside swayed lazily by, clickety-click, kilometre after endless kilometre. There was something alluring about the Ukrainian landscape – perhaps it was the enormity of the sky – and I wondered if one day I would return, after we had won the war perhaps. When the warm, velvety darkness at last cloaked the landscape, I took my place among my *Kameraden* who were already asleep on straw filled sacks – heavenly beds in comparison to the broken bricks of some wrecked house or the confinement of cold bunkers shuddering under an artillery barrage.

✤·✤

A mist of golden straw dust swirled in the almost horizontal shaft of morning sunlight that struck in from the ventilation opening high in the wall of the wagon. Gradually, I came to my senses after what must have been at least eight hours of unbroken sleep.

'*Morgen* Erwin,' chirped a voice.

The words came from a silhouette leaning nonchalantly, hands in trouser pockets, against the open door of the wagon. I recognised the voice as that of the medic, a veteran of the Battle at Dunkirk. Still drowsy, I rose unsteadily to my feet and brushed the straw from my uniform. '*Morgen* Hans.' I stepped carefully over my still sleeping *Kameraden* to reach the doorway and shaded my eyes with a hand to peer into the sunlit countryside. 'Shouldn't we keep inside in case there are partisans in the area?'

'*Nah*, we're too far from the front – relax.'

I let my hand drop from my face and drew the fresh morning air deep into my lungs. 'It's a beautiful morning.'

'Sleep well?'

I yawned widely. 'Too well,' I ran my hand through my hair, 'I was dreaming – about France.'

'Ah France – you'll like France. I had the chance to visit Paris after Dunkirk.'

'Do you think the British will try another landing?'

'It's possible. I doubt we're being moved there simply to give us a holiday.'

A woman waved to us as she hung out washing in her back yard. We returned her greeting.

'The British – they shouldn't be hard to push back into the sea,' I offered.

'Don't underestimate the British. They have brave and capable officers. Sepp Dietrich respects them. He even ordered a military funeral for a British major who resisted capture by grabbing the rifle from one of our men's hands then clubbing him with it – a fellow called Tichatzki, from Oberallgäu if my memory serves me well. He found the major hiding in a burnt out tank. Unfortunately, he was killed after a struggle. The guard of honour was from *1.Kompanie*, they fired the salute over the grave.'

There was a tap on my shoulder. It was Boris, our Romanian *Kamerad*.

'Stand clear Erwin – I need a piss.' He stood at the edge of the open wagon door and unbuttoned his fly.

After travelling for several days – trains carrying military personnel seldom took a direct route – we came to siding in a rail yard somewhere in Saarland, Germany, where we jumped out to stretch our legs. A two-metre high timber fence, which Hans immediately started to clamber over, obscured our view of the other side.

'I'm choking for a beer – anyone coming with me?'

I looked at him in astonishment wondering how he had the nerve to leave the yard without permission. 'What if the train leaves?'

'Ha. Just tell them to hang on a bit,' he laughed.

Sitting on top of the fence, the medic paused to wave to a couple of his mates who, having also found their thirst for beer overwhelming, were already on the other side.

'They're crazy,' said Boris, 'if the train leaves without them they'll be in shot for desertion.'

Time passed. Now and then, one or other of us stood on our tiptoes to peer longingly at a bar on a street corner, not too far away.

'The sly old dog,' said Boris, 'he must have known there was a pub close by.'

When the locomotive's whistle blew, faces red with drink appeared along the top edge of the fence, among them that of our medic, Hans.

'I've got something for you,' he chuckled.

There was the chinking of glass against glass and four bottles of *Weissbier* appeared above the line of the fence, one after the other. Welcoming hands on our side rescued them.

'The locals donated them – now help me over before that train gets going.'

12

The Beauties of Paris

We were posted a village lying to the south east of Paris where we slept soundly on the floor of the village hall, our minds free at last from thoughts of sudden death or the horrific wounds the following day might bring. Training began as usual with roll call at 6 am but, except for nights spent on sentry duty, there was plenty of free time to play cards or chess. Disappointingly, there was still no opportunity for the keenly anticipated encounters with attractive young French women.

On a glorious summer's morning, a few days after settling into our new billet, an *Unterscharführer,* a ruddy-faced farmer's son from Austria, called out a list of names at roll call, ordering those mentioned to remain behind. My name was amongst those called. When the remainder of the *Kompanie* had been dismissed, I looked around and recognised faces I had seen on the *Ostfront*, each one carrying a look of bewilderment.

A smile broke across the *Uscha*'s naturally ruddy face. 'I have a pleasant surprise for you old hares from the *Ostfront*,' he announced in a voice that boomed like alpine thunder. 'Today, you will see the sights of Paris.' His arm swung elegantly in the direction of a truck waiting at the edge of the assembly area. 'Gentlemen, take your seats.'

The truck's engine revved impatiently as we clambered into the back. As we sped through a village, a pretty girl about eighteen years old stood on a street corner shielding her eyes against the sun. She smiled and waved as we passed. Of course, as young men do, we returned her favour with raucous yells of approval and loud whistles as she shrank into the distance holding her long brown hair against the side of her face in the turbulent air.

Dazzling little white clouds sailed across the deep-blue summer sky as we travelled the long straight roads. Barely a word passed between us as the sun beat down on our heads. We were warm, happy, feeling more like tourists than soldiers.

As we approached the Seine the streets became wider, the buildings more pleasing to the eye. It was a pleasure to drive along well-made roads free of rubble, to see the citizens go about their everyday life. Thankfully this beautiful city, Paris, had been largely spared the attention of our *Stukas*.

A wide bridge lined with ornate street lamps carried us over the Seine. Boris squealed like an excited child, pointing into the distance. 'Look, look, the Eiffel Tower.'

Most of us had seen the newsreels showing Hitler admiring this spectacular feat of engineering and we were disappointed to see it slip behind a row of trees without fist paying a visit. Soon, we came to a halt on an immense plaza, at the edge, I thought, of some extensive park. The passenger door of the cab slammed and our *Uscha* appeared at the side of the truck.

'Everybody out.'

We jumped down and stood wide-eyed, drinking in the beauty of our surroundings.

'Come,' said our *Uscha*, 'there is something I wish to show you.'

We followed like obedient schoolboys on a day trip as our *Uscha* marched us briskly towards a tall stone obelisk at the edge of the plaza.

'Granite,' announced the *Uscha* on reaching the base of the obelisk, 'from Luxor.'

I let my gaze drift over the mysterious symbols carved into its surface, towards the pointed pinnacle.

'The hieroglyphs tell the story of Ramses the First and Second, Pharoes of ancient Egypt,' continued our *Uscha*. 'The inscriptions are more than 3000 years old. Now turn around.'

We had stopped not at the edge of a park, as I had at first thought, but near the entrance to a magnificent boulevard lined either side by rows of trees.

'The Avenue des Champs Elysée,' declared our *Uscha* like a pompous tour guide. 'Those splendid marble statues at either side of the road are the Horses of Marly – as you see their strength is subdued by their grooms, a wonderful metaphor for man's power over the forces of nature. In the distance you can see the Arc de Triomphe, the tallest archway in the world – you will soon get a closer look at that,' he said turning back towards the waiting truck, 'but not today.'

Leaving the leafy boulevards behind, we drove along narrow streets with blocks of flats forming cliff faces on either side. Every window was open, shutters flung back against the wall, to capture any breeze that might temper the rising heat. The name of the street stuck in my memory, probably because of its surprising name, Rue d'Amsterdam. A turn took us into a generous boulevard with a central reservation thick with trees, welcome shade for citizens who went about their business without showing the slightest inclination to concede that their country was under enemy occupation.

'*Die Rote Mühle.*' exclaimed Boris pointing to an incongruous red windmill perched on top of a low building, the famed *Moulin Rouge*.

Our truck's tyres squealed as we came to an abrupt standstill on the hot cobblestones. At the side of the truck, stood a man astride a tricycle laden with baguettes a metre long, his eyes silently scolding us with a look that said, 'Watch where you're going why don't you.'

To our delight, we spent the rest of the afternoon in the *Moulin Rouge* watching the shapely chorus girls dance as we sipped cool beer.

❦·❦

Several days after our visit to the *Moulin Rouge*, we revisited Paris. It was pleasant enough just to be able to stroll in the shade of the trees but inevitably it seemed, we found ourselves in a bar close to a *Soldatenheim* set up by the *Wehrmacht*. As soon as we sat at a table, the girls in the bar swooped on us, pressing their lithe bodies against our backs, pulling up chairs to sit with their arms around our shoulders. Of course they were prostitutes, but their scent, the cool stroke of their soft fingers on my cheek, enflamed the innate urge that obliges young men to seek the company of young women. We bought them drinks, laughed at their broken German until one of the girls, young and beautiful, began to sing *J'attendrai*. My spine seemed to melt, shivers of pleasure surged across my skin. Desire and nostalgia merged into a single glorious emotion for which I have no name.

A faint blush came to the girl's pale cheeks as the last note left her lips. A burst of loud applause from everyone in the bar shattered an appreciative moment of silence. The girl smiled demurely and lowered her eyes as we broke into our own song, *Das ist Berlin*.

Suddenly the door of the bar crashed open to reveal our Austrian *Uscha* carrying a girl under his arm, her legs flailing the air. None of us had noticed him leave but we laughed heartily at his reappearance. The girl shrieked something in French as he lowered her to her feet. Her companions, sitting with us at the table, gasped as if some miracle had been revealed to them.

'What is it?' I asked them.

The girls looked at each other then burst into squeals of delight. One of them, rushed up to our giant *Unterscharführer*, slipped a hand over his crotch, and gasped, '*Mon Dieu.*'

Though I knew she was a prostitute, my dreams for the next few nights took me back to the bar in Paris, to the girl who sang so beautifully. What was a nice girl doing working in such a place? A cliché of course, but I was too young at the time to realise the foolishness of my infatuation. I imagined holding her hand, kissing her lips. Even in daytime, my thoughts returned to the bar where she worked.

❦ ❦

A *Rottenführer* from the quartermaster's store turned up at evening roll call with a measuring tape over his shoulder. Beside him, an assistant stood holding a clipboard.

'Today I have the pleasure of measuring you for the new black dress uniforms you will wear at the victory parade in Berlin – when we have won the war,' boasted the *Rottenführer*. 'You must all look impeccable in front of the *Führer*. It will be a very special day for the whole world.'

Since I had never had one of these smart uniforms, I looked forward to visiting the photographer's studio where my mother now worked, to have my photograph taken while wearing it.

Having completed his measurements, the *Rottenführer* made a further announcement. 'As you might have heard, *Hauptsturmführer* Springer has been transferred from *3.Kompanie* to *1.Kompanie*. As a mark of respect and thanks for his men, he and a few fellow officers have, at some risk to themselves, travelled unarmed into the unoccupied zone while posing as businessmen to acquire some of those items that are, for the moment, unavailable in the shops back home. You may purchase these at the *Kompanie* shop when off duty.'

It was an offer most of us accepted. I bought a silk scarf and two pairs of silk stockings, treasures to send home to my mother who I had not seen since I left for the *Ostfront* the previous summer.

❦ ❦

Reinforcements, their young and eager faces bronzed by the strong French sunshine, were arriving in droves but none had yet found their way to our *Kompanietrupp*. Fresh combat uniforms were issued and we cleaned our vehicles, including the new ones that had just arrived, until not a single speck of mud or dust remained on them. An air of excitement enveloped the whole *Kompanie*.

At morning roll call, an officer made a proclamation, 'As you may have suspected, over the last few days preparations have been in progress for a special occasion. In a few days, the whole of the *Leibstandarte* will gather in Paris to take part in a grand parade on the Champs Elysée. Nothing will be allowed to interrupt this event, not even a bombing raid by the British. Every man must look his best for this event – boots and weapons must be polished till they gleam – no dirt under the fingernails.'

A few days later, with our equipment and personal possessions stowed in our truck, we set off for Paris to join with the other battalions of the *Leibstandarte*, which now consisted of around 20,000 men and dozens of new tanks, artillery pieces and *Flak* batteries – everything that a fully equipped Panzer division should have.

We arrived in the assembly area and waited to take our place in the column of vehicles now stretching along the entire length of the sun-drenched Avenue des Champs Elysée. At last, our truck joined the parade. We stiffened our shoulders and looked straight ahead, determined to look our best for our leader, 'Super Sepp Dietrich'. Soon we were passing between the magnificent Horses of Marly.

Wehrmacht soldiers lined the roadsides. Behind them, rows of French civilians looked on from the shade of the trees. To our right, as we approached the Arc de Triomphe, stood *Generalfeldmarshall* von Rundstedt, Commanding Officer of the Army in France, with our diminutive steel-helmeted Sepp Dietrich by his side. At the precise moment we came alongside them, our heads turned smartly towards the admiring generals. Von Rundstedt acknowledged our passing with a nod of his Field Marshal's baton. After the terrible battering we had taken in Russia, the *Leibstandarte* was once more a force capable of executing the Will of our *Führer*.

⁂

After the parade, we drove to a field on the outskirts of Paris where it seemed every high-ranking German in France had assembled – Generals of the *Waffen SS* and *Wehrmacht*, Admirals of the *Kriegsmarine* and Chiefs of the *Luftwaffe* – to witness a demonstration of our assault tactics using live ammunition.

At the end of the manoeuvres, we packed our equipment. As I passed a telephone box to Boris – stripped to the waist as he stood on the back of our truck – he rolled his eyes in warning. I glanced over my shoulder to see Sepp Dietrich in the company of several high-ranking officers. Although they remained too far away to hear exactly the words that passed between them, it was clear that praise was gushing from their smiling mouths.

'They love our Sepp,' said Boris, hands on hips, watching the entourage pass between the rows of vehicles.

'We all do,' I chirped, 'he's the pride of Germany – I don't know if we could have survived Russia without him.'

'He's so small compared to us,' said Boris. 'Who would expect that a little man could be such a fine leader?'

'Boris,' I said patiently, 'Napoleon was no giant.'

'No, but they say our Austrian *Unterscharführer* is – in more ways than one,' he laughed.

The story of our Austrian *Uscha* amusing the prostitute in Paris by hanging a bucket full of water on his erect penis had done the rounds.

'Well, sometimes size does matter,' I conceded.

13
Transfer to Normandy

After packing our equipment onto our trucks, we drove to the west, to a village near Francheville in Normandy where we took up quarters in a large room above the restaurant of a hotel set in an idyllic leafy spot close to a stream. A few days later, news came of my promotion to *Sturmmann*, the first step on the promotion ladder. Sepp Dietrich himself signed the relevant documents in Saint Quentin. Immediately, I wrote to my parents to tell them my news.

The perpetually dejected look on the hotel proprietor's face betrayed the dismay he felt at our presence but, no doubt hoping we soon leave, he never complained and we more or less kept out of his way. A delivery of proper bunk beds and lockers, which we installed in our room, served only to darken his mood. As in the Lichterfelde barracks, each locker was shared by two men, an affirmation of the mutual trust that extended to the battlefield. We arranged everything in the room so that a gable end was free to allow one of our *Kameraden*, who was handy with a paintbrush, to decorate the wall with an enormous eagle grasping a swastika in its talons, similar in design to the badges sewn onto the sleeves of our tunics. This artwork was a sight that brought an involuntary grunt of disapproval to the proprietor's throat when he first saw it but it made us feel more at home.

The hotel proprietor's mood slumped further when we welcomed fresh recruits to our *Kompanietrupp*. Among them Heinz Ellers, Heinz König, a chap called Warnicke and another by the name of Bruder who was to become our driver. These were all the type of men we expected to welcome as *Kameraden*, tall and in prime physical condition, but there was one chap who didn't fit the bill at all.

'You must have got yourself lost my friend,' remarked Boris.

The recruit looked at him accusingly. 'What do you mean?'

'This is the *Leibstandarte*,' said Boris, as if no further explanation was required.

'What are you talking about?' challenged the misfit.

'Well,' said Boris, 'you're so – how can I put this – hmm, small.'

'Sepp Dietrich's not much taller than me,' said the recruit indignantly.

'You can hardly compare yourself with him,' retorted Boris striking an aggressive pose with his square chin thrust towards the little man.

Not wishing to get off to a bad start with the new arrival, I struck up a more friendly tone. 'What's your name?'

'Heuss,' answered the recruit aloofly.

Boris, annoyed by the arrogant attitude of the little man, was growing red in the face. 'Heuss – is that supposed to tell me something?'

'My father is a professor at the University of Stuttgart.'

'Ah, pulling strings,' said Boris slowly shaking his head.

Once their excitement had quietened down, the new arrivals started to blend well with the rest of the *Kompanietrupp*. Although training and guard duty filled most of our days, morning roll call took place later than usual, sometimes not until 8 am. It quickly became our custom during fine weather to take our evening meal – sandwiches usually – sitting stripped to the waist at a long wooden picnic table under a tree in the grounds of the hotel. On one such sunny evening, we were discussing whether we should complete a form issued earlier in the day. Signing this form would release us from our membership of the church and therefore of the payment of *Kirchensteuer* – a small tax deducted from our wages to help pay for the upkeep of the churches in Germany. Though I did, and still do, believe in an ultimate Creator of the Universe, I decided the money would be better in my pocket than in the coffers of the church and duly signed the release form. Every Catholic in the *Kompanietrupp* declined this opportunity, deciding to remain faithful to his church.

As the sun sank behind the trees lining the nearby roadway, our conversation turned inevitably to girls, girls we had seen in the streets or in shops but had remained, as always, out of reach. To my immediate right was Heinz Ellers and sitting beyond him was Ferch, the handsomest man in our troop, if not the whole of *4.Kompanie*.

'I tell you,' said Ellers, turning to Ferch, 'they were looking straight at me – right into my eyes – they were practically begging me to speak to them.'

I ruffled his hair as he spoke. 'It's the blond hair Benjamin, and the youthful looks.' Because Heinz Ellers was the youngest member of our *Kompanietrupp*, I had given him the nickname 'Benjamin' after the youngest of the twelve sons of the biblical Joseph.

A car drew up, out of sight behind the hedge that ran along the edge of the hotel's gardens. Two doors slammed. The lazy metallic squeak of the rusty gates to the yard brought us instinctively to attention. An unfamiliar high-ranking officer strolled towards us, hands clasped behind his back. At his side was a familiar face, an *Untersturmführer* from our own *Bataillon*.

'I've seen that officer before,' I whispered to Heinz Ellers, 'at *Kompanie* headquarters – a *Sturmbannführer* from Berlin.'

'What he's after with us?'

We fell silent as the two officers approached. The leaves of the trees rustled in the warm breeze.

'*Sturmbannführer* Linge is looking for personnel to assist him,' announced our *Untersturmführer*.

Linge looked us up and down, one after the other. After a moment of thought, he nodded curtly in Ferch's direction.

'What is your name?'

Ferch's body stiffened. '*Schütze* Ferch, *Sturmbannführer*.'

'Come out from behind that table to allow *Sturmbannführer* Linge to get a better look at you,' said the *Untersturmführer*.

Ferch, his cheeks reddening, shuffled from behind the table and strode up to the two officers.

Linge eyed Ferch slowly from head to toe then nodded curtly before turning to march back towards the gateway and the waiting car. I slapped Ferch on the shoulders. 'You lucky devil – do you know who that was?' I asked.

Ferch, puzzled, shook his head.

'Linge is Hitler's chief valet. You'll be back in Berlin, in the *Reichkanzlei*, before you can say *bon jour*.'

A few days later Ferch was told to collect his equipment and report to *Bataillon* HQ. That was the last I saw of him.

In mid August 1942, the Allies stormed ashore at Dieppe, about 100 kilometres to the north. We prepared for battle and moved out of our comfortable billet above the restaurant. Fortunately for us, the landing turned into a disaster for the Allies. They tried to create bridgeheads at several places along the coast but their tanks had floundered in the deep shingle on the beaches. Only one tank managed to get onto the esplanade and our artillery sank one of their warships. After taking heavy casualties, the survivors – mostly Canadians – were taken prisoner by *Wehrmacht* units. The mood amongst our men was one of elation – for the second time German forces had easily repelled an enemy force from the beaches of France.

Although the *Leibstandarte* was never called to defend against the raid on Dieppe, we were shortly afterwards sent to a nearby camp that had been set up to handle the many prisoners that had been taken. A handful of prisoners had set fire to the huts in the camp and had threatened to break out but our presence was required only for a few hours.

When we returned to our old billet above the restaurant by the river, we discovered that our painting of the eagle had been scraped from the wall. Of course, we were annoyed about this and promptly summoned the proprietor.

'I meant no offence gentlemen but surely you can understand my position,' he said shrugging his shoulders in Gallic fashion with the palms of his shaking hands upturned.

'Let's not make a big thing of this,' I said taking pity on the Frenchman. 'Find us some paint and that will be an end to the matter.'

We repainted the wall with our *SS* insignia but moved out of that billet only a few days later to a gardener's house in the grounds of an elegant château surrounded by rich apple orchards. In front of the château, standing in the idyllic gardens, was an enormous tree. Nearby, on the lawn, lay a broken flagpole, which we soon repaired. Every morning at 8 am our *Kompanie* gathered there for roll call as our flag was hoisted. However, I did not benefit from this late start to the day. I had to get up more than hour earlier than the rest of the men to collect the latest weather report from the radio post. After wakening *Hauptsturmführer* Waldmüller – now our *Kompanie* leader – at 7 am for his morning coffee and croissant, I read the weather report to him as he ate. It was around this time that I learned I had been awarded the *Ostmedaille*, a medal issued to those would had endured the hard winter on the *Ostfront*.

Heinz Ellers and I were appointed batmen to *Hauptsturmführer* Waldmüller who was very strict but always correct in his treatment of us. After roll call, we brushed down his uniform, cleaned his boots, and did any other little chores that came our way. This was not as tedious as it sounds because he had a radio and we could listen to German stations as we worked. On several occasions, we were present when Waldmüller was listening to the BBC and he warned us to guard our conversation against ever mentioning this.

Another of our tasks was to steam open letters written by the men in our *Kompanie*. Waldmüller examined every one in detail. If they contained information relating to our location in France, he simply tossed them into a waste paper bin, the contents of which we would later burn.

As Waldmüller's batman, one of my more unpleasant duties was to sort through the belongings of fallen *Kameraden* and it happened that amongst those of a soldier killed at the start of the Russian campaign, was a Belgian FN 7.65 calibre pistol. Having been stored for about a year in one of our trucks, the weapon was in a sad state with the barrel badly rusted. To free it off, I took it into the garden at the rear of the *Hauptsturmführer*'s quarters and fired a couple of rounds into the earth.

Hauptsturmführer Waldmüller was taking roll call the following Saturday. When it came to my name, his broad forehead creased into a heavy frown as he announced that with immediate effect I was to be punished with three days in the 'bunker' – a hut in a nearby wood with little more than four walls and a leaky roof. Somehow, Waldmüller had learned that I had taken a shortcut in cleaning the pistol by firing it into the ground.

There was a window in the 'bunker' but no glass to keep out the rain. The 'bed' was a plank of wood and a blanket and I settled down to serve my three days detention. Apart from being chilly at night, my time in the 'bunker' was not unpleasant. The fine summer weather brought many passers-by, some of whom were Flemish nationals. Often, they stopped to chat and gave me things to eat and drink. On Sunday evening, the *UvD* came to tell me that I was a free man – a day early. This was not an altruistic act of remission by *Hauptsturmführer* Waldmüller, he had simply missed my services and there was no record made of the 'offence' in my *Soldbuch*. On resuming my duties as batman, Waldmüller said nothing of the matter and our relationship promptly returned to normal.

Hauptsturmführer Waldmüller celebrated his thirtieth birthday the following Saturday – a day early – an event well attended by his many officer friends from *Bataillon* and *Kompanie* HQ. The merriment, fuelled by the consumption of large amounts of wine and cognac, continued in his office in the château for most of the afternoon. To round off the party Waldmüller led his guests to the gardens where he fired off a whole magazine from his P38 machine pistol at the nearby church tower. There was a loud ringing sound and a few sparks as the rounds struck the bell. Soon the priest appeared at the château, his stern face glowing with anger, but Waldmüller managed to placate him with his explanation that he was only having a bit of fun because it was his birthday. The following day I delivered Waldmüller's written apology to the church authorities.

꙳

At weekends, we came off duty after the evening meal and were free to do as we pleased but still there was no opportunity to get to know the local girls. Not that it mattered a great deal since the scant contact we did have left us in no doubt that there was little chance of striking up a friendship with them. We were young men reaching the peak of sexual desire and the situation was driving us insane.

As a distraction from thoughts of girls, a few of us from the *Kompanietrupp* took the opportunity to make a Saturday evening trip to the nearby village pub for a beer or two. Already in the bar were several Flemish chaps who were friendly towards us. One of our *Kompanietrupp* was from Cologne and spoke a dialect of German that our new friends could understand without great difficulty. Soon we were sitting round a table sharing tales as we sipped our beer, taking turns to buy rounds of drinks.

One of the Flemish chaps called out from the bar, 'Coffee for everyone?'

Not wishing to offend our new friends, we accepted the offer. The second cup seemed to taste better than the first, the third more pleasing than the second. Before long, I had lost count of the number of cupfuls I had taken. At last, after an enjoyable evening, it was time leave. We thanked our Flemish companions for their warm hospitality and, wishing them well for the future, stepped into the cool night air. It hit us like a sledgehammer. As we found out later, our Flemish friends had laced their, and our, coffee with Calvados, an apple brandy distilled locally.

Under the combined effect of caffeine and alcohol, we staggered down the road, holding each other up. Somehow Ellers and I became separated from the rest of our *Kameraden* and eventually realised we were lost. A railway embankment seemed familiar so we climbed up to the track and tried to focus on the surrounding landmarks to get our bearings. A whistle blew. Ellers thumped into me from behind and I found myself rolling down the embankment, arms and legs flailing the air.

'Erwin,' Ellers slurred when we came to a halt, 'watch out for trains.'

On Sunday morning, I woke with a pounding headache. How Ellers and I managed to find our way back to the gardener's house I shall never know. At breakfast, embarrassing stories of our exploits in the village, none of which I was able to recall, passed among our *Kameraden*. Some of these stories were, I dearly hope, fabrications of their vivid imaginations intended to cause us the maximum embarrassment.

We had heard the drone of enemy aircraft engines, even the hiss of wings cutting through the moist night air, but had never seen the aircraft themselves. Skilful pilots must have flown them as they came in low under cover of darkness with feathered engines to make their approach as quiet as possible. Despite our many patrols in the surrounding countryside, their landing strip remained undiscovered though we were certain each flight brought in agents and instructors for the French Underground fighters.

In an effort to track the incoming enemy aircraft, *Hauptsturmführer* Waldmüller had an observation platform installed high up in an ancient oak tree in the garden of the château. A ladder, secured by a rope, led up to the stout, almost horizontal, lower branches. Higher branches had been cut to allow a person to use the stumps to climb to a second ladder leading to the platform constructed in the sawn-off crown. It was a nerve-wracking experience to climb up to that tiny platform – large enough for just one person – but it offered excellent views of the surrounding countryside. A telephone allowed the rapid communication of any intelligence gathered by an observer perched up there. It was manned day and night.

One evening when I was on guard duty at the château, a party of high-ranking officers and their wives arrived to marvel at the platform. Among them was the recently appointed commander of our *Bataillon*, *Sturmbannführer* Albert Frey. Frey was from Heidelberg and the son of a master baker so at least I shared something in common with our highly decorated leader. His wife, Lotte, was a particularly fine-looking and vivacious woman with a marvellous figure. She insisted on clambering up to the observation platform 'just to see how the world looks from up there'. This was a courageous act for a woman. Even during daytime, it required a cool head to climb up to the platform and an even cooler head to tackle the descent. Having been on observation duty there on several occasions I can personally testify to that.

My stint as batman to Waldmüller came to and end when I was appointed courier to the *Kompanie*. Every evening, including the weekends, I carried written communications between *Bataillon* and *Kompanie* headquarters, a journey that took two hours on foot. One particularly wet evening, soon after I had heard the news that our divisional commander, Fritz Witt, had been to Paris to select girls for bordellos for the exclusive use of the *Leibstandarte*, I passed the local inn as usual. A bike was leaning unattended against the wall. I paused to stare at it for a moment thinking it would at least halve my journey time. However, it would be risky to remove the bike without the owner's consent and if caught, I would certainly be fined and, perhaps, stripped of my recent promotion. I looked to the sky; the grey sheet of cloud showed no sign of lifting. I grabbed the handlebars, swung my leg over the bar and pedalled hard, hoping to avoid being spotted. Having completed my journey to *Bataillon* HQ, I pedalled back to the inn as fast as I could thinking that, if the bike had been reported missing, the military police would already be waiting there for me. Luckily, the bike's temporary absence passed unnoticed so I put it back exactly where I had found it and, having worked up a good thirst, called into the inn for a beer. Standing at the bar was one of our Flemish friends. I bought him a drink and told him my tale about the bike.

'Ah, that would be my bike you're speaking about,' he chuckled. He slapped my shoulder. 'Don't worry about it – the state I'm in I don't think I could manage to ride it anyway.'

14

Little Diversions for the Young Men of the *Leibstandarte*

Fritz Witt's trip had not been in vain. The prostitutes he found in Paris were installed in a hotel close to *Kompanie* HQ. Evidently he had reached the conclusion that it would be better for his soldiers to visit a properly run establishment rather than pick up local prostitutes and risk infection with a sexually transmitted disease – after all, a sick soldier is not a fighting soldier.

With my nineteenth birthday only a few months away, I decided it was time to lose my virginity. By the time I turned into the street where the hotel was located, my nerves were jangling, my legs turning to jelly. Two men from another *Kompanie* were hanging around the door of the hotel smoking cigarettes. They spotted me – it was too late to turn back.

I handed my rifle to the *UvD* inside the doorway and went into the restaurant. Girls milled around, exchanging touches and smiles with the *Waffen SS* men sitting at the tables. The atmosphere was relaxed, the room filled with the over-loud babbling of the intoxicated visitors. I went to the bar to order a beer.

The full-bosomed barmaid smiled. 'Ah, a new customer -how old are you?'

'Eighteen.'

As she leaned forward to fetch a bottle of beer from beneath the counter, she caught me staring at her décolleté. 'Are you looking for a girl?'

The words sent a tingle of excitement surging through every nerve in my body. All I had to do now was say *ja*. I looked her straight in the eyes to give my reply but all that came out of my mouth was a frog-like croak.

A wave of the barmaid's hand brought a woman of about thirty to my side.

'This is the *Puffmutter*,' said the barmaid, 'she'll fix you up with a girl.'

Hands on hips, the *Puffmutter* looked me up and down. 'I have just the right girl for you,' she said beckoning me to follow, 'you don't need to look any further.'

In a whirl, I found myself paying the fee for a green ticket on which was written a room number and a girl's name, 'Yvonne'. The *Puffmutter* ushered me to a medical orderly sitting at a desk at the foot of a flight of stairs. He thrust a freshly laundered towel into my hand.

'Show me your ticket,' he yawned. He glanced at it and granted himself a lazy smile. 'Ah, Yvonne, she's nice,' he said, recording her name on a form. 'First time?'

I nodded.

'Show me your condom.'

I fumbled inside my tunic and pulled out one of my three standard issue condoms.

'When you're finished I want to see that filled. Don't throw it away.'

I nodded again, this time noticing a shallow tray draped with a white cloth on the desk.

'Room nine – you have fifteen minutes,' he said and, with a sideways jerk of his head, signaled for me to go upstairs.

Hardly enough time, I thought, as I made every effort to refrain from running up the steps. Breathless with excitement I hurried along the dimly lit corridor looking for the designated number. With white knuckles, I rattled on the door of room 9. The lock clicked and the door opened to reveal a pretty young woman. I showed her my ticket wondering if I was in a dream. It was the girl who had sung so beautifully in the bar in Paris but, naïvely, I was disappointed when she showed no sign that she had recognized me. I mumbled, 'Yvonne?'

'*Oui,*' she said reaching out to take my hand to lead me to a double bed in the corner of the dingy room. 'Give me your condom and take off your clothes,' she said in a way that suggested this was no more than a perfectly rehearsed stock phrase in a language that was completely foreign to her.

As I undressed, Yvonne undid the tie of her chiffon nightdress to reveal her small conical breasts. I had never seen a naked woman before let alone stripped off in front of one. Even before I had removed my underwear I was fully primed, ready to enjoy my first sexual encounter.

Yvonne sat on the edge of the bed and took the condom from its packing. With cool fingertips she slowly unrolled the rubber over my penis – the only prelude to an act of mating that was otherwise without the usual rituals of love.

In less than five minutes, I had performed the deed that broke my virginity. But, as they say, you never forget your first time. At the foot of the stairs, I held the used condom between my thumb and forefinger to allow the medic to peer at it. Satisfied it had been properly used, he reached under his desk to fetch a small bucket and raised it towards me. I let the thing drop to join the slimy mass of rubber already lining the bottom of the container.

'Now drop your trousers,' ordered the medic as he slipped the bucket under the desk. With a deft movement of his hand, he whisked away the cloth covering the waiting tray to reveal a large syringe filled with an ominous brown liquid. Before I had time to think, he gripped my penis and thrust the blunt needle deep into my urethra. I winced as he slowly squeezed the plunger of the syringe, forcing the liquid, a sulphonamide solution, into me. It was a most unpleasant feeling.

'You'll be fine in an hour or so,' assured the medic when the procedure was complete. He franked the form on his desk with the date and location of the bordello. Handing it to me he said, 'Now listen carefully, don't lose this – put it in your *Soldbuch* – it proves you have been properly sanitized. If you come down with anything nasty, you must show it to your *Kompanie* doctor. Keep it for ten weeks.'

❧·❧

Just days before Christmas 1942, Ellers and I were ordered to report to a local garage late in the evening where we were to work through the night to avoid disrupting the garage's usual work. We arrived to find half a dozen vehicles belonging to our *Kompanie* parked in the yard. Inside the garage, the owner stood impatiently beside one of our trucks, its lights and windows taped over, ready to give a ten-minute lesson in spray-painting.

'It looks like we're heading for Africa,' said Ellers as we sprayed the first truck with sand-coloured paint.

'Well Benjamin, they say it gets hot enough to fry eggs on the tank turrets,' I quipped, 'but at least we won't be tortured and killed if we are captured by the British.'

Our work in the garage lasted several nights. Intoxicated by the fumes of the cellulose paint thinners and the thought of the heat of North Africa, we sprayed the final vehicle. As we cleaned the spray guns, the growl of a truck engine outside rattled the rusting corrugated iron sheets that formed the door of the garage. The driver came in carrying the first of a dozen canisters of paint. 'The colour's been changed. You've to start repainting the trucks white – without delay – looks like it's back to the *Ostfront* for us.'

The men in our *Kompanie* treated the news of our impending return to the *Ostfront* with magnanimity – after all, we were the *Führer's* elite regiment, the *Leibstandarte SS Adolf Hitler*, we took orders without complaint, fought with honour.

❧·❧

My brother and his fiancée had decided to hold their wedding on Christmas day 1942. I had been granted leave to attend the ceremony in Berlin and was looking forward to the event. However, my fame as a baker had evidently spread among the officers and Waldmüller asked if I would mind preparing a Christmas treat for the whole of *4.Kompanie*. It seemed fate had me marked out as a baker and once more, I 'agreed' to a 'request'. Being a very fair man, Hans Waldmüller assured me that my leave had been deferred rather than lost.

During the three days in the run up to Christmas, I prepared a treat of cakes and cookies for the men in *4.Kompanie* while the French bakers carried on their work at night, as usual. Unfortunately, I developed a rash on my hands from the exposure to yeast and dough. Knowing that soldiers with an infection of any sort were not allowed home leave, I put this prospect to the back of my mind and enjoyed the most memorable Christmas party of my life – a happy time spent in the company of *Kameraden* with whom I had shared so many dangers. We dined like royalty in the château with roast piglet and plenty of accompaniments such as roast potatoes and vegetables on offer. Heinz König, we discovered to our surprise, was an excellent piano player and provided non-stop entertainment.

The day after Christmas, I reported to the *Kompanie* doctor. Although the rash had improved with only a slight redness remaining between my fingers, he refused to sign my pass. I had already missed Horst's wedding and the prospect of having no leave at all, I knew, would break my mother's heart. She had not seen me since I left Lichterfelde barracks in the summer of 1941. When I mentioned my lost leave to *Hauptsturmführer* Waldmüller, he was sympathetic to my plight.

'Give me the pass – and don't mention this to anyone,' he said. 'I was once a police detective.' With a satisfied grin, he handed me the pass with the forged signature of the doctor without explaining anything of the circumstances in which this devious skill would be necessary in the course of his duties as a detective.

I bought a bottle of Calvados at the canteen before making my way to the rail station in Evreux on the evening of Monday 28 December. It seemed half the *Wehrmacht* garrison had gathered to there to catch the same train. It was a struggle to push my way into a carriage and I had to stand all the way to Berlin, a journey that took more than twelve hours.

❧·❧

By chance, my mother was looking out the open window of our flat as I made my way along Strausberger Strasse. She slammed the window down and, despite the icy breeze, reappeared on the street without her coat.

'Oh Erwi, it's been such a long time,' she sobbed through tears of joy as she ran to me. 'You're father and I were so worried about you. I hope that phone call from Horst didn't get you into trouble – I put him up to it you know.'

'No Mama, it didn't.' When in Taganrog, more than a year earlier, I had been assigned to telephone duties at *Kompanie* HQ when Horst had made the call. Because of the helter-skelter nature of our advance, I had not had the opportunity to write home and my parents, fearing the worst, had asked Horst to use his position as a telephonist with the Air Ministry to try to get in touch with our *Kompanie*. By a miracle of effort, he managed to arrange the necessary connections. When I picked up the telephone I handed it to one of our officers saying, 'A call from Berlin.' I almost fell from my stool when he handed the phone back saying the call was for me. To have heard Horst's voice from so far away, to know that he had taken so much trouble to get in contact with me, touched my heart and for a few moments, I had been overcome by a longing to be back in Berlin with my family. I put my arm around her shoulder and squeezed gently. '*Mutti* – it's good to be home.'

I spent a quiet New Year's Eve with my parents. On New Year's Day, we travelled in light snow to Erkner, on the south side of Berlin, to visit the home of Horst's new in-laws. Unfortunately, I had left my billet in France too soon to receive the usual Christmas gift of *Schnapps* that the *Führer*, at his own expense, gave to every man in the *Leibstandarte* – a gesture of thanks repeated at Easter. However, I had a bottle of Calvados I had purchased before leaving France and took it with me as a present to our hosts. Horst, on leave from the Air Ministry, and his new wife arrived shortly after us with a present of biscuits and cakes. We spent a fine day exchanging family tales before returning to Berlin.

'Son, son, waken up, there's an urgent telegram for you.'

I rubbed my eyes. It was already half-way through the first day of 1943. 'What does it say?'

'You have to return to your *Kompanie* on 4 January.'

Did that mean I had to leave for France on that date, or did I have to be there in three days? My father and I were of the opinion that I should leave immediately but my brother Horst, who visited later that afternoon, said I should wait until the fourth since there would be hardly any trains running over the weekend.

In the end, I decided there was enough ambiguity in the instruction for me to remain with my family for three more days.

⚜ ⚜

I reported to the guard at the *Schlesischer Bahnhof* on the morning of 4 January and was relieved to see another soldier from our *Kompanie* already waiting on the platform. Soon another turned up, then another. Finally, there were eight of us looking for transport back to our unit in France. Since there were no trains available, we reported to our barracks in Lichterfelde where we hung around for a day before being sent to the Magdeburg barracks where a *Totenkopf* unit was awaiting transport to Russia.

On arrival in Magdeburg, we made sure our papers were made up to date to prevent any difficulties that might arise if we were stopped by the police, an important issue because we had to account for our whereabouts at all times. Again, we were forced to hang around for a few hours before being told we could catch a train that was due to leave from Berlin the following day.

We were in a sort of limbo where no one was responsible for us and had had nothing to eat or drink the whole day. In desperation, we took our packs to my parents' home for safekeeping before deciding to make our way to the Oranienburg concentration camp, about an hour's train-ride to the north, where we knew of a canteen that served meals to the guards from the *Totenkopf* division. We made our presence known to the officers there and explained that we needed provisions for our trip back to our unit. They gave us food and drink, including bottles of *Schnapps*, and two large cartons of cigarettes. Since we had no money, we had to sign for the provisions, but who eventually paid for them, I shall never know.

We left Oranienburg to spend the night at my family home where we pushed my parents' beds together – it was not unusual at that time for married couples to sleep in separate beds – and four of us slept head to tail across them while the remainder of my *Kameraden*, and my parents, spent the night on the floor.

The next day we travelled to Evreux and arrived there to see a train loaded with white-camouflaged vehicles departing from a platform on the opposite side of the station. A few enquires soon revealed that it was the train taking our regiment back to Russia. Luckily, we were able to hitch a ride with another train that left a few days later.

15

Return to Russia

As the days dragged by, the landscape grew inexorably whiter until sometime around the middle of January 1943, our train came to a halt at Poltava, in the Ukraine. Without leaving the station, I managed to find another train carrying a *Panzer* unit heading for the sector where *4.Kompanie* was in position. After a few hours, it came to a halt at a desolate little station where the *Panzer* unit unloaded their vehicles, many of which, as if in complaint against the bitter cold, were reluctant to start. I went from vehicle to vehicle asking the drivers if they were heading for the sector where *4.Kompanie* was stationed but was out of luck. As the trucks and armoured vehicles disappeared down a snowy track I was left with no choice but to wait until morning with the remaining fifty or so men from the *Panzer* unit. A hard frost set in as the sun, as pale as a full moon, sank into the thin cloud that had settled over the vast dazzling landscape. My cheeks tingled in the cold air, a familiar feeling, as the encroaching darkness brought its icy stillness.

The angry zip-zip of bullets shattered the wintry silence. Only the flashes of light from the muzzles of their weapons betrayed the position of our attackers. Suddenly, we found ourselves in a battle zone without a secure front line.

'The bastards are less than half a kilometre away,' yelled our only officer. 'Set up a perimeter in the rail yard – we're sitting ducks on the platform.'

Somehow, we managed to reach the cover offered by some crates scattered in the rail yard without taking any casualties. After a few minutes, the enemy gunfire stopped as suddenly as it had begun. We waited, shivering, every German eye peering into the deepening gloom.

A shout went up. 'Ivans – by the track.'

I could just make out groups of ghost-like figures in white camouflage suits. Less than a hundred metres away, they were manoeuvring towards us through the deep snow. Our two machine guns opened up, breaking the silence of the night with their mechanical rattle. With no shortage of ammunition, we continued firing until there was no sign of movement near the track. Frost glittered on every surface as wolves, eyes glowing like white fire, ventured ever closer to the scent of spilled Russian blood. Pitiable whimpers followed the sharp crack of a rifle shot. Our faces blue with cold, we welcomed the return of the *Panzer* unit the following morning. A radio link was quickly established with *4.Kompanie* and, an hour later, a truck arrived to carry me to my unit.

❦·❦

Despite the Russian attack at the rail station, I managed to hang on to the bottle of *Schnapps* and several cartons of cigarettes I had picked up in Oranienburg, most of which I sold when I arrived at the *Kompanie* command post. I lodged my gains for safekeeping at the orderly's hut but held on to a few packs of cigarettes and the bottle of *Schnapps* to share with my *Kameraden*. Finally, I located my *Kompanietrupp* in a well-made bunker.

'Couldn't drag yourself away from that little French tart in the hotel, eh Erwin?'

'How are things back in Berlin?'

One after the other, my *Kameraden* shook my hand, slapped my back, laughed like excited schoolboys. At last I was 'home' and relieved to find there had been no further losses while I played catch up. I passed round the bottle of *Schnapps*, each man taking a hefty swig to fend off the cold, then rummaged under my camouflage jacket to find a full pack of cigarettes to press into Boris' hand.

A wide grin flashed across his face, 'I was beginning to think the Tommy bombers had dropped one on your head.'

'We were messed about in Berlin,' I explained, 'sent here, there, everywhere, before I managed to get a train to Evreux – finally got a lift with a train carrying a *Panzer* unit but you wouldn't believe how slow it was.'

❦·❦

Thinly spread on the hills overlooking the frozen River Donets, *4.Kompanie* defended a sector of the eastern approaches to Kharkov. I laid the necessary telephone connections – 'puppet strings' as we called them – to link the scattered machine-gun crews with the *Kompanie* command post. *Alles gut!*

Within a few days of settling into my new position, the Russians began an artillery barrage during which the telephone connection with the command post was broken. It was my duty to repair the damage as quickly as possible, a dangerous task when under fire. I followed the cable from the front-line telephone through deep snow, my footsteps breaking unpredictably through the crusty surface. Rivulets of sweat trickled down my back and brow. Panting out white clouds of breathed air that hung around my face in the still air, I came to the broken end of the cable but the section leading to the command post was lost in the shell-churned snow. With bullets buzzing too close for comfort, I began a systematic search until I found the missing cable-end but it was too short to reach the wire from the front line and I had to repair the gap with a length of cable taken from the drum I carried. I took the wire strippers from the leather pouch on my belt, knelt beside the broken cable, and took off my gloves. Before I had completed the first connection, my fingers were numb. I dropped the strippers, fumbled for them in the crystalline snow. As I worked on the second connection, my fingers were already blue and painful, almost too painful to manipulate my tools. When I completed the repair, I looked around to get my bearings and noticed a squad of Russians at a distance of around a hundred metres. One of them called to me. I could hardly believe my eyes – the soldier was wearing a steel helmet and a skirt. And she wasn't the only one – the whole squad wore skirts. For some reason they withheld their fire though I must have presented a tempting target. Yet again, my guardian angel had been by my side.

Back in our cosy bunker, my *Kameraden* greeted the news of my encounter with a troop of women with calls of derision. The clever remarks came thick and fast.

'You must be desperate for a girl Erwin – that little maid from Paris has gone to your head.'

'Did you ask them for a date?'

'I said you would go blind.'

Everyone laughed and to tell the truth I was beginning to doubt my own eyes. However, the following day they saw for themselves that I hadn't been spinning a crazy tale.

Flares hissed into the deep black of the night sky then burst with the radiance of a million stars. Beneath the falling flares, the snowfields by the River Donets teemed with the ominous dark shadows of Russian infantry.

Our platoon leader yelled, '*Feuerfrei!*'

Firing at will, our machine gunners put their recently issued MG42s to lethal work. With their high rate of fire, they mowed down another night attack. By day, we came under constant artillery bombardment from the '*Ratsch-Bumms*', as we called the Russian howitzers because of the characteristic sound of their fire. We feared these weapons because they fired high velocity rounds that exploded a fraction of a second after the sound of the discharge reached our lines, allowing no time to dive for cover. Even more threatening was the sight of endless columns of Russian infantry, slithering like black snakes across the snowfields on the far side of the Donets, day after day, working their way around our southern flank to complete a deadly noose.

Exhausted after days without proper sleep and very little food, it was clear we would not be able to hold out against the anticipated onslaught. In darkness, with temperatures below minus-thirty degrees, we abandoned our well-prepared defence positions and made our way towards Rogan, a satellite town a few kilometres to the southeast of Kharkov.

We had only just set up our defence perimeter through the centre of Rogan when the Russians appeared in force. At times, the storm of bullets was so thick it was impossible to look out over a window ledge or wall without risking a bullet through the head. T-34 tanks supported by infantry broke through our defences. After three days of continual fighting – it might have been four – we withdrew to the open, hilly ground between Kharkov and Rogan, every one of us staggering on the very limits of endurance. On our right flank, across a ravine, *1.Kompanie* was taking a terrible pounding on a hill overlooking the main road to Kharkov. Gradually, the Russians were pressing us closer to the city centre for the *coup de grâce*.

Fortunately, we were under the command of 'Papa' Hausser. Having taken the lesson of Stalingrad taken to heart, he gave the order to pull back from the city. Just after midday on the 15 February – a date I remember because it was the day after my parents' wedding anniversary – we escaped through a corridor only a few hundred metres wide, on the western edge of the city.

Word spread soon after that Hausser, risking the severest of punishments, had saved our skins by his courageous decision to defy Hitler's order to hold Kharkov to the last man. To have a leader who cared about the men under his command was a great comfort to us. We knew he would never sacrifice us, *'seinen Jungs'*, 'his boys', to fulfil some futile order from above.

※･※

By the beginning of March 1943, the situation had improved. A growing Russian threat to the south had been eliminated. We were on the move to retake Kharkov, desperate to inflict a telling wound on the enemy, resolute in our will to repay 'Papa' Hausser for the loyalty he had shown us, determined to repay the Russians for our humiliating retreat just a few weeks earlier.

With our fellow *Waffen SS* formations *Das Reich* and *Totenkopf* on our flanks we pushed through a milky mist that obliterated the horizon, blurred the distinction between sky and ground. Every solid object took on a shade of grey, floated in a world without perspective or colour. Onwards we pushed, day and night, stopping only to shovel snow from the wheels of vehicles that had lost the road. Where the Russians had offered resistance their dead lay, ice caked around their eyes and mouths, faces locked in anguish by death's cold embrace. Here and there, frozen arms thrust stiffly through the snow as if summoning help. To me, they were no longer Bolsheviks – simply poor sods who had died defending their country.

A flash came from the barrel of one of our new Tiger tanks, only a few metres to my right. Suddenly, the frenzied roar of battle disappeared. I had learned the hard way that the blast from a Tiger's powerful gun leaves through side vents, the recoil brake. The supersonic blast battered my eardrums, leaving me unable to hear the approach of vehicles, incoming shells or the warning shouts of my *Kameraden* – a dangerous handicap on the battlefield. I was thankful when, after a few hours, my hearing slowly returned.

Over snow-covered fields, red with the reflected light of ferocious combat, our *Kampfgruppe* 'Frey' closed in on Kharkov along the main road connecting the city with Belgorod. Tracer bullets ignited the thatched roofs of cottages where we encountered resistance, the heat of the flames melting the ice on nearby picket fences. Steam rose from my uniform as I passed a burning windmill, its blades spinning madly as it flayed itself to death in a storm of swirling sparks.

At first light, the Russians made a determined effort to stop our progress with a surprise attack across the open spaces of an airfield on the northern edge of the city. A few kilometres to my right, our *Nebelwerfers* showered the defenders with a storm of rockets. Ahead, our Tigers clashed with Russian T-34s, throwing off their attack with ease. Draped in the vivid red of our swastika flags, our half-tracks pushed closer to the city centre.

Crouching at street corners, we watched our tank shells burst open buildings that served as nests of Russian resistance. Couriers on motorcycles raced back and forth with vital messages, their wheels churning the dirty, compacted snow. Deeper into the city, we found the defenders had barricaded the streets with burnt out vehicles and tank traps, forcing our *Panzers* to queue on the approach roads until our *Pionierkorps* cleared the blockages.

Street combat in winter was always a dangerous undertaking but in Kharkov the perils were exceptional. Perhaps this had something to do with the layout of the town or perhaps the enemy had developed new combat strategies. In either case, the Russians doggedly contested every house, every street corner. In places, knee-deep snow slowed our movement adding to the danger on streets where sniper fire was a constant threat.

As we fought from building to building, led by a wily *Oberscharführer* with whom we had fought many times, we came under small-arms fire from a handful of Russians sheltering in the entrance of an apartment block. Our *Oberscharführer* was on the opposite side of the road and opened fire on them, forcing the Russians to scarper down the road. We gave chase and managed to loose off a few rounds as they disappeared into a building that might have been a factory or warehouse. Our *Oberscharführer* followed them into the building. We dashed across the road to catch up and found ourselves at the foot of a stairwell. Leaping several steps with every stride, we began a mad rush up the stairs. A metallic crash from above brought us to an abrupt halt. We looked at each other, our eyes silently agreeing to continue our charge irrespective of the danger.

At the top of the stairwell, a heavy metal door barred our progress. Frantically, I tried the handle but the door was locked. A *Kamerad* pushed me to the side and kicked at the door. I joined in the assault, timing the blows of my rifle butt to coincide with his kicks but the heavily built door remained steadfastly shut. With the push into the centre of the city still going on outside, we had no choice but to abandon our rescue attempt. I can only guess at the fate of our *Oberscharführer*. We lost a fine *Kamerad* that day.

⚜

On the second day in Kharkov, I received an order to report to the *Kompanie* command post.

'*Sturmmann* Bartmann,' said the officer in charge, 'I have a little task for you.' He handed me an envelope saying earnestly, 'This letter concerns the movement of ammunition, make sure it gets to the supply depot. I'm sure you will understand that this mission is vital to our success in this battle.'

I had only a vague idea of the whereabouts of the supply unit from what I had seen as we fought our way into the city. '*Untersturmführer*, where exactly should I deliver the letter?'

The *Untersturmführer* screwed up his face and shook his head then, without any further words of explanation, gave a vague wave of his hand. 'I trust you'll find it.'

Darkness was falling as I began my journey along streets where vicious fighting had raged the whole day. Time after time – so it seemed to me – I got the risky jobs. I swallowed my irritation – an order had been issued and it was my duty to execute it irrespective of the risk.

Keeping to any cover that was at hand, I passed by buildings with blown out windows, good vantage points for lurking snipers. After several kilometres, following in reverse the route we took earlier in the day, I reached the outskirts of the city. A dim light came from a lonely house set back from the roadside and I wondered whether I should knock on the door to ask the occupants for directions. A moment's consideration led me to the conclusion that such exploration would be too perilous for a solitary soldier. I decided to press on through the darkness until I eventually came to a fork in the road. Which branch should I take? I hesitated for a moment before deciding to carry on to the right. After walking another kilometre along the deserted road, the dark figures of soldiers formed in the gloom. Were they Russians or Germans? I stood rooted to the spot. One of the figures moved towards me, waving a hand, signalling for me to come forward. A Russian voice called. A cold shiver rippled through my spine. Though my heart was pounding, I kept quiet and turned as nonchalantly as possible, to make my escape on shaking legs. The Russian called once more but I ignored him and carried on back the way I had come. Yet again, my guardian angel had been by my side.

When I reached the junction, I took the left fork. Before long, the outlines of vehicles formed in the eerie, faint blue light thrown up by the snow. This time I was more careful and crept forward until I could identify them as German. I shouted the password, '*Morgenstund.*'

A nervous sentry let me advance then an adjutant escorted me to the commanding officer's quarters where we found him fast asleep. The adjutant shook the officer's shoulder. '*Obersturmführer*, I'm sorry to have to waken you but there's an urgent message for you concerning the supply of ammunition.'

Bleary eyed, the *Obersturmführer* took the letter from my outstretched hand and began to read. '*Scheisse,*' he cursed, 'I'll have to move the whole garrison.' Staggering from his bed to grab his tunic, he turned on his adjutant. 'Well don't just stand there – get the men ready to move.'

I hitched a lift with them to the junction then returned on foot to my *Kompanie* command post. When I recounted my adventure to the officer who had sent me on this dangerous errand he simply replied, 'You were lucky.'

A board the size of a tabletop hung on a lamppost in Kharkov's town square. It carried the neatly hand painted words: *Platz der Leibstandarte.* That the renaming of a town square in the Ukraine in this manner – an apparently meagre token – should have filled me with pride may seem absurd now but it represented praise from commanders for whom I had the greatest respect, commanders who did not hide from the dangers their men faced.

Though the *Leibstandarte* had suffered thousands of casualties, I had come through the battle for Kharkov unscathed. The notion of a 'guardian angel' was no longer simply a synonym for 'good luck'. I was convinced such entities existed and that one of them had chosen me as a companion.

❧·❧

After our victory in Kharkov, we withdrew to the west, to Olshany where our *Pionierkorps* set up piping hot showers and a delousing facility. Just to feel clean was one of life's great pleasures for a soldier on the *Ostfront*. A period of rest and recovery followed – a sure sign we were being fattened up for yet another titanic struggle.

On one occasion, we had the choice of visiting the *Soldatenheim* in Kharkov where girls plied their trade, or the opera house. I elected to visit the opera where Mussorgsky's *Boris Godunov* was playing. Performed by an excellent cast, and well attended by our troops, it was a welcome respite from the hazards of war.

❧·❧

As a break from normal routine, our officers arranged a shooting competition between teams from different platoons. A nearby ravine with a cliff at one end provided a safe site to test our shooting skills – stray shots would cause no damage here. Targets were set up at 100, 200 and 500 metres. The prize was a box of cigars donated by an officer. Only the six best marksmen from each platoon were allowed to compete for this prize. *Obersturmführer* Fritz Lotter, our youthful *Kompanie* chief at that time, was the first to demonstrate his skills before the competition got properly underway. Then, one by one, the members of each team took their turn. I was pleasantly surprised to find that I came second, behind Lotter, with my score for 500 metres being particularly good. A football match pitting NCOs against officers extended the spirit of friendly competition. Having no football strips to identify the teams, the NCOs played stripped to their waists and long johns.

❧·❧

Our Berlin family home. 38 Strausberger Strasse is the opening under the round archway.

Showing off my new uniform, July 1941.

Time for a smoke, October 1941. I only started smoking after I arrived on the Eastern Front.

Winter begins to bite, October 1941.

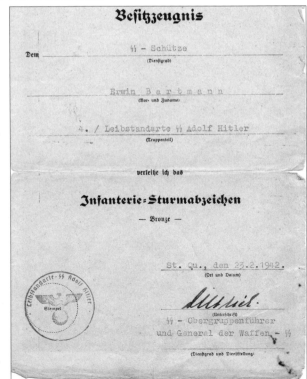

IM NAMEN DES FÜHRERS
UND
OBERSTEN BEFEHLSHABERS
DER WEHRMACHT
IST DEM

ᛋᛋ-Unterscharführer

Erwin Bartmann

AM 25.8.1942

DIE MEDAILLE
WINTERSCHLACHT IM OSTEN
1941/42
(OSTMEDAILLE)

VERLIEHEN WORDEN.

FÜR DIE RICHTIGKEIT:

ᛋᛋ-Sturmbannführer
und Kommandeur

This certificate, for the 1941/42 *Ostmedaille*, arrived shortly after my promotion to *Unterscharführer* in 1943 although I received the medal much earlier, while still a *Sturmmann*.

Besitzeugnis

Dem   ᛋᛋ - Schütze
(Dienstgrad)

Erwin Bartmann
(Vor- und Zuname)

4. / Leibstandarte ᛋᛋ Adolf Hitler
(Truppenteil)

verleihe ich das

Infanterie-Sturmabzeichen

— Bronze —

St. Qu., den 25.2.1942.
(Ort und Datum)

(Unterschrift)
ᛋᛋ - Obergruppenführer
und General der Waffen - ᛋᛋ
(Dienstgrad und Dienststellung)

Signed by Sepp Dietrich, commander of the *Leibstandarte*.

Spring 1942 by the Black Sea, after our withdrawal from Sambek.

Sojourn in France. The *Kompanietrupp* enjoy a meal in the shade of a
tree - a pleasant break from the rigours of the Eastern Front.

Taken shortly after my promotion to *Sturmmann*, a proud moment for me.

The star belonging to the cap badge given to me by a Russian POW.

Sunshine in Olshany. Our Russian hostess looked after us like a mother.

Larking about in the sunshine, Olshany 1943.

Testing our connections while keeping a look-out for the enemy.

On the road to Kharkov.

Myself with Horst dressed in his *Luftwaffe* uniform.

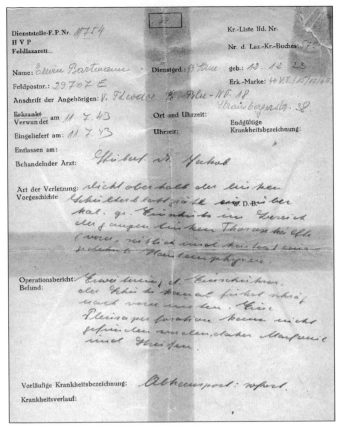

Medical report on my wound at Prokhorovka, written the day it happened.

The shrapnel that passed through my lung in Prokhorovka, small but so nearly deadly.

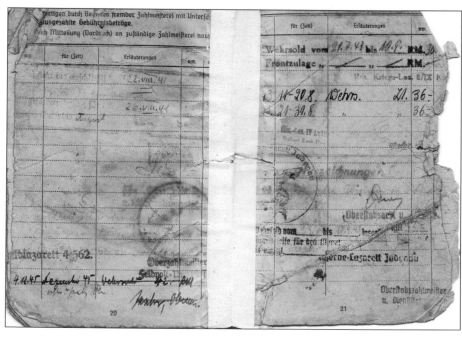

Besitzeugnis

Dem

SS.Stm. Erwin B a r t m a n n

(Name, Dienstgrad)

4./ I.Leibstandarte SS Adolf Hitler

(Truppenteil, Dienststelle)

ist auf Grund

seiner am 11.Juli 1943 erlittenen

ein maligen Verwundung — Beschädigung

das

Verwundetenabzeichen

in "S c h w a r z"

verliehen worden.

Judenau , den 30.August 19 43

(Unterschrift)

Oberstabsarzt u. Chefarzt

(Dienstgrad und Dienststelle)

The documentation accompanying my Wound Badge in Black.

Pages from my *Soldbuch* with details of my pay and the
stamp of the hospital in Judenau, near Vienna.

A fellow veteran informed me that a window-sized version of this picture looked down from the photographer's studio as the Russians entered Potsdamer Platz.

'The Three Musketeers' - with Gunter Schmidt, who worked on the *Reichsbahn*, and Horst Musch, who enlisted in the *Kriegsmarine*.

A girlfriend posing outside the Radio Station in Berlin at the last of their annual floral displays, 1943. I didn't meet her until about a year after this was taken.

My new cap with the wire removed, as was the fashion, taken autumn 1943.

Sharing a smile with a fellow machine-gun instructor while
stationed in Alt Hartmannsdorf, March 1945.

Horst and me, taken shortly after the birth of his first child.

POW camp near Aldershot. I'm fourth from the left, top
row. It seems I was fated to be a baker.

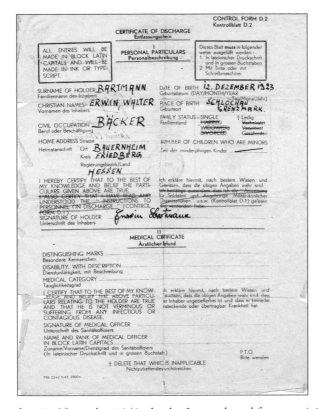

Paperwork issued on 27 November 1948, the day I was released from captivity in Scotland.
It entitled me to claim a German military pension for more than seven years' service.

Certificate No. **BNA** 39437   Home Office No.   B.84423.

BRITISH NATIONALITY ACT, 1948.

CERTIFICATE OF NATURALISATION

Whereas   Erwin Walter Bartmann

has applied to one of Her Majesty's Principal Secretaries of State for a certificate of naturalisation, alleging with respect to   himself the particulars set out below, and has satisfied the Secretary of State that the conditions laid down in the British Nationality Act, 1948, for the grant of a certificate of naturalisation are fulfilled :

    Now, therefore, the Secretary of State, in pursuance of the powers conferred upon him by the said Act, grants to the said

Erwin Walter Bartmann

this Certificate of Naturalisation, and declares that upon taking the Oath of Allegiance within the time and in the manner required by the regulations made in that behalf he   shall be a citizen of the United Kingdom and Colonies as from the date of this certificate.

In witness whereof I have hereto subscribed my name this *5th* day of *November*, 19 *55*.

HOME OFFICE,
LONDON.
                                      J a Newsam
                                    UNDER SECRETARY OF STATE.

PARTICULARS RELATING TO APPLICANT.

Full Name	Erwin Walter BARTMANN.
Address	13, Annandale Street, Edinburgh, 7, Midlothian.
Profession or Occupation	Baker.
Place and date of birth	Schlochau, Germany. 12th December, 1923.
Nationality	German.
Single, married, etc.	Married.
Name of wife or husband	Erika Ruth Edith.
Names and nationalities of parents	Theodor Friedrich and Katharine BARTMANN (German).

I took my Oath of Allegiance to the Queen on 5
November 1955 and became a British citizen.

An attractive Ukrainian woman in colourful traditional headdress welcomed Ellers, Bruder, König and me into her house – our billet – with the customary offering of bread and salt. Although still young with a complexion as fresh as a sunflower, she looked after us like a mother, preparing our meals and washing our clothes. Her German was good enough for her to be able to tell us that her husband was a pilot in the Soviet Air Force. She slept in the only bedroom while we shared the front room, the window of which looked out to the house where our battalion headquarters had been set up, on the other side of the road.

Though at first he contrived secretly to be alone with her, it soon became obvious that a relationship was developing between Bruder, our driver, and our Ukrainian hostess. As he was leaving the house one morning to carry out some routine maintenance work on the truck, he announced that he would be spending the night in the bedroom with her. 'Promise me – all of you – that you won't disturb us tonight,' he pleaded.

We chanted in unison, 'We promise.'

As soon as Bruder left, Ellers began a search of the cupboards. 'What luck – our pretty little hostess makes jam,' he declared, gleefully grabbing a handful of empty jars. 'All I need now is a ball of string to tie them to the bedsprings.'

That evening, Bruder smiled broadly as he went hand in hand with our hostess into the bedroom. Ellers threatened to giggle but König slapped a hand over Ellers' mouth before he lost control. Hardly able to contain our mirth, we listened and waited. Before too long, a single 'chink' of glass against glass came from the bedroom, then silence.

'*Scheisse* – he's found them,' whispered Ellers whose disappointment was quickly dispelled by a chorus of splendid chimes as jars containing differing amounts of water struck each other under the bed next door.

Bruder burst angrily from the bedroom but his protests drowned in our howls of laughter. It took our driver several days to see the funny side of Eller's prank.

Life was good in Olshany until tragedy struck one afternoon as I took a message into the battalion headquarters. Attracted by frantic screams, I turned to see two women amidst a crowd of children, grappling with a heavy German motorcycle that had fallen over. The dispatch rider, who happened to be leaving the headquarters, pushed past me and stormed into the crowd where two women, hands pressed to their cheeks, looked on in horror. I followed on behind to see what had happened.

'*Verdammt* – there's a kid under it,' groaned the dispatch rider as he hoisted the motorcycle onto its parking stand.

A woman lunged towards the child, a boy of six or seven, and in a frantic effort to revive the youngster, slapped his face. Her fruitless efforts ended with a cry of grief that struck into my heart like a sword. She took the limp body in her arms and rocked it like a baby, crying, 'Kolya, Kolya.'

Attracted by the commotion, women from the houses nearby quickly gathered around the dispatch rider, screaming at the tops of their voices as they flung their fists at him. In vain, he tried to explain that his machine must have fallen while the boy was playing on it.

Sturmbannführer Frey, organised a coffin for the youngster and issued orders for us to keep off the streets while the funeral took place in a nearby Catholic church.

16

Friendly Fire

As we drove northwards towards Bjelgorod, the ecstasy of victory shone in the faces of my *Kameraden*. Seduced into a delusion of invulnerability by mere survival, we had forgotten with ease the ghosts left to roam the ruins of Kharkov, forgotten too that capricious fortune was the arbiter of life and death.

Our column came to a halt in the shelter of a deep ravine. Clouds of dust settled around us as an *Oberscharführer* made his way to the side of our truck and called, '*Sturmmann* Bartmann – and you, König – scout out to the end of this ravine and tell us if Ivan is waiting for us – we don't want to drive straight into a trap. It's not suitable terrain for laying telephone cable. If you spot anything get your arses back here at the double.' There was a mocking quality to his voice, as if he took delight in assigning this dangerous task to my young companion and me.

We trotted along the road, glancing back occasionally to judge the distance we had travelled. Soon our column was lost behind the lush buttresses sweeping down from the high ridges on either side of the ravine. We were alone in enemy territory, ambush territory. After a couple of kilometres, we stopped to recover our breath at a spot where the rift in the landscape opened into a wide valley.

'No sign of Ivan,' said König pushing his helmet to the back of his head to wipe the sweat from his brow with the sleeve of his tunic.

'No sign – but they have snipers that have had plenty practice. We'd never be able to spot them – too well camouflaged.' I pointed to a lonely haystack in an open field. 'We'll take cover in there and make some observations.'

König, now twenty metres ahead of me, was near the haystack when the sound of an approaching aircraft came from behind. He turned to look at the sky.

'Don't worry,' I shouted casually, 'you'll soon get to know the sound of Russian engines.'

'I don't recognize the type,' yelled König, ducking.

The knee-high grass swayed in the wake of the plane. 'Heinkel 112.'

After swooping in a wide curve, the Heinkel made a second, head on approach. König waved but instinct warned me the pilot was lining up to attack. 'Take cover,' I screamed as I threw myself to the ground. König dived into the haystack so that only his feet were visible. 'Bloody ostrich,' I thought, laughing aloud.

The Heinkel's machine guns flashed. Spurts of dirt kicked up from the ground. The whirr of ricochets with different notes was almost musical. Then something whipped against my leg, high up at the front of my thigh, which was odd because I was lying face down on the ground. As the din of the aircraft's engine faded there was movement in the haystack. König's feet disappeared and a moment later, his head popped out from the straw.

'*Meine Fresse* – that was close.' He let go a whistle of relief.

'Closer than you think,' I said easing myself to my feet. My legs trembled but there was no pain. The impossible had happened – I had been hit.

König, covered in straw, ran over to me. He fumbled inside his tunic pocket for a first-aid dressing. 'It's not too bad – it doesn't look too bad.'

He sounded even more scared than I felt. I reached down to the wound and pressed gently. 'The bullet must have hit a rock and travelled parallel to the ground,' I said subduing the shock. My fingers found a reassuring bulge – the bullet had lodged under my skin without striking the thighbone. Blood now ran freely down my right leg, soaking the front of my uniform trousers. I took the dressing from König and bound the wound as best I could before we made our way back to the ravine.

Spooked by the Heinkel's machine gun fire, our unit was in a state of high alert with every gun pointing in our direction as we approached. König shouted the password. When the *Oberscharführer* saw my blood-soaked leg, he immediately summoned the ambulance from rear of our column.

Inside the ambulance, I gritted my teeth as the medical orderly swabbed the gash with a liberal dose of iodine solution. I tried not to wince as his forceps probed inside my leg – after all, it had been drilled into us in Lichterfelde: *pain is in the brain.*

'Just a flesh wound,' said the medic holding up a bullet for me to see. 'It'll heal in a few days – keep it covered to cut down the risk of infection. Now, how did it happen?'

I recounted the details of the Heinkel's attack.

'Ah, that's a pity – you can't put your name forward for a wound badge because it wasn't caused by enemy fire. I'll write that in my report.'

My *Kameraden* in the *Kompanietrupp* found the site of my wound highly amusing. A few centimetres to the side and it could have destroyed my ability to father children but for me it was certainly no laughing matter. It caused considerable pain and made it impossible for me to sit comfortably in a moving vehicle. A pain in the groin, I discovered, was certainly not in the brain – and guardian angels are not in constant attendance.

A week or so after my wound, an *Oberscharführer* assembled a reconnaissance unit to establish the exact whereabouts of the Russian defences. Under a clear blue sky, we set off into the unknown, beyond our front lines. I sat in the sidecar of a motorcycle driven by a *Rottenführer*. With his machine pistol on my knees and an expensive camera and telephoto lens between my feet, we led the way along a winding road with three of our cars following a half a kilometre behind. At the crest of a steep rise in the road, the *Rottenführer* slammed on the brakes bringing the motorcycle to an abrupt halt. For a moment we sat in silence, our eyes and mouths wide open as we stared at an anti-tank gun pointing threateningly in our direction.

The *Rottenführer* cut the engine. 'They would have let us have one by now if it was manned,' he said. 'Let's take a look.'

I glanced back to see our three cars motionless at the bottom of the slope and handed my companion his machine pistol as I stepped from the sidecar. As we approached the anti-tank gun, a movement in a field to the side of the road caught my eye. I tapped the *Rottenführer* on the shoulder and pointed into the field.

'*Verdammt* – they're having a brew up.'

At that moment, the astonished faces of six Russians turned to gape at us for an instant before they realised we were German. We spun on our heels to make a dash for the motorbike as the Russians made a dash for their gun. It was a race against time with another lucky escape as first prize.

Panting with the effort of running uphill, I jumped into the sidecar. The *Rottenführer* heaved on the kick-start. The engine gave a token 'chug-chug' then stopped. Still the Russians had not managed to loose off a shell. Again, the *Rottenführer* stamped on the kick-start but the engine steadfastly refused to show the slightest sign of life.

His strength ebbing, the *Rottenführer* gave a grunt of defeat and dismounted the motorcycle. Without a word of warning, he turned to run towards the waiting cars, leaving me alone in the sidecar. It would be fair to say that I was beginning to panic when I followed his example. As we ran down the hill, one of our cars, an open top affair, sped up to meet us. It braked sharply and spun round to face downhill, engine racing. The anxious driver moved off before we had the chance to climb in but the men in the back pulled us aboard as we ran alongside.

At the *Kompanie* command post, the *Rottenführer* and I reported the loss of our vehicle and expensive camera. I was not at all surprised when an officer ordered us to attempt to recover the equipment later that night.

❧ ❦

Two *Kameraden* from another platoon waited in the front seats of the car that rescued us earlier in the day. 'In this moonlight we won't need lights,' said the driver. 'The Russians won't see us coming.'

We drove through the inky blue shadows cast by the hills, until we came to the rise beyond which we hoped our motorcycle still stood. The driver switched off the engine as we neared the crest of the hill, allowing the incline to bring the car to a quiet halt. The clicks of the handbrake as it pulled over its ratchet, shot through the silence like rifle fire.

'We should turn the car,' whispered the driver, 'we don't want to make more noise by starting the engine.'

The *Rottenführer* and I clambered out of the back seat and heaved the car back and forth across the width of the road until it pointed downhill, ready to make our getaway. Breathless from the effort of pushing the car, we made our way to the crest of the hill to see our motorcycle still exactly where we had abandoned it. Had it been booby-trapped? Were the Russians waiting, ready to fire at us as soon as we reached the motorcycle? These were my thoughts as I climbed into the sidecar with the *Rottenführer* already heaving on the kick-start. A throaty roar ripped into the stillness of the night. The *Rottenführer* spun the machine around and we sped off, unscathed. My guardian angel had returned.

17

On a Summer's Day

With shirtsleeves rolled neatly to the elbows, we passed an isolated farmhouse before continuing across a rolling meadow inhabited by twittering larks. Only a few months earlier, in the deepest cold of winter, these handsome little birds flocked around roads and tracks picking at the tiniest morsels uncovered by our passing vehicles. Boris whistled a melody he had grown fond of while stationed in France: *Du hast Glück bei den Frau'n, Bel Ami*.

The sudden zip of bullets brought grunts from unlucky *Kameraden*. I dived for cover. The *Oberscharführer* in charge of the patrol, the red-faced farmer from Austria who had shown us the beauties of Paris, risked everything to get a fix on the enemy through his binoculars. Our sharpshooters began to trouble the enemy machine gunners with rifle fire.

As if immersed in a lurid nightmare, I crawled towards the spot where I had last seen Boris. My heart sank when I found him lying on his back in the long grass. Bright red blood drenched his legs; his fingers trembled. Bullets had shattered both thighbones. I called out '*Sani, Sani.*' Moments later, though it seemed an age, two medics arrived with a stretcher.

The machine-gun fire stopped as suddenly as it began. Perhaps our marksmen had scored a decisive hit. During the lull, we set up a defensive line while the medics evacuated our wounded to the farmhouse. Soon, Russian infantry arrived on the scene and began firing on us with rifles and mortars from the safety of a low ridge. The Russian machine gun found a new lease of life, harassing us with a stream of explosive bullets. We were in a vulnerable position. Our *Oberscharführer* gave the order to fall back to the farmhouse where a large room served as a temporary hospital. Before long, the approach of Russian infantry with tank support interrupted the treatment of our wounded. Without anti-tank weapons or armour of our own, we were sitting ducks. The *Oberscharführer* made the agonising decision to evacuate the farmhouse without taking the badly wounded with us. A few of us offered to hold the building until reinforcements arrived but our *Oberscharführer* took the view that we would be quickly overwhelmed by the superior strength of the Russians. It was with a feeling of abject helplessness that I said goodbye to Boris.

❦

At first light, we set off with the support of machine guns and mortars and soon retook the ground lost the previous day. News soon spread that the Russians had murdered the wounded we had left behind. Since Boris and I were in the same *Kompanietrupp*, the call to report to the farmhouse to identify his body came as no surprise.

In the makeshift hospital ward, the sickly smell of stale blood hung in the warm air. Flies buzzed in zig-zag flight, waiting for their chance to feed or lay their eggs. A *Kamerad* from a mortar crew was already present. For a moment, we stood together in a festering silence, staring at the bodies, at the squashed testicles scattered across the floor. 'The bastards – the fucking bastards,' he snarled. His anger overflowing, he kicked out at a table sending the basin on top crashing to the floor. 'Look,' he said pointing to a body, naked from the waist down, 'the bastards sliced off his bollocks, everything. Look at the amount of blood – they were still alive when they were mutilated.'

'I can see it as if I was there,' I said. 'The Russians forced them to witness the torture of their *Kameraden* until their own turn came along.'

In the corner of the room was a heap of men, their heads cleaved open to the eyes by a blow that might have come from a heavy axe.

'At least they didn't suffer too long,' said my companion.

'They were in a hurry when they did that,' I speculated. Then I found Boris. The handles of the pliers from his tool kit, just visible inside his gaping mouth, stretched his cheeks into a gruesome smile. The tips of the metal jaws penetrated his windpipe and were visible through the stretched skin of his neck. He must have slowly, and painfully, choked to death.

Such are the horrors of war but still, after all these years, an icy shudder runs down my spine when I think of the torture of my *Kameraden*.

18

Sewing Machines and T-34s

We laughed when we first saw them, the Polikarpov Po-2 biplanes – crop dusters, nothing but cloth stretched over a slight timber frame braced by strands of wire and powered by engines that clattered as if cobbled together from parts scavenged from a junkyard. When I first heard them, they brought to mind an image of my mother, her feet working the treadle of her sewing machine and hands industriously feeding the work piece under the needle. We came to dread the sound of these '*Nähmaschinen*' (sewing machines) as we called them. They were tough little birds that could take rifle or machine-gun fire with apparent impunity. In a favourable wind, they flew so slowly they appeared to hover. Surprisingly, the low airspeed of the *Nähmaschinen* was no great disadvantage – our Me109s risked stalling if they tried to match their speed and flashed past before they were able to take proper aim. By the time they returned for a second pass, the Russian pilots had often skilfully manoeuvred their aircraft out of harm's way. At night, the rattle of their engines would stop suddenly, as if the aircraft had been spirited from the darkness. Then, like hunting owls, they swooped, their bracing wires hissing through the air, a prelude to a storm of shrapnel from fragmentation bombs that burst without first whistling a warning. These attacks drained our strength not only by inflicting casualties, but also by denying us precious sleep. The female pilots of these infernal machines soon earned the epithet '*Nachthexen*' – witches of the night.

At dawn, we found ourselves at the exposed edge of a high plateau overlooking a road junction defended by two of the omnipresent T-34s. As we waited for our next orders, three black specks appeared in the sky beyond the tanks. Dipping close to the treetops, they disappeared from sight, hidden by their camouflage.

'The bitches will be on top of us soon,' cursed a *Kamerad*.

Expecting a fragmentation bomb attack, we took what cover we could. The tinny rattle of the planes' engines took on a laboured note, dragging the aircraft above the plateau, before easing back to a contented purr. Our sporadic rifle and machine-gun fire did nothing to deter the attack. A liquid, poured from canisters, fell from the planes. It turned first to white smoke, then to cascading pellets of fire. Where they landed, the dry grass caught light. The cry went up, 'Phosphorus.'

Several pellets hit a fellow close by. He screamed dreadfully as the inextinguishable fire sizzled into his skin. Experience had taught us that even relatively minor phosphorus burns could bring a lingering death.

As the rattling of the Russian planes' engines faded into the distance, our *Oberscharführer* called for volunteers to tackle the tanks at the road junction. I immediately stepped forward with the *Rottenführer* and *Unterscharführer*, both from the same *Kompanietrupp* to which I belonged. These chaps were a few years older and kept themselves apart from the rest of us less experienced soldiers, probably as a survival ploy.

Equipped with machine pistols and stick grenades pushed into our belts, we set off towards the tanks on a Zündapp motorcycle and sidecar. As a recently promoted *Sturmmann*, I held the lowest rank and could only listen as my two companions discussed their strategy to deal with the tanks as we rolled downhill.

'We should keep it simple,' shouted the *Rottenführer* into the ear of the driver, 'Park the motorbike out of sight of the tanks and move in on foot to get a closer look.'

As the *Unterscharführer* guided the motorcycle round a sharp bend, he looked at me and gave a crazy cackle. 'At last, a chance to earn the tank destruction stripe – I'll stay with the bike in case we need to make a quick getaway,' he offered generously. 'You two can deal with the tanks.'

The *Rottenführer* and I left the motorcycle sitting under a copse of small trees and made our way to within fifty metres of the tanks. We listened for Russian voices but heard only the lazy hum of flying insects as the air around the two 'Mickey Mouse' T-34 tanks shimmered in the sunshine. Likening this model of Russian tank to Mickey Mouse was no criticism of their quality of construction, it was simply an amusing reference to their appearance when they had both turret hatches open.

'Remember,' the *Rottenführer* whispered, 'we have to time this perfectly – take out both tanks at the same time.'

I nodded then wiped the sweat from my brow with the back of my hand.

'We'll work our way round the rear to make sure there are no footsloggers nearby – stick close to me.'

Keeping to natural dips in the ground and the cover of long grass, we crawled on our bellies until only a twenty-metre stretch of open road separated us from our goal. Resting on one knee, the *Rottenführer* slung the strap of his machine pistol across his shoulder and calmly pushed his two stick grenades deeper between his belt and body. 'Make sure you don't drop them,' he said, couching now like a cat about to spring on an unsuspecting mouse.

Instinctively, I followed his example. For a brief moment, his pale blue eyes fixed on mine as if to confirm that I had the courage to follow.

'The one on the other side of the road's yours – see you back at the motorbike,' said the *Rottenführer* before leaping from our hiding place.

I sprinted to my appointed target. Heart pounding, I grabbed a handle on the sloping rear of the tank and clambered up to the flat area above the engine, behind the turret. My fingers trembled as I unscrewed the metal cap on the end of the grenade handle to expose the porcelain tug ball and lanyard that would ignite the delay fuse. With the grenade in one hand, I grasped the handle of a turret hatch with the other, yanking it forward. The tank crew had become careless; they were fast asleep at their posts. I tugged the lanyard and let the grenade fall into the tank. It landed on the lap of a crewmember. Mouth agape, he looked up at me as I slammed down the hatch. I can only imagine the panic he must have felt as the grenade's delay fuse marked down his final few seconds.

A rocket of flame shot from the turret of the *Rottenführer's* tank as I leapt to the ground. A blast of sound and heat from behind sent me staggering forwards as my own target exploded from within. Everything had gone exactly to plan and it was with a feeling of intense elation that I arrived back at the waiting Zündapp. I had fulfilled the criteria required to earn the tank destruction stripe – the annihilation, without assistance, of an enemy tank.

Pleased with our work, we returned to *Kompanie* headquarters to report the details our successful exploit to an officer. But, he explained, there was a problem – there had been only two Russian tanks and three of us had been involved in their destruction. The rules stated quite clearly, he said, that only one *Panzer Vernichtungs Abzeichen* (a cloth stripe carrying a metal symbol of a tank) could be granted for the destruction of each tank. I learned shortly afterwards that the *Rottenfürhrer* and *Unterscharfürhrer* were awarded these coveted stripes while I was given only a vague hint that my role in the demolition of the tanks would be duly recognised.

On a particularly hot day in early June, a message circulated by field telephone warned that our *Pionierkorps* had neutralised a poison gas shell. As a precaution, we put on the gasmasks we carried in aluminium cylinders. Since the shell had landed only a short distance from where I had dug in, I decided to take a closer look at it. Split in half along its length, it oozed a brown liquid but, as far as I know, no one was harmed by it. Nevertheless, our commanders radioed the Russians to complain about their use of gas. By the strange etiquette of war on the *Ostfront*, they received a prompt apology for the erroneous use of the gas shell. We in turn declared our displeasure with a storm of rockets from our *Nebelwerfers*. On arching trails of smoke, our rockets screamed towards a hill a few kilometres ahead of our front lines. The six rockets from a single launcher would strike a small area at one-second intervals with devastating consequences for anyone caught in the open. When we advanced through the enemy position, I saw at first hand the devastating effect of our bombardment. Russian soldiers wearing the smart blue uniforms and gold-buckled boots of Stalin's elite guard slumped against their artillery pieces in poses that suggested they might continue loading their weapons at any moment. There was no blood, no mutilated corpses. The concussive effect of the high explosive in the *Nebelwerfer* rockets had killed them as they stood.

A few days later, I took command of two machine-gun crews. Ellers and König were also transferred to machine-gun duties so I didn't feel too much like a stranger among the *Kameraden* of my new platoon.

19

Prokhorovka

We were making made good progress through a cutting in a forest when a Russian fighter plane screamed low over the trees. The engine noise faded into a dull, distant drone and it seemed the pilot had elected to ignore us. But the drone, took on a higher pitch as the plane, now a growing black dot, wheeled across the sky. I ordered the two machine-gun crews under my command to prepare for an air attack. As was the custom in such circumstances, a designated machine-gun crewmember, *Schütze Zwei,* acted as a human stand by supporting the barrel of the weapon on his shoulder while facing the attacking aircraft. As the plane's guns flashed, *Schütze Zwei*'s nerve deserted him at a crucial moment and he grabbed at the barrel of the machine gun as he ducked. Somehow, it slipped behind his head as the weapon fired a burst of bullets. He slumped forward, hitting the ground face first with half his head missing though still alive. The *Kamerad* who had fired the machine gun called out a sorrowful wail, '*Sani, Sani.*'

Within seconds, a medical orderly was attending the horribly wounded man. He summoned a motorcycle and sidecar coming up from behind to hurry. White faced, the machine-gunner could only watch as the motorcycle turned for the first-aid station with his *Kamerad* slumped in the seat of the sidecar. Once more, the difference between life and death was determined by a fleeting moment of misfortune.

We generally worked in small groups held together by immutable bonds of trust and confidence, each group keeping largely to itself. To lose a *Kamerad* in such a way must have been a devastating experience for the man who pulled the trigger. From then on, to avoid repetitions of this type of accident, the soldier supporting the machine gun on his shoulder always faced the gunner. By avoiding sight of the attacking aircraft, he was less likely to flinch and cause an accident.

It must have been the 3 or 4 July when we took up positions in ditches made muddy by heavy rain. Though well hidden from the enemy, our battalion endured a spell of heavy artillery fire before things quietened down. Under a sky shining with stars indifferent to the fate of men, we waited for the signal to advance. It was by no means cold, but occasional shivers of uneasiness coursed through my body. As was usual before a major engagement, an officer arrived to give encouragement and final instructions. 'Our initial target is Teterovino,' he announced. 'Good luck and remember whose name we carry on our sleeves – we fight for the *Führer*, for Germany.' Soon afterwards, the grunts and growls of heavy engines shattered the silence of the night – our *Panzers* were preparing for battle.

The hours passed slowly. I was getting edgy, impatient for our turn to advance. Hunger and fear, hand in clammy hand, worked together on my stomach, squeezing it into a tight knot. I was more nervous than usual, spooked perhaps by the terrible accident that had killed the fellow in the machine-gun crew. At last, shortly before first light, the order came to move forward.

By late afternoon of the first day, we reached a secure position close to a village. Thankful that a hard day's fighting was over, we threw ourselves into a ditch and settled down for the night, impervious to the flashes and thuds of an artillery bombardment that continued into the night, just a few kilometres to the east.

The following day, in good light, we followed three or four kilometres behind a *Panzerkeil* – a wedge-shaped formation of advancing tanks – towards Teterevino, overcoming successive lines of Russian defences each with its own entrenched infantry units, treacherous minefields and anti-tank artillery. As we advanced, a *Kamerad* to my right twisted towards me. His face wore a look of utter horror. His lips moved but his words were lost in the crescendo of battle. A shell – probably fired by one of our own anti-tank guns judging from the low trajectory – had punched a hole the thickness of a man's arm clean through his chest. After staggering a few steps, he fell to the ground – just another body.

A squadron of Soviet tanks appeared on the ridge of a low hill and came to a standstill. Immediately, they came under fire from our Tigers. One of the T-34s took a direct hit, its turret flying high into the air on top of a pillar of flame before tumbling to the battlefield. Above the wrecked tank hung a perfectly circular smoke ring, a characteristic sign that the tank had exploded violently from the inside. The Soviet tanks now rushed to engage our *Panzerkeil* – the beginning of a feverish contest that the Russians lost.

As we advanced towards the ridge under clouds of black smoke, we came across a trail of spent shell casings leading to the smouldering hulk of a Tiger tank. The sickening stench of hot steel and roasted flesh stuck at the back of my throat. The tank's turret, pockmarked with craters where Soviet tank shells had struck, had shrugged off dozens of hits, each one of which must have stretched the crew's nerves to snapping point. Near the base of the turret was a circular hole surrounded by silvery metallic globules where the Tiger's armour had melted like candle wax. A Russian shell had finally found a weak spot. In the surrounding fields, half a dozen Soviet tanks burned, each ringed by scorched grass. It appeared to me that the crew of the Tiger, tormented by the swarm of T-34s, had fought heroically until it took the fatal shot. With no sign of a massive internal explosion, it had probably run out of ammunition.

We were a dwindling, exhausted force by the time we reached a forest close to Prokhorovka on 11 July 1943 – a day I was destined to remember well. It was a thoroughly unpleasant morning with lashing rain and gusting winds. Shortly before midday, *4.Kompanie* received the order to assist in the clearance of Russian defenders dug in amongst the trees. A fearsome artillery barrage hindered our progress through the dripping foliage. Desperately, we searched for cover as we pushed forward, always forward, until we chanced upon a zigzag of abandoned Russian slit trenches, welcome protection from the exploding shells. By now there were only seven men left of the initial twelve of my two machine-gun crews. The constant boom of ear-splitting detonations left no room for words, no room for fear, no room for thoughts of past or future as we crouched in the trench.

Shells screamed above our heads. A shower of stones and soil followed a dangerously close detonation that pounded the air from my lungs. Fragments of hot metal cascaded onto the wet grass where they spat and sizzled. To the side, the trunk of a tree as thick as a man, took a direct hit. It disappeared in blinding burst of light. Clouds of wood splinters, no bigger than kindling, showered the forest floor. A shell exploded directly above. I felt something strike my left shoulder. Overwhelmed by a sudden dizziness, I slumped to the bottom of the trench. My vision was blurred and the voices of my *Kameraden* had a ghastly hollow quality.

'Erwin's hit.' called Ellers.

There was the sound of ripping cloth followed by the pressure of a hand at the nape of my neck – Ellers was applying a field dressing.

'It's bad – better get him to the collection point. Erwin, can you stand?'

My *Kameraden* pulled me to my feet and hooked my fingers over the back of Ellers' belt.

As I stumbled along a forest path behind Ellers, everything seemed smothered in a smoky haze. I could make out colours and shadows but every now and then, darkness fell like a soft cloak over my eyes.

We came to an abrupt halt. There was alarm in Eller's voice. '*Verdammt* – the wood's crawling with Russians.'

I managed to grunt, to show Ellers that his efforts to save me were still worthwhile.

'We'll rest here until they pass.'

Strangely, there was still no pain. Perhaps the constant repetition of the maxim 'pain is in the brain' while I trained in Lichterfelde was working, a sort of self-hypnosis.

At the first-aid post, the medics added me to the rows of wounded already lying on the grass. How long it took to get to there, I shall never know but I remain eternally grateful to *Kamerad* Ellers who risked so much to save my life. The sounds around me were no longer those of the battlefront but the groans and cries of wounded men. My head spun with every gasp for air. Incapable of the slightest movement, I stared at the shafts of sunlight cutting through forest canopy.

'This one's gone, won't make it – this one too,' said a distant, disembodied voice.

A boot kicked lightly against my leg. I winced.

'This one's still alive.'

A blurred face loomed before my eyes.

'Now then, let's have a look at you.'

The medic yanked me brusquely into a sitting position and removed the blood-soaked field dressing applied earlier by Ellers, replacing it with a fresh one before lowering me the ground and nimbly unbuttoning my tunic. His cool hands ran over my chest.

'No exit wound – it's a puzzle – I've never seen anything like this before. Don't worry my friend, I'll send you to the field surgical unit when transport becomes available.'

As I lay waiting for the ambulance, strange, chaotic, dreamlike thoughts came to me. I was a child walking by the lakeside in Schlochau, place of my birth. We stopped and I looked up to the ragged stonework of the ruins we called the Witches' Tower. Mother crouched beside me. 'Somewhere, deep under the water,' she whispered in my ear, 'is the golden dome from the Witches' Tower.' She smiled. 'Who knows, when you grow up you might be the one who finds it.'

'How did it get there Mama?'

'One night, long, long ago, there was a terrible storm. The wind lifted the dome into the sky and threw it into the water.'

I giggled expectantly as she reached the climax of her story, which always ended with her mimicking the rush of a great wind in my ear. Shivers of delight ran down my spine.

Then, his face blue with rage, my father looked me in the eye. 'How could you do this to me Erwin? I'm an elder of the church and my *son* resigns his membership.'

The ambulances arrived. Medics ran around shouting instructions. 'Get the worst cases on board. Leave the others – we'll try to fit them in later.'

Though still in no great pain, I was conscious enough to realise what was happening and shocked to find myself loaded onto the floor of the ambulance among the seriously injured, heaps of torn flesh oozing blood that mingled on the floor of the vehicle. A medic found a space between bodies and did what he could to ease the discomfort of the wounded as the ambulance sped through the forest. Every bump in the dirt track brought a chorus of agony yet nobody begged the driver to slow down. For those losing blood from missing limbs every second saved was precious, no pain too great to bear.

We had not travelled far when the sound of rifle shots rang out. Bullets tore through the canvas cover of the ambulance but they whizzed straight over our heads without causing further casualties.

Though none of us were capable of moving without assistance, the driver's mate turned and screamed, 'Keep your heads down.'

As we picked up speed, machine-gun bullets pattered across the metal skin of the ambulance. The medical orderly, sitting at the rear, slumped to the floor with blood pumping from a chest wound. I later learned that some of the wounded in other ambulances had also been hit.

At the *Hauptverbandplatz* (main dressing station), we, the wounded, were lain on the straw covered floor of a large tent, to wait our turn to be examined by a surgeon. Every now and then, medical orderlies came in to ascertain who among us were still alive. With the dead promptly removed, newly arriving casualties soon filled the empty places.

Darkness fell. By now the left side of my chest was badly swollen and every intake of breath a burning agony. Worse still, a great heaviness seemed to pull at my eyelids. It would have been easy to submit to the desire to sleep, to escape the sensation that my chest was about to burst. Fearing sleep would bring death I fought hard to remain awake.

Eventually – it must have been after several hours – the orderlies took me on a stretcher to the operation tent where Dr. Jakob, a high-ranking officer in charge of the surgical unit, examined my wound. (For those readers interested in such historical details, the *Feldpost Nummer* of the *Hauptverbandplatz* was 19754 and my case number in the records 5794). Dr. Jakob concluded that a fragment of shrapnel had entered high on my left shoulder blade and passed into my chest. He could find no evidence of any puncture in the pleural membrane and the absence of an exit wound, he said, indicated that the shrapnel was still inside my body.

'There's not much I can do except tidy up the wound,' said Dr. Jakob. 'It's a bit ragged so I'll remove the uneven tears in the skin and stitch it together to reduce the chance of infection.'

Before I had time to contemplate the doctor's words, an orderly placed an ether-soaked mask over my mouth and nose.

'Breathe in,' said the doctor.

I drew in the pungent fumes as deeply as my aching chest allowed but the anaesthetic had no effect.

'Now, now, we don't have time to waste – breath deeper,' demanded Dr. Jakob.

Redoubling my effort comply with the doctor's instructions I took a long slow intake of the fumes but experienced no more than a faint drowsiness.

Dr. Jakob, exasperated with my failure to succumb to the ether, turned me onto my right side and said curtly, 'I'll have to go ahead without anaesthetic.'

I clenched my teeth, felt the caress of a disinfectant-soaked swab on my shoulder, cool at first, then stinging.

'You must remain absolutely still,' ordered the doctor.

A scalpel blade sliced into my shoulder. Ragged slivers of skin dropped from the doctor's forceps into a white enamelled dish close to my face. As Dr Jakob inserted the stitches, the skin around the repair tightened until the raw flesh came together. My ordeal was over in just a few minutes and I was given an hour to rest on the floor before being driven with other wounded men to a railway station to await evacuation.

❧·❧

The day passed – as did the night – but still we lay patiently on the platform waiting for the promised train. A friendly medical orderly made heroic efforts to console us. His frequent reassurances that a train was on the way gave us hope that we would soon see the inside of a proper hospital. Apart from some weak soup and water, no nourishment was provided. After about two days – though I am not certain of this since I had lost all track of time – a goods train drew alongside the platform and we were loaded into cattle wagons to begin our journey away from the front line.

Lulled by the gentle rocking of the wagon and metronomic rhythm of its wheels on the track, sleep brought its welcome respite from the burning sensation raging through my chest. How long I travelled in that train I cannot say but when wakened by the sound of voices, I found myself in a ward of a small hospital in Kharkov with a handful of *Waffen SS Kameraden*. The wounded from various *Wehrmacht* units occupied adjacent wards. After several days, I began to feel much better and was able to socialise with my fellow patients.

An officer wearing gold-rimmed glasses visited to pep up the moral of the wounded. He moved from bed to bed asking about wives and children. His commiserations were genuine enough and when learning of some tragic circumstance he would grasp the complainant's hand – if he had one – or pat him on the shoulder without the slightest sign of reserve one might expect in an officer. When he arrived at my bedside, I re-lived the incident that brought me to the hospital. He said a few kind words and asked how my family were bearing up and was about to move on to the next bed when he paused for a moment to ask, 'Is there anything I can do for you?'

At that time, I was an avid smoker and it had been quite a while since I had enjoyed a cigarette. 'A smoke would be good,' I replied.

The officer smiled as he reached into his tunic pocket and took out a wrapped cigar. He held it, vertically, in front of my eyes. 'Would this do?' he asked sliding the cigar from its wrapping. 'Here take it,' he said, 'I have a handy little set of cigar scissors somewhere.' His hand searched a trouser pocket until it found the instrument and, with the dexterity of an expert, he snipped off the end of the cigar as I held it in my hand. 'All these wounded – it must have been tough at Prokhorovka,' he said sympathetically. His hand reached once more into his pocket. 'We mustn't forget these,' he said rattling a blue and yellow matchbox.

Attracted by the rattling matches, the matron shook her head and pointed to a notice, which read: *RAUCHEN VERBOTEN!* She was not the sort one would cross so, when the officer left, I went into the corridor and leaned against the wall. I held the cigar before my eyes, admiring its form. I caressed it, ran it slowly under my nose to savour the rich aroma of fresh tobacco. Holding the cigar between my teeth, I struck a match, applied it to the tip and sipped in the cool smoke. A tender, sensual thrill filtered right down to my heels. I closed my eyes and thought of...absolutely nothing.

A despairing moan interrupted my moment of bliss. I tried to ignore it but its pitiful tone demanded investigation. Irritated by the intrusion, I waved the cloud of friendly smoke away from my face and pushed from the wall with my good shoulder. Cigar in hand, I followed the sorry wailing to a side room where, propped up by pillows, a *Wehrmacht Leutnant* lay in bed. 'Do you need a doctor?'

The *Leutnant*, his face a ghastly grey, opened his eyes and groaned, 'I'm dying, I'm dying.'

'What happened to you?' I asked.

'A bullet,' he gasped in a weak, rasping voice, 'through the lung.'

Without thinking, I found myself repeating the mantra drummed into me during training at Lichterfelde, 'Pain is in the brain.' I put the cigar to my lips and drew in the smoke once more then offered him a drag, which he refused. Not wishing to provide an audience for the *Leutnant's* constant moaning I made my excuse to leave. 'I'd better get out of here with this cigar before the matron spots me. I'll pop in again later to see how you are.'

As I left he wailed, 'I'm dying, I'm dying.'

When I called in later that day, he was dead.

❧⋅☙

Perhaps I should not have given in to my craving for a smoke because a few days later, I suffered a setback with the pain in my lung getting worse by the minute. A doctor diagnosed the build up of fluid then disappeared from the ward. Shortly afterwards, he returned with a fearsome-looking device that consisted of a long needle attached to a machine which, I presume, was designed to apply suction.

'This might be a little uncomfortable,' declared the doctor from behind my back.

I felt the needle press hard against the skin, between my ribs. Suddenly the skin gave way and the needle sank deep into my lung. The tiniest manipulation of the probe brought involuntary yelps of agony from my throat.

The device made a rhythmical light popping sound as the doctor cranked its handle. 'It's no good,' he eventually conceded. 'I'll have to try something else.' He called for a nurse to bring a syringe.

I could hardly believe my eyes when the nurse returned with a syringe equipped with a needle that looked more like a six-inch nail than a medical instrument. I bit my lip hard as the needle poked around inside my lung.

'Hmm, there doesn't appear to be any fluid there after all,' the doctor concluded as he withdrew the probe.

Suddenly I was fighting for breath, gasping like a fish out of water.

Unable to deal with the situation, the doctor sent me to a *Wehrmacht* surgical unit in Kraków where my uniform was removed leaving me wearing only my long johns and shirt before being escorted to a crowded ward with beds in tiers of three. Being one of the more mobile patients, I took my place on the topmost bunk. My stay at this hospital was brief and I was soon on my travels once more, this time aboard a train with wagons fully equipped with beds, attractive Danish nurses, and all the proper medical paraphernalia. The train travelled through Silesia and stopped at Kattowitz, where every wounded man on board was given a present from the local Nazi Party – wine or beer or chocolate – before continuing onwards to a convalescent establishment in Austria .

Strauss waltzes played by an orchestra on the platform greeted our arrival in Judenau, a village not far from Vienna. Locals lined the sunny streets, clapping their hands to welcome those who had sacrificed youth and limb for the protection of the *Reich* and European culture. Those of us who could still walk – and I was among these though I had to parade in my underwear – filed past the appreciative onlookers. The more seriously wounded lay on flat-back carts pulled by horses lucky enough to have escaped conscription. Unfortunately, the convalescent hospital was at the other end of the town and for some time afterwards, dreams of wandering the streets of Berlin in my underwear disturbed my sleep.

20

The Scarecrow of Prokhorovka

L et's get you out of these filthy clothes,' said one of the two nurses dressed in rubber overalls in the porch of a monastery that now served as a hospital. Before I realised what was happening, they stripped me of my shabby underwear – my last vestige of dignity – then washed my naked body with warm soapy water. Just as I began to relax and enjoy the experience, they wrapped me in a dressing gown and led me to a bed with sheets as white as the billowing clouds of heaven. Only those denied a clean and comfortable bed could know the absolute pleasure one feels when this privilege is restored. What a change from trying to grab some sleep in a rain soaked trench. Because there were insufficient facilities to feed all the patients at once, meals were served according to a rota but, having teetered on the verge of starvation many times on the *Ostfront*, this was no great annoyance to me.

After a few days in Judenau, I learned there was an SS hospital in nearby Vienna. I suggested to the duty doctor that it would be better for me if I were transferred there. 'But there is a problem,' I added, 'I seem to have lost my uniform. I wonder if you could make enquiries about a replacement.'

'I'll make some telephone calls,' he offered, 'but no promises.'

A few days later, the doctor returned with a bundle of rags over his arm and a document in his hand.

'This is your pass,' he said, handing me the document, 'you are to travel to the SS hospital as soon as possible. I managed to get you this uniform,' he said, placing the bundle of rags on the edge of my bed.

I looked at the tattered heap of cloth in dismay. Patches of light grey material taken from a First World War uniform covered the knees and elbows in makeshift repairs.

'It's all they could find in your size,' the doctor explained.

I pulled on the uniform. The tunic arms were five centimetres too short, the trousers ten centimetres too long. 'I'll look like a scarecrow in this,' I complained.

Subduing a smirk, the doctor replied, 'I'm sorry, but it's the best I could do.'

'If I bump into a *Gendarmerie* patrol they'll arrest me as a deserter and send me to a punishment battalion.' I was only half-joking – the Military Police were always keen to justify their place away from the dangers of the front line.

The doctor rubbed his tired eyes and, with a sigh of irritation, took a pad of forms from the side pocket of his white coat. 'Hmm, I understand that might be a problem for you. I'll write a note explaining the circumstances.'

I still harbour the suspicion that presenting me with such a hideous garment was a deliberate act of humiliation by some *Wehrmacht* quartermaster who, unlike his comrades on the front line who always said they felt safer with the *Leibstandarte* nearby, harboured a grudge against the *Waffen SS*.

The guard at the *SS* hospital in Vienna laughed raucously. 'Wait right here – and don't move. I'll be right back – by the way, where were you wounded?'

'Prokhorovka,' I answered.

He returned a few minutes later with two colleagues. 'Look,' he exclaimed pointing at me, 'it's the scarecrow of Prokhorovka.'

Soon everyone in the hospital that could walk had come to laugh at the sorry sight. It is a pity no one took a photograph of me in that cobbled together uniform that raised so many smiles amongst my *SS Kameraden*.

I was allocated to a ward populated mainly by *Leibstandarte* wounded who asked endless questions about this or that member of the *Leibstandarte* still at the front. For the most part, I was unable to provide any information but at least their questions offered a means of becoming acquainted with my new companions.

Before I had time to settle in properly, a doctor took me to a room equipped with an X–Ray machine. As I lay on an operating table, he swung the apparatus into position and took an image of my chest. The following day he returned to the ward with the developed photographic plate, which he held up to the window. 'This Röntograph shows a pellet of shrapnel lodged between two ribs on the left side.' He pointed to the image. 'There it is, at front of your chest,' he explained. 'We'll dig it out for you tomorrow morning.'

When I came round from the anaesthetic, I was alone in a room. I waited patiently but when no one appeared, I decided to make my way downstairs to the ward. Soon there was a gaggle of nurses chasing after me. They scolded me mercilessly as they led me back to my bed. Shortly afterwards the doctor who performed the operation appeared holding a pea-sized piece of bronze-coloured metal between his thumb and forefinger. 'You have indeed been very fortunate,' he said. 'This entered at the top of your shoulder blade and travelled right through your lung. It must have passed within millimetres of your heart.'

My recovery progressed well and I was presented with a brand new uniform, a proper *Waffen SS* uniform that fitted perfectly. My only complaint was that it lacked the regimental cuff band carrying the words: Adolf Hitler.

To break the monotony of hospital life, a group of us were driven by car to the Prater, a large area of parkland where we ate a packed lunch in the dappled shade of trees close to the riverbank. We visited the *Ruprectskirche*, the city's most ancient place of Christian worship, before taking a stroll through narrow alleyways that suddenly gave way to a wide street on the other side of which stood a building of astonishing beauty. Intricate stone carvings surrounded the arched windows, resplendent Gothic spires pierced the sky and the roof, decked with tiles of gold, green, and white in great zigzag patterns, dazzled the eye. Despite the magnificence of the interior of the building, it is the *Fenstergucker* that I recall with pleasure. Carved into the stonework of the steps leading to the pulpit, a mason, chisel in hand, looks out from a window, an eternal greeting to visitors to Saint Stephen's Cathredral.

As a soldier, I had seen the towns and cities of Ukraine and Russia but had never travelled within the German speaking parts of Europe. To have the chance to visit Vienna was a real privilege for a young chap from Berlin.

To complete my recovery I was sent to Bad Vöslau, a pretty *Kurort* that before the war had been dedicated to pampering wealthy visitors with massages and hot mud baths. My quarters were in an elegant old hotel, commandeered by the *Wehrmacht* for the recuperation of wounded soldiers. It stood close to the entrance to the thermal baths, just a stone's throw away. A first floor room with a veranda behind a wrought iron balustrade, freshly painted in white, offered a fine view onto the surrounding mountains. Once more, I was the only *Waffen SS* man present.

I spent the daylight hours exploring the surrounding Viennese countryside. A narrow track through a forest took me to an ivy-clad archway, the entrance to Burg Merkenstein, a fortress reduced to ruins by the Turks centuries beforehand. Close by were two beautiful villages, Gainfarn and Grossau, with dainty buildings and picturesque churches. For hours, I lay in the sunshine in the *Schlosspark* close to the hotel, watching the birds fly in and out of the foliage of an ancient plane tree or hunt for insects in square of grass. In this idyllic spot, it was difficult to believe that bloody conflict still raged on the *Ostfront*.

The doctor in charge of the hospital, a high-ranking *Oberstabartz*, came to me shortly after breakfast one day and handed over my release papers, a travel pass and a letter carrying the frank of the *Leibstandarte* headquarters at Lichterfelde. As I read the letter, an irrepressible smile came to my lips. I had been granted three weeks home leave, promoted *two* grades (from *Sturmmann* to *Unterscharführer*) and awarded both the Iron Cross Second Class *and* the Wound Badge in black (awarded to those who had been twice wounded or frostbitten). At last, my successful completion of the dangerous mission in Kharkov and my role in the destruction of two Russian tanks had been officially rewarded. But what was I to do now? I had a uniform but no insignia to show off my new rank. For a *Waffen SS* man it would have been completely embarrassing to have encountered a *Wehrmacht* patrol without this and, at worst, I might have been mistaken for a deserter because the insignia on my uniform didn't match my papers.

As luck would have it, I discovered there was a shop for soldiers in the town where, on presentation of one's papers, items of uniform could be purchased. Fortunately, the shop had in stock the silver braid and collar pip that would display my new rank. With my train due to leave Bad Vöslau later that day, I hurried back to the hotel to sew my purchases onto the 'mirrors' of my tunic collar.

21

A New Life in Berlin

At the exit of Schlesischer Bahnhof, the probing stare of policemen looking for deserters or spies searched the faces of departing passengers for signs of guilt. I continued past them without making eye contact.

'May I commend you on your smart appearance?'

The words, superficially polite, were cold and threatening and somehow, I knew they were directed at me. '*Danke*,' I called over my shoulder without stopping.

'Halt!'

My stomach quivered.

'Papers, if you please.'

I took my *Soldbuch* with the enclosed leave pass from my tunic pocket and presented it to the open hand stretched towards me. The policeman examined the documents closely then looked me in the eye before waving me past. Perhaps my brand new uniform had aroused his suspicion.

Taking the most direct route to my parents' flat, I came to Grosse Frankfurter Strasse. The traffic was as heavy as ever and the white lines marking the edge of the pavements – added at the beginning of the war to make driving without lights easier during blackouts – freshly painted. On crossing over to Strausberger Strasse, the feeling of belonging that draws the traveller home brought a lump to my throat.

I paused on the pavement opposite our flat and breathed a long sigh of pleasure. My mother had just finished cleaning the close and was standing with her back to me, mop in hand and bucket of steaming water at her feet, admiring her work. As I made to cross the road, the merrily ringing bell of a tram warned of its approach. The moment it passed, I hurried across the road calling out, 'Mama, I'm home,' She turned and stood for a moment as if stunned then wiped her hands on her apron before throwing her arms around my neck, pulling my face close to hers.

'Oh Erwin, I was so worried when I heard about your wound.'

'I'm fine Mama, the wound's healing well.'

She let go my neck and, stepping back a pace, mopped her cheeks with a corner of her apron. I put my hand in my pocket to find the pellet of metal that had almost taken my life. 'Look Mama,' I said holding it between my thumb and forefinger, 'you see – it's tiny, hardly anything to worry about.'

Father appeared at the entrance of the close. His lips fluttered a little before he spoke. 'Ah Erwin, I saw you from the window, you must tell me about your adventures. Here, let me have a look at that.'

I placed the shell fragment in the palm of his hand and he rolled it back and forth a few times, weighing its significance. It was good to be home.

·❦·❦·

Somewhere between sleep and wakefulness, I lay in a pool of blood in the back of an ambulance clattering over a dirt track in a forest. Around me were bodies with missing arms and feet. Mother's voice dispelled the horror of the dream.

'Erwin, this is the third time I've called – are you ever going to get up?'

I opened my eyes, eased my feet over the side of the bed, and pulled off my sweat-soaked vest. My legs throbbed, the legacy of a freezing night in the back of a truck on the run from Rostov. Still groggy, I answered, '*Morgen Mama.*' The first day of my leave was already half gone.

It was a hot day, too hot to spend in the sweltering company of the ovens of the Glaser bakery. News of Fritz could wait. Instead, I made my way to Friedrichshain where the *Flakturm* – a concrete parody of a medieval castle – loomed far above the park's tallest chestnut trees. On top, the barrels of 88mm anti-aircraft guns pointed skywards. It was the first time I had seen this structure. Its ominous presence sent a shudder of disquiet across my shoulders.

Keeping to a path running parallel to Frieden Strasse, I came to the cascading pools of the *Märchenbrunnen*, the fairytale fountains. Surrounding the pools, on a low wall, were sculptures of characters from Grimms' fairy stories. As a child, I loved to sit here with my father on the stone benches overlooking the fountains while he repeated the stories of Jacob and Wilhelm Grimm until I knew them by heart. Now, as I stared into the gushing waters, my childhood seemed impossibly remote, as if it too had been nothing more than a fairy tale. I took a deep breath and turned for Lichtenberger Strasse to visit the Horst Wessel *Sturmlokal* with the intention of enjoying a quiet drink.

As I sipped my beer, I mentioned the *Flakturm* in conversation with the chap in charge, an *Unteroffizier* from the *Luftwaffe*, which prompted him to lead me on a guided tour of the cellars where piles of blankets and other supplies were stored against the walls.

'This speaks for itself – emergency bedding and Dixie cans for use in the bomb shelters – a lesson from Hamburg. You don't need to be a genius to work out who's next in line.'

Images of burning buildings flitted through my mind. Of course, as a soldier, burning buildings were nothing new to me – but these ones were German.

'Why don't you come along this evening? We have a gipsy trio – good music – take your mind off things for a few hours. You won't be disappointed, they're talented musicians. Fiddle, clarinet, accordion – you name it, they can play it.'

After leaving the *Sturmlokal*, I took a stroll down to Memeler Strasse to visit the Glaser bakery where I learned that my journeyman, Fritz, had fallen for *'Volk und Vaterland'*.

At the end of my three weeks sick leave, I reported for duty at the Lichterfelde barracks where an *Obersturmführer*, sitting at a large polished desk, questioned me about my experiences on the *Ostfront*. As I was about to leave his office, I asked the *Obersturmführer* if he knew what had happened to my battalion.

The *Obersturmführer*'s face took on a thin-lipped serious look. He placed his pen on the desk and, elbows resting on the shiny surface said, 'I cannot give you exact details of course, but I can tell you they are in northern Italy. As you know, the Italians have deserted us. Your *Kameraden* are assisting with the disarmament of the Italian Army and keeping order in the towns and countryside. The cowardly ways of the Italians will be no great loss to us. Let the Americans see what they can do with these traitors. However, as far as you are concerned *Unterscharführer* Bartmann, I have to tell you that we have no specific role for you at this moment. In the meantime, you will remain here at Lichterfelde but, of course, this situation may change suddenly. Now, is there anything further you wish to ask?'

Being a Berliner, I took full advantage of this situation. 'My parents live in the Friedrichshain district,' I said, forgetting for a moment that it was now called Horst Wessel. 'It would please them if I was allowed to stay with them.' To my surprise, the *Oberstrurmführer* showed no sign of resistance to my request.

'On two conditions – you must report here, in person, twice a week and at all times be prepared to return to the barracks at a moment's notice.'

As I made my way to the *Strassenbahn* stop near the gates of the barracks, I was already pining to join my *Kameraden* in the Italian sunshine. On my next visit to Lichterfelde, I made a request to return to my unit.

The conditions for remaining with my parents were soon relaxed with my personal appearance required only once a week, providing I kept in contact by telephone. Each time I reported to the barracks in person, I received food rations to last until my next visit. This was a great relief to my parents who must have found it something of a trial during my three weeks at home when they had to share their meagre rations with me.

On the evening of 22 November 1943, I was at home with my parents when we received the happy news that my brother's wife had given birth to a baby girl, Angelika. I was an uncle. Within hours of receiving this news, the city's air raid sirens drew a resigned breath before wailing their weary warning across the city, a cruel antidote to my brief period of delight. It was the second massive air raid within a week. The systematic destruction of Berlin had begun.

My parents took shelter in the basement while against my mother's protests, I watched the battle unfold from an open skylight in the attic of our block of flats. The British were targeting the central parts of the city so there was little to fear in here, in Strausberger Strasse.

The drone of heavy bombers grew louder, like a drum roll before an execution. Searchlight beams probed the darkness, crisscrossing in their hunt for the intruders. Then the 'Christmas lights' appeared – hundreds of coloured flares dropped from British pathfinder aircraft that spread out as they fell on parachutes, a prelude to a night of bombing designed to strip the city of civilians and their homes. Wave after wave of bombers passed over central Berlin. To the west of Alexanderplatz, high explosive bombs exploded in a continuous thunder that rolled over the night sky. Then the incendiaries fell and Berlin caught fire. Clouds of smoke, lit blood-red from below, hung over the city.

It was already mid afternoon when I took the *Strassenbahn* to Alexanderplatz. I continued on foot past the Stock Exchange, heading west to get a closer look at the previous night's damage. Beyond the *Tiergarten,* smoke still billowed from stricken buildings. Ambulances dodged the rubble strewn across the roads. Crews of workers on mobile gantries repaired the overhead electrical lines serving the *Strassenbahn*. Civilians with shovels, their backs bent by work and dismay, cleared the tracks. Between the debris on the pavements, tables, chairs, and other items of rescued furniture were stacked. Clumps of dishevelled women and children, refugees in their own city, pushed prams filled with household treasures along streets lined, not by flats and shops, but by labyrinths of crumbling buildings.

A few cast disparaging glances in my direction, the first occasion on which I detected civilian resentment towards the *Waffen SS*.

On Oranienburger Strasse, *Wehrmacht* personnel toiled among the ruins of the *Neue Synagogue*. Remnants of its dome lay scattered on the pavement, the original golden colour showing through the scratched grey camouflage paint. I stopped to speak to a *Wehrmacht Feldwebel* directing passers-by around the rubble on the pavement, to ask if he knew any details about the severity of the attack.

'The worst so far, by far,' said the *Feld*. 'Two thousand dead – a battlefield – never seen such injuries, even on the *Ostfront* – women and children mostly – zoo took it hard – all the elephants killed – it's a shame, when I was a kid I loved it when we visited the zoo – and *Potsdamer Bahnhof* – no trains in or out.'

'It's a pity about the Synagogue, it was a beautiful building,' I ventured.

'What are you talking about,' corrected the *Feld*, 'it's been an army store for about three years.'

I had often walked past this building as an apprentice baker on my way home from twice-weekly classes at the trade college in Friedrich Strasse. The last time I passed it, in the spring of 1940, it was still a centre for Jewish prayer. Though it was a listed building, its demise, unlike the destruction of the Kaiser Wilhelm Memorial Church and the Charlottenburg Palace, escaped comment in the radio report that followed later in the day.

My father was sitting in his armchair behind a copy of the *Völkischer Beobachter* when I arrived home, a hard-faced silence his only welcome. On an occasional table by his chair was the church's copy of notification of my release from membership. I had overlooked the possibility that as an elder, the church authorities would inform my father of my decision to resign from the congregation.

The *Völkischer Beobachter* snapped shut. Father picked up the letter and screwed it into a ball. He tossed it in my direction. 'How could you embarrass me like this?'

There was no point in mentioning the small saving I would make by not having to pay the church tax, the *Kirchensteuer*, or assuring him that I still believed in a Supreme Being even if I felt disinclined to follow the teachings of a particular church.

To give my father's anger time to cool, I took a walk to the *Sturmlokal* in Lichtenberger Strasse where I was now a frequent visitor. I had become friendly with the *Luftwaffe Unteroffizier* in charge of the establishment and we often spent time sitting opposite each other at a table to discuss the deteriorating war situation over a few beers. This time was a little different.

'The Russians are at the Dnjepr – where did we go wrong Erwin?'

Anything that that hinted of defeatist talk could easily have got us both into trouble with the police but I had grown to trust the man from the *Luftwaffe*, a little. 'We lost a great opportunity at Dunkirk,' I said. 'My cousin, Theo Gerlach, was a machine gunner with a *Wehrmacht* unit there. They watched the British troops gather on the beach but even though they were easily within range, he was ordered not to fire on them. The British were sitting ducks but we let them escape.'

'*Naja* – even our boys more or less left them alone,' said my friend from the *Luftwaffe*.

'I also think we lost a great opportunity when we decided not to invade England,' I added. 'With the Atlantic to cross, Hamburg and Berlin would have been out of range of the American bombers.'

'The British – could we have defeated them on their home ground?'

'We were better prepared for war than the British, it might not have been easy but we could have done it. I've heard it said that the Scots would side with us – they've always hated the English.'

'Ah,' said the *Luftwaffe Unteroffizier* thoughtfully, 'more Ukrainians might also have joined us if we played our cards right.'

The *Unteroffizier* had a point. From my conversations with Ukrainians while stationed on the *Ostfront*, I was convinced many more of them would have sided with us against the communists were it not for the harsh treatment dished out by the *SD* but this was too risky a topic to pursue.

The resident gipsy trio struck up their music. Off-duty *Luftwaffe* personnel drifted in, shivering after their vigil on the *Flakturm* in Friedrichshain Park. As the evening wore on, alcohol declared its inevitable victory with the shameless squeals of women and the loud guffaws of men on the hunt for an amorous encounter.

A slim, youngish woman with light-brown hair sat at a table near the bar. My friend from the *Luftwaffe*, who had an eye for a pretty woman, twisted his neck to smile at her before turning his attention back to his beer.

'Not a bad looker,' he said in an admiring tone. 'How old do you reckon she is?'

'Thirty,' I replied, 'about your age.'

The *Unteroffizier* finished off his beer in a long gulp then ran his fingers through his dark curly hair. 'Things to do,' he said getting up from his seat and putting on his cap. 'I'll leave you to her – see you later.'

I was left thinking that my companion's words had been disordered by drink. What did he mean 'leave *you* to her'? As I finished my beer, the woman, now in the company of some older men, caught my eye.

'See something you like soldier?' she called across the room as she stubbed her cigarette into a metal ashtray.

Before I could think of some smart response, she was sitting on the seat vacated by my companion. Close up, the lines of strain on her face spoiled her beauty. I offered her a cigarette. She took it and hung it between her lips, bright red with lipstick, as she rummaged in her handbag.

'Here, let me.' I offered, striking a flame on my cigarette lighter.

She pulled her seat closer and leaned forward, left forearm and right elbow resting on the table. Our knees touched as the glowing tobacco ate into the white cigarette paper.

The gipsy band struck up with fiddle, tambourine and clarinet, playing music that had a frenetic, eastern flavour – 'music for the ears' as my *Luftwaffe* friend called it. Gradually, I had come to understand what he meant by this. Their music was joyful, sensual and totally without pretension, a welcome change from the austere works of Wagner or military marches designed to stir afresh feelings of loyalty to the Fatherland.

We exchanged names and potted histories of our lives, the usual sort of chitchat that resonates between a man and a woman when they first meet. As she told me about her work as a typist, she slid her hand under the table, to adjust her stockings I thought, but her fingers found the inside of my knee and made pleasant drumming movements.

'I hate the bombing,' she said. 'I get so frightened at home, alone.' As if reading my thoughts she added, 'Don't worry, I'm not a prostitute. All I want is a bit of fun to help me forget about the mess we're in. Who knows, we could be burned to a cinder tomorrow.' Her fingers worked their way onto my thigh.

I was nearly twenty years old and my sexual experience amounted to nothing more than a few minutes in a bordello in France a year earlier. Though she was not exactly the girl of my dreams, the woman had a fine figure and pleasant features. We both wanted sex, perhaps for different reasons, and the starving are willing to dine at any table.

When I next visited the *Sturmlokal* my friend from the *Luftwaffe* smiled broadly and said, 'Good in bed, isn't she?'

I had learned that a young man from the *Leibstandarte*, in a city lacking young men, would have no trouble attracting girls. Almost everywhere I went, opportunities for striking up relationships with women popped up and I resorted to keeping a diary to prevent my 'dates' clashing. Berlin, I realized, had become a city where many of the young and not so young women were on the hunt for sex. All a young chap wearing the uniform of the *Leibstandarte* – the elite regiment of the armed forces – had to do was cast a glance towards a likely looking girl. A slight nod of the head, a knowing smile, was all that was required to launch an affair.

22

New Year Celebrations, 1944

There was a large, elegant villa in the grounds of Lichterfelde barracks. A wide but short run of steps, flanked in summer by pots of pink and white petunias, led to a set of French doors sheltering under an arcade of three round-topped arches. This was the officers' mess and a venue for their frequent parties. On several occasions during my training in 1941, I served there as a waiter, keeping the guests supplied with the best *Sekt* and *Cognac*. The parties, which frequently ran through to the early hours of morning, often included entertainers among the guests, some of whom were famous throughout the *Reich*. At the start of the war, ambitious people from every walk of life were eager to curry favour with Hitler's *Leibstandarte* from whose ranks the rulers of the *Reich* would arise after our inevitable victory. Such guests were never in short supply, particularly during the high points of the year such as Christmas and New Year.

Though there was little opportunity for the level of privacy our officers enjoyed when entertaining female guests, NCOs were permitted to invite girlfriends to their quarters provided they were signed in and out at the guardhouse by the main entrance. Under normal circumstances, guests of the NCOs could remain until midnight but at New Year, this limit was extended to 1 am to allow some time for celebration. To entertain a girl in barracks after the permitted time would have risked loss of rank and a consequential reduction of pay.

Around the time of my twentieth birthday – just before Christmas 1943 – the frostbitten areas of my legs began to play up badly. Even the slightest brush against some everyday object – easily done because of the loss of sensitivity in the skin – caused the wounds to ooze yellow fluid and blood. This would have been hard to bear in the Russian winter and I secretly thanked the foresight of the doctors for not allowing my return to the *Ostfront*. After tolerating the irritation for several days, I decided to pay a visit to the *Waffen SS* hospital on Unter den Eichen, a wide, straight street lined by oak trees, not far from the Lichterfelde barracks.

A fellow *Unterscharführer* from the *Leibstandarte* was already sitting in the waiting room when I arrived, the only other patient. He stood up as I crossed the room and offered his hand in comradeship.

'Schimanski,' he announced, his eyes sparkling and mischievous.

'Bartmann,' I replied shaking his huge hand. With shoulders as square as a wardrobe Schimanski, a giant of a man, loomed over me. 'Haven't seen you about,' I remarked. On reflection, my quip was rather silly since such a tall man would have been conspicuous even in a regiment that selected only tall men.

'Just arrived in Berlin,' he replied in a deep, rumbling voice.

As we waited to see the doctor, we exchanged medical notes so to speak. He had taken a bad stomach wound in Italy, the aftermath of which was a tendency to break wind with a stink that could instantly dispel the appetite of a starving man.

'The bullet was spinning,' explained my new friend, 'caught hold of my guts and twisted them like a rope caught in a propeller.'

He was first to see the doctor and came from the examination room waving a piece of paper. 'Permission to fart, anywhere, anytime,' he boomed as he left the waiting room.

After a thorough examination, the doctor advised that I should check in to the *Krankenrevier* (sickbay) at the barracks to have the dressings on my legs changed regularly. Little did I realise this was the start of a routine that would last my entire life.

※·※

Celebrations in the medical orderlies' mess were reaching their climax in the final hours of 1943. Wary of exposing the slowly healing sores on my legs to accidental damage, I decided to spend a quiet night in bed and fell into a deep sleep with ease. I wakened with a start. Someone was shaking my shoulder.

'Shh, it's me – Schimanski.'

'What time is it?' I asked.

Schimanski's finger went to his lips. 'Shh – not so loud – I've got a little problem. Get dressed – it's about three o'clock.'

Schimanski already had my uniform laid out at the end of my bed. Still fuzzyheaded from my unwelcome awakening, I struggled into it and staggered after Schimanski as he led the way upstairs.

'The medics left me in the shit,' Schimanski complained as we entered the mess, 'buggered off while I was having a piss.'

On a fur coat spread across a table, a beautiful young woman – completely naked except for a pair of red shoes – posed with the grace of a professional model in the flickering yellow light of the candles at the four corners of the table.

'Who is she?' I asked.

'An extra from the film studios in Babelberg.'

'She should have left by now.'

'I know – that's the problem – how do we get out of this one Bartmann?'

The 'we' startled me into full wakefulness. 'You lot got yourself into this.' I hissed. 'Who brought her in?'

'I did.'

'Her clothes?'

'Can't find them- maybe she wasn't wearing anything under her fur coat when she arrived. We'll have to get her out before the *UvD* turns up or we're in the shit,'

'You mean *you* are in the shit,' I retorted angrily.

'Bartmann you *have* to help me get her out'.

I would certainly be apportioned a good share of the guilt if caught helping Schimanski but I gave way to his pleas.

'Thanks Bartmann.'

We wrapped the woman in the fur coat and tried to get her to stand, a skill that had all but abandoned her in her intoxicated state. 'We'll have to support her,' I said in exasperation. My recent promotion lurched on the lip of an abyss. 'How do we get her out of the barracks?'

'I'll think of that later,' replied Schimanski.

Suddenly, the girl flung her head back and began to sing. Schimanski's massive hand stemmed the flow of slurred lyrics.

'For God's sake Schimanski, don't smother her.'

We managed to get the girl through the corridors and outside without arousing suspicion. A frosty stillness welcomed in the first morning of 1944.

'There's a place near the officers' mess,' Schimanski explained, 'out of sight – we'll get her over the railings there.'

Keeping to the side of a low wall surmounted by a fence of pointed iron railings, we managed to get the girl to the 'quiet spot' behind a clump of bushes close to the officers' mess. Squeals of delight came from a room upstairs – a girl's voice. A fleeting image of a drunken chase came to mind.

'I wish I was an officer,' sighed Schimanski.

'Stop dreaming and help me get her over the fence,' I scolded.

We heaved the girl level with the top of the fence but her limp body was in danger of impalement on the spiked railings.

'It's no use,' I whispered, 'even if she was sober she would get hurt if we let her fall on the other side.' We lowered her to her feet.

'Stay here,' said Schimanski disappearing into the undergrowth, 'I won't be long.'

When he returned there was a broad smile on Schimanski's face. 'We're in luck,' he announced. 'The sentry on duty owes me a favour. We can slip her through the gate without signing her out.'

We took the girl through the guardhouse while the sentry looked the other way. I helped the girl to the seat at the nearby *Strassenbahn* stop and buttoned her fur coat against the cold night air. Meanwhile, Schimanski chatted to the guard.

A few weeks later, I was travelling on a crowded tram from Lichterfelde to the centre of Berlin when I noticed an attractive young woman boarding at the other end of the carriage. Our eyes met and I smiled. Her reaction was not one I expected. Her brows furrowed as she looked at me through squinting eyes. As if possessed by a sudden revelation her mouth dropped open and with nostrils flaring, she pushed the other passengers aside to make her way towards me. It was then I recognised her as the naked girl with the fur coat.

'You thoughtless swine,' she screamed as she aimed a slap at my face. 'I could have frozen to death.'

Luckily I was near the door of the tram and though it was travelling at speed, I managed to spring to the safety of the pavement before she had the chance to mount a full-scale attack.

23

Snobbery and Rebellion

Schimanski was having trouble with his stomach and a swelling behind my knee made walking painful. To set us on the road to recovery, an *SS* doctor prescribed a spell at a convalescent unit in Konitz, just across the Polish border and close to Schlochau where I was born. The *SS* presence there consisted mainly of *Sicherheitsdienst* and *Gestapo* personnel who spent their time monitoring the host of refugees flooding in from the east.

On arrival at the convalescent unit, we reported to the *UvD* who directed us to a barrack room occupied by a solitary soldier who told us that the entire *Kompanie*, led by *Hauptsscharführer* Grebarsche, consisted of only eight men. Grebarsche, as it happened, was the holder of the Knight's Cross, the only bearer of this prestigious award in the area despite the abundance of *Wehrmacht* generals.

There was a hotel in the town centre with a large lounge where men of all ranks spent their free time. One evening *Hauptscharführer* Grebarsche, in the company of another chap from the convalescent *Kompanie*, had gone on ahead. Schimanski and I arranged to follow later and meet up with them at the hotel. As we opened the door of the lounge, a *Wehrmacht* officer with gold-braided shoulder boards, a general, sitting at a table close to the door looked up. I glanced around the room and saw that Grebarsche and his companion had already occupied their usual seat in the far corner. As *Waffen SS* men we played everything by the book and, as per protocol, we turned to salute Grebarsche, the Knight's Cross holder.

The *Wehrmacht* general stormed from his seat. 'What's the meaning of this disgraceful behaviour in public,' he said curtly. You *completely* ignored me. Stand to attention when I speak to you. What sort of soldiers are you? *Waffen SS*, huh, when will you people ever learn how to behave?'

As the onlookers in the lounge stared at the unfolding drama, I wondered if the pompous little officer had ever seen action on the front line. The plain fact of the matter was that he was digging a hole for himself with his antagonistic attitude.

'*Herr General*,' I said angling my eyes to the corner where *Hauptscharführer* Grebarsche sat, 'perhaps you didn't notice the presence of a Knight's Cross recipient.'

Hauptsturmführer Gebarsche, overhearing what was going on, stood up at the side of his table, clicked his heels and bowed smartly in the direction of the general before introducing himself.

Blood rushed to the general's cheeks. At that moment, I caught the whiff of one of Schimanski's silent farts. The general sniffed the air.

'What's that terrible smell? This is outrageous, this is, is...' for a moment, the general was lost for words. 'Who did this?'

'I did *Herr General*, I can explain,' said Schimanski.

I may be wrong but I thought detected the hint of a smirk on Schimanski's lips.

'This is an affront, a *total* affront to military practice – gross insubordination,' the general blubbered through his fat cheeks. 'You won't get away with this, oh no. To show disrespect for an officer, *especially* in public, is a serious offence.'

Schimanski smartly took the medical certificate issued by the *SS* hospital from his tunic pocket and presented it to the general.

'*Herr General*, I apologise, but as you will see from this medical certificate, the inability to control my flatulence is the result of a serious wound to the intestines.'

The general's face turned from bright pink to fiery red as he read Schimanski's certificate.

I had no time for pompous oafs like this *Wehrmacht* general. He was one of those high-ranking officers who, in their outdated military snobbery, always seemed willing to pick on *Waffen SS* men. I must confess that it was with pleasure that I watched him squirm like a caterpillar impaled on a fishhook when he realised his mistake. We laughed about the incident as we drank our beer but the encounter with the general left me with a vague feeling of disquiet. There was something more rotten than Schimanski's flatulence lurking at the heart of the German military establishment – a social elitism alien to those of us in the ranks of the *Waffen SS*. The ordinary *Wehrmacht* soldier harboured no such antagonism. In an open display of *Kameradschaft*, a *Wehrmacht* unit based on the outskirts of Konitz invited the whole of our convalescent *Kompanie* – all ten of us – to a sailing club at a nearby lake. It was a fine breezy day and we looked forward to an exciting day's sailing.

'Please gentlemen, make yourselves at home,' said a *Feldwebel* as he ushered us into the clubhouse where a handful of his men waited to greet us. His hand stretched out towards a long table. 'Help yourself to some coffee and biscuits – or a glass of

Schnapps or beer if you prefer.'

One of the *Wehrmacht* soldiers reached into a brown paper bag on the table and pulled out several packs of cigarettes. 'A little present for our visitors,' he said sliding them across the tabletop.

Being polite, we opened a packet to offer each of our new friends a cigarette before lighting up ourselves. When we finished our coffee and *Schnapps*, our hosts led us to a timber jetty where sailing dinghies jostled against each other in the breeze. The *Feld* divided us into groups, allocating each to a different vessel.

As my confidence in our 'captain' grew, I began to enjoy the exhilaration of skimming across the choppy water – and the happy panic that gripped me as we tacked towards a heavily wooded shore on the far side of the lake. Suddenly, bullets hissed above our heads, perforating the billowing main sail. Though there was little chance of hitting a target from the heeling boat, I drew my pistol from its holster and fired several shots into the woods. Our 'captain' turned the dinghy and, with the wind now behind us, we made a rapid run to the safety of the clubhouse. Once ashore, I learned that we had survived the adventure without as much as a scratch between us.

'Damned partisans,' cursed the *Feld*, 'they've been causing more and more trouble lately – a real thorn in the flesh – getting bolder by the day. God knows, it's an effort to keep on top of the situation.'

Shortly after our lucky escape on the lake, Schimanski and I took a trip from Konitz to Warsaw where we had discovered a small chocolate factory willing to accept cigarettes in exchange for their produce. We lodged at the *SS* barracks on Narutowicz Square until we began to run short of money, then switched to cheaper accommodation in a *Soldatenheim* ran by the Red Cross. With the main railway station just across the street, we always took the table by the window and watched the world go by as we ate lunch. As we chatted about the occasion when Schimanski had taken me to a *Luftwaffe* establishment in Dahlem – not far from the Lichterfelde barracks – where we somehow managed to land up in changing rooms for the showers used by the girls that worked there, I noticed four monks crossing the road towards us. Dressed in habits, they formed a conspicuous group among the civilians going about their everyday business. The thought had just crossed my mind that they might pose a threat when a *Wehrmacht* patrol happened to pass by. Their sharp-eyed leader must also have had misgivings about the monks because, only a few metres from our viewpoint behind the window of the *Soldatenheim*, he stopped them.

Although I could not hear the exchange of words, it was clear that the monks were protesting vehemently. The *Wehrmacht* officer pulled open the robe of one of the men. The hair at the nape of my neck stood on end when I saw the array of weapons – pistols and hand grenades – hanging on the inside of the robes. The other 'monks', forced to open their habits at the point of *Wehrmacht* guns, revealed a similar cache of weapons. With hands on their heads, the imposters waited on the pavement until a car screeched to a halt outside our window.

'*Gestapo*,' said Schimanski coolly as the black uniformed men slammed the car doors behind them. 'Serves them right – these partisans are bastards,' he continued, 'blew up the *Wehrmacht* brothel not long ago – killed a few of the girls, nice girls, fond of opera. You would have liked them Bartmann. Never mind, it's been repaired. Fancy a visit?'

Schimanski knew the best places no matter where we went. '*Naja*, I agreed, 'but just for a beer.'

Of course I cannot be certain, but it is possible that the 'monks' had planned to attack the *Soldatenheim* in which case we had a lucky escape, our second in less than a week. We were no longer secure in Warsaw.

⚜·⚜

The guards at the brothel unlocked the door and let us in. A second set of doors opened into a hall where cigarette smoke hung in the air. When a table became vacant Schimanski, a towering hulk, pushed the competition out of the way. No sooner had we sat down when two girls latched onto us and sat on our knees. Though not bad looking, their behaviour was too brazen for my liking. We chatted about everyday things – the weather and the Russian push towards the west – before I put Schimanski's claim to the test. 'Do you like opera?' I asked the girl on my knee.

'Opera? Oh, I can't say I do – but surely you haven't come to a place like this to speak about opera,' she giggled as she grabbed my cap.

I almost managed to retrieve it but she squirmed to the side and thrust it up her skirt, between the top of her thighs.

'Give me back my cap,' I demanded. It was relatively new and I didn't want it messed up.

'Get it yourself,' laughed the girl.

I slid my hand up her skirt – there were no knickers – and tugged at my cap. Her thighs squeezed tight on my hand then, realising I wasn't playing a silly game, the girl suddenly got up from my knees and slapped my face.

'Tosser,' she yelled as she beat me on the head with her fists.

Everyone in the hall turned to look as I held up my arms to fend off the blows. Schimanski pushed 'his' girl away. 'Time for a tactical retreat my friend.'

The girls were still screaming at us as we reached the exit doors at the rear of the hall. Once outside, Schimanski laughed a deep and glorious laugh. 'The next time I'll take you to the *SS* brothel. I promise you Bartmann, the girls there *are* cultured – you can speak to them about opera to your heart's content.'

❦·❦

When our stay in Konitz came to an end, Schimanski and I travelled back to Lichterfelde barracks. By this time, the swelling behind my knee had made walking painful. I reported to the sickbay where a doctor ordered an urgent operation to remove a varicose vein.

Within a day or two of my operation in the *SS* hospital on Unter den Eichen, I was back on my feet and given the task of supervising an electrician, a member of the work party that arrived under guard each morning from the nearby Tempelhof concentration camp, to assist with the construction of an underground operating theatre. He was a friendly chap who openly confessed to being a habitual petty criminal since the start of the war. We had many interesting conversations about his former 'career' as he installed the wiring to the new X-Ray apparatus.

On the 17 July 1944, a truck raced into the hospital yard. The officer in charge jumped from the cab and called to me, '*Unterscharführer* – tell everyone that can walk to assemble here immediately.'

I hobbled as quickly as my bandaged knee allowed to spread the news through the wards. When I returned to the yard, I joined the queue of walking wounded waiting to receive rifles and pistols distributed from the rear of the truck.

'Until further notice we must be vigilant,' ordered the officer. 'The perimeter must be guarded in case anything out of the ordinary happens. No one is to enter without permission. Be prepared to defend yourselves – there are sufficient weapons for those confined to bed – everyone capable of handling a weapon is to be armed.'

Without any further explanation, the truck left the hospital and I was left wondering what was going on. I speculated that the panic had something to do with the inmates from the concentration camp. Whatever the reason for the state of high alert, the event added a flash of excitement to my time in hospital.

On the morning of the 21 July 1944, a hot sunny Friday, I was playing cards with a fellow patient in a side room when there was a *Sondermeldung* (special report) on the radio. The previous day, it announced, a clique of *Wehrmacht* officers had made an attempt on the *Führer's* life at the *Wolfsschanze* (Wolf's Lair, Hitler's headquarters in East Prussia) from which he conducted the war on the *Ostfront*. A bomb had detonated under a table killing four high-ranking officers. Hitler escaped with relatively minor injuries and took the whole affair as sign that, protected by Providence, he had been saved to complete his task of crushing Bolshevism. I realised then that the state of alert in the hospital had been to prepare us to resist any attempted coup by the *Wehrmacht* in Berlin. It appears then, that the commander of the *SS*, Heinrich Himmler, must have got wind of the plot against Hitler at least three days in advance of the bombing in the *Wolfsschanze*.

For me, the capture of the conspirators was welcome news. In a rising against Hitler, German would have fought German causing great loss life in my home city. At that time, the *Waffen SS* had recently slowed the British and Canadian advance on Caen and, thinking that Germany could still win the war, I viewed the attempt on Hitler's life as an act of treachery that would undermine our prospects of repelling the Allies on the Western Front.

❦

When released from hospital, I got in touch with Schimanski. We had become good friends and frequently spent time together in the Horst Wessel *Sturmlokal* in Lichtenberger Strasse, listening to the gipsy trio play their music while enjoying a few beers together.

On an evening in late summer 1944, Schimanski and I were standing at the bar when my friend from the *Luftwaffe,* the fellow in charge of the establishment, took us aside. 'There's something funny going on here,' he whispered. 'I think pistols are changing hands.' He rolled his eyes to indicate a hefty blond man sitting at a nearby table. 'That Dutchman – he works for the postal service – he receives the pistols.'

'Who supplies them?' I enquired.

'It's hard to credit this but I'm sure it's an *Oberfeldwebel* from the *Wehrmacht*. Lately, he's been in here every other evening.'

A few days later, I popped in for a beer. When I finished my drink, I made a visit to the toilet. As I opened the door, I was shocked to see an *Oberfeldwebel* from the *Grossdeutschland* division handing a pistol over to the Dutchman. Suspecting that the weapon was destined for the increasingly active Dutch underground fighters, I was unable to contain my anger. 'You bastard.' I raged, 'I hope that will be the pistol that kills you.' But there were two of them and, without proof, there was little I could do about the incident.

A week later I was sitting at a table with *Kamerad* Schimanski when in came the same *Wehrmacht Oberfeldwebel*. I looked him in the eye as he passed. 'Only a traitor sells contraband weapons to an enemy.'

He staggered to an abrupt halt to cast a dirty look in my direction. 'I want an apology for that remark,' he demanded. 'You have no right to address a soldier of superior rank in such a disrespectful way.'

Schimanski rose to his feet and looked the *Oberfeldwebel* in the eye. 'And just what are you going to do about it?'

Confronted by Schimanski's towering bulk, the *Oberfeldwebel*'s face went blank. He turned on his heels and left the premises without a word. That was the last time we saw him in our *Sturmlokal*. Although this was this trivial occurrence, at least in comparison to the great events in history taking place on our doorstep, it finally made clear to me the desperate situation facing the *Reich*. A rot had begun from within, an abject acceptance that we would lose the war which traitors were happy to exploit for their own personal gain. Shortly after this incident – I had just returned from collecting my rations from the barracks in Lichterfelde and was about to enter my parents' flat – I heard the screech of brakes from a car. I thought nothing of it and went into the flat. As I slipped off my uniform jacket, there was the loud banging of fists on the door. I opened it to see a *Hauptman* and *Feldwebel* from the *Wehrmacht*.

'Papers.' demanded the *Hauptman* in a stern voice.

I showed them my *Soldbuch* and the letter from my *Kompanie* commander giving permission for me to stay with my parents.

The *Hauptman* examined the documents then announced, 'You are under arrest.'

I was shocked. As far as I was aware, I had done nothing wrong. 'Why am I being arrested?' I asked.

'You don't have an official pass stating you are on leave.'

I had no idea what would become of me as we sped through the streets of Berlin. If an officer in the *Wehrmacht* decided I was a deserter, I would be in deep trouble and possibly shot without trial. At the *Wehrmacht* barracks, my captors flung me into a cell already occupied by other detainees. Time passed, slowly. Darkness fell and still no one came to take me for interrogation. In exasperation, I called through the bars of the cell door, 'I demand to see an officer.'

The *UvD* appeared. 'What's all the noise about?'

I tugged at the 'mirror' on my tunic collar with the *SS* runes. 'Look – I'm a member of the *Leibstandarte*. You've no right to hold me here. I demand to see an officer as soon as possible.'

Fortunately, the *UvD* saw sense and granted my appeal. Eventually the officer in charge showed up to listen to my story. His eyes rolled in their sockets as I harangued him mercilessly. 'I am a member of the *Waffen SS*. We have our own court in Berlin,' I explained, 'any disciplinary action levelled against me should be conducted by an *SS* court and not by the *Wehrmacht*'

He pursed his lips and tilted his head slightly, as if he were a child trying to work out the solution to a mathematical problem that was too difficult for him. 'Oh, very well then, I'll call Lichterfelde to ask them to send someone over to collect you.'

Several hours later, the *UvD* appeared at my cell door with none other than my old friend Schimanski. By the time the *Wehrmacht* formally passed me into Schimanski's tender care, it was well after midnight. At such a late hour, the buses and trams were running an hourly service so it took us quite a while to get back to the Lichterfelde barracks where I reported the incident to an officer who dismissed the matter without recording anything of it in my *Soldbuch*. The following morning I returned to my parents' flat. Though I have no proof, I still harbour the suspicion of a connection between the incident with the gunrunning *Oberfeldwebel* and my arrest by the *Wehrmacht*.

24

First Love and Final Gatherings

The year was on the wane, as was my enthusiasm for casual sexual encounters, which though superficially pleasurable, lacked lasting satisfaction. I was twenty years old and had enjoyed easy sex for months but had never met a girl with whom I had considered sharing my life. However, as the fortunes of war dictated, this situation was about to change.

I was returning to my parents' flat after a visit to the bakery in Memeler Strasse, when I chanced across a girl that had been in my year at school and was now a typist in the office of the nearby fire station. We chatted for a while, asking each other about the fate of mutual friends and acquaintances from our schooldays.

'I remember you had two friends – you always hung about with them – called yourselves the "Three Musketeers" – ah, yes Horst and Gunter – are they married?'

'I can't say – I haven't seen them for ages,' I replied.

'Ah,' she sighed, 'that's a pity – you three were such good buddies too – and what about you, do you have a regular girlfriend?'

'Never come across the right one,' I confessed.

She pressed an index finger to her cheek and thought for a moment. 'I have a friend you might like to meet. Her name is Ingeborg.'

Though she lived in Palisaden Strasse – a short distance from my parents' flat – I had never seen Ingeborg before. She had been married to an *Unterscharführer* in the 2nd Regiment of the *Leibstandarte*. He had fallen as a hero in Russia leaving her with a six-month-old baby daughter that he had seen only in snaps sent to him while he served on the *Ostfront*, a situation that was at this stage of the war far from uncommon. She was everything I could have hoped for, attractive, intelligent and considerate – and her eyes, their sparkling blueness, shone through the despair that war had heaped upon her.

At first we were just good friends, sharing time together because we enjoyed each other's company. Gradually, our relationship became more serious and at last, I had the chance to enjoy the pleasures of courtship. We went to the cinema or theatre together before the Allies' bombing ended such outings. Despite the war situation, this was a joyous episode in my life. I treasure the memories of the mornings I woke up beside her in her flat, or shared a stroll with her and her daughter in Friedrichshain.

❦·❦

A few weeks after the start of my liaison with Ingeborg, I arrived at my parents' flat to see my mother on her knees, filling a cardboard box with old shoes of mine that I thought she had thrown away. She looked up with a broad smile.

'It's lucky I held on to these,' she said. 'I had a visitor while you were out – someone you haven't seen in ages.'

'Why have you been digging all these old shoes out Mama?'

'As I was saying, we had a visitor, someone you know well.'

'Oh, who was it?'

'Horst Musch – you're pal from school – you just missed him.'

I was astonished. I had met Horst's mother in Palisaden Strasse shop only a few days earlier and she had said nothing of Horst's impending return.

'Did he say where he was going?'

'Home, I think – he was desperate for a pair of shoes.'

'Thanks Mama,' I said turning for the door.

Horst Musch's parents lived only a few blocks away. He had enlisted in the *Kriegsmarine* in 1941 and I had not met up with him since the spring of that year. I walked quickly, my steps sometimes breaking into short runs, until I reached his parents' flat.

'Ah Erwin – it's such a shame – you just missed him,' said *Frau* Musch. 'He's gone round to the Schmidti's pub – Gunter's home on leave.'

At last the 'Three Musketeers' were back together. We spent the evening revelling in shared memories. Gunter was now an engineer with the railway, home on leave from serving in Russia. Horst, who was wearing a pair of my old shoes, had just arrived after walking home from Greece to escape the advancing Soviet Army.

❦·❦

Soon after the final meeting of the 'Three Musketeers', my brother Horst and I managed to fix up a date to visit our parents' flat at the same time. It was a quiet day, free from the chilling wail of air-raid sirens and I looked forward to our family get-together.

'Horst and your father will be here soon,' *Mutti* said as I entered the flat. 'They've just gone over to the pub across the road for a beer. Have a seat on Papa's chair until they get back. I've got a little surprise for you.' She turned to the gramophone on the occasional table in the front room. 'It's your favourite,' she said holding up a shiny black disc. 'Do you remember how you used to pester me to play you this when you were a child?'

'*Naja*, I found it in a box under your bed – I must have been about five.'

'You were enthralled by the music – you take after your father – the love of opera must be in your blood.'

Taking care not to scratch its surface with the needle, *Mutti* carefully lowered the pickup arm to the record as it rose and fell with the uneven motion of the turntable. A hiss came from the gramophone's brass horn. I closed my eyes to allow the music to transport me to another realm. 'Belle nuit, o nuit d'amour' always sent ripples of pleasure coursing over my skin. Horst and Papa arrived. They had enjoyed more than one drink judging by their jovial mood. As we sat together at the table in the front room enjoying a rare cup of coffee, Papa retold his favourite tale about the burial that went wrong in Schlochau.

'They were lowering the coffin into the grave – somebody let go the end and it tipped up. What a shock – the lid came off and the body lurched forward with its hands stretched out as if it was about to grab the priest.'

Mama giggled, girlishly. 'He got such a scare – I've never seen an old man run so fast.'

To add to the jovial atmosphere, I did my Hitler impression, building up to a crescendo as I spoke. 'Everyone must do their duty to the *Reich*. Victory is in our grasp but it is to the women of the *Reich* that I wish to speak to today. We need more soldiers and we need them quickly. For that reason, pregnancy is cut to six months. Every woman is expected to do her duty to the Fatherland.'

'Not too loud Erwin, anyone on the stairs could hear you,' warned Horst. Then, glancing over his shoulder as if checking for the presence of uninvited visitors, he continued in a low voice. 'What I am about to tell you is top secret – you must not repeat this – tell no one.'

Wide-eyed with expectation, Papa and I nodded.

Mama's brows furled. 'Then perhaps you shouldn't tell us, Horst.'

'I trust my own family Mama,' replied Horst, brushing aside her concerns. He leaned forward in his seat and whispered, 'As you know, I am responsible for making the telephone connections when calls are made to and from the Air Ministry. Listen to this – the other day I made a connection between Göring and the *Führer*.'

Mama gasped. 'Oh Horst.'

'Göring asked the *Führer* for permission to use three special bombs but he refused. "If I use them in the east they will get us from the west," said the *Führer*.'

Papa pulled his chair closer to the table. 'What were these special bombs?'

'I don't know for sure but they must be powerful – although Göring clearly mentioned three I got the impression there might be more.'

'This is the *Wunderwaffe*,' exclaimed my father. 'Our scientists have done well with their rockets – who would put it past them to come up with something like this? It would really surprise the British if they put one of these special bombs in a rocket.'

25

Fond Farewells

Towards the end of November 1944, I took up duties as an instructor with a heavy machine-gun training *Kompanie* attached to the *Leibstandarte Ausbildung und Ersatz Bataillon* (Training and Replacement Battalion) based around Spreenhagen, the same training *Kompanie* I had volunteered to help earlier in the year when having a leg infection treated. I was posted to nearby Alt Hartmannsdorf, a tiny village consisting of nothing more than a few streets around two inns and a slaughterhouse. One of the inns, nicknamed the *Drei Mädel Haus* (Three Maidens) because the woman who ran the establishment had three daughters, stood at the end of the main street. With a hall boasting a raised stage, the *Drei Mädel Haus* had been popular amongst Berliners as a venue for wedding receptions and family parties. A second inn was located in the centre of the village, on a street corner opposite the slaughterhouse where our field kitchens stood in the yard. The *Kompanie* leader was a young officer about my age, *Untersturmführer* Schenk. He took up quarters in a large private house but always ate his meals in the company of the instructors at the inn opposite the slaughterhouse.

I shared a billet with a fellow *Unterscharführer* in the house of a local farmer who treated him as if he were a long lost Joseph, newly found. He worked in the *Kompanie* office and somehow managed to supply our hosts with little gifts of cake or wine but they looked at me with different eyes, making it very clear that I was not a welcome guest. They even filed a false complaint against me for messing the outside toilet during a party in the run up to Christmas. Hardly a pleasant word passed between us and, despite the onset of winter, I was always relieved to get out of that house in the morning.

The accommodation provided for the recruits – mostly young lads of sixteen or seventeen – was rather more primitive. They were crowded into bunkers half-buried in a nearby field. My squad occupied four of these bunkers, each one accommodating fifteen recruits. Their toilet was nothing more than a pit scraped in the sandy soil found in that area of Germany. Above the pit, a wooden batten with holes cut out – a *Donnerbalken* (thunderboard) – served as a communal toilet seat. With no hot water available, washing was a brief and uncomfortable experience for the youngsters. To enable them to bathe properly I took them to the nearby Oder-Spree canal when weather conditions allowed. They collected their meals – often no more than a slice of bread and boiled potatoes with the skins still on – from the field kitchen and took them back to the bunkers to eat. In just six weeks, the recruits would have to learn the tips that might help them survive at least their first day fighting the Russians. Field training and weapons practice were the chief activities. At night, and in the thick mists that settled over the wintery countryside, they practised map reading and navigation. Life was hard for the recruits who until then had enjoyed all the comforts of a home life such as they were in these difficult times. Still, their living conditions were no worse than those I experienced during two cruel winters on the *Ostfront*.

Starting early each Wednesday morning, I marched a troop of blood donors drawn from the ranks of the recruits approximately twelve kilometres to Erkner, to board the electric train to central Berlin. Because each donor received a generous portion of salami and a bottle of red wine, there was never a shortage of volunteers. After arriving at the *SS* surgical unit on Unter den Eichen before noon, I left them in the hands of the attractive nurses, many of whom were Scandinavian volunteers. With only a couple of bays where the nurses collected blood, it took the whole afternoon to process my squad. This allowed time for me to visit my parents' flat in Strausberger Strasse before returning to pick up the blood donors in the evening.

One day, after dropping off a squad of blood donors in a miserable winter drizzle, I was about to enter the close of my parents' flat when a tapping on glass attracted my attention. The younger daughter of the Jewish family that lived next door was at the widow of her flat, her face ghostly white against the black interior.

I pointed to my chest.

She nodded, pointed downward then disappeared from view.

I went into the close, out of sight of passers-by, to wait for her. The hurried steps of dainty feet followed the metallic click of a door latch echoing down the stairwell. When she came into sight, she hesitated on the final flight of steps.

'Erwin, I don't know who else to turn to, and I don't want to put you in a difficult situation, but I have a favour to ask.' She said the words deliberately, calmly, though her eyes glistened with tears. Her nimble feet brought her quickly down the last few steps. In her hand was an envelope. 'My father died – he was a prisoner in Oranienburg Concentration Camp – it's about the body,' she said offering the brown envelope to me.

I took a letter from the envelope and read that the body of the girl's father would be released only if a representative reported to Oranienburg to sign the relevant papers. Oranienburg was not exactly round the corner and with Jews banned from public transport, how could she possibly get there before the authorities disposed of the body?

'You're the only one who can help us Erwin. I'll come straight to the point – would you sign the papers on our family's behalf?'

'I'll have to get permission from my commanding officer at Lichterfelde,' I said. 'I can't promise he will allow me to do this for you.' For a moment, I thought she would embrace me but that would have violated the etiquette of the times, we both realised that.

Her eyelids lowered over her deep-brown eyes. She sighed deeply and said, 'Thank you, Erwin. That's a great comfort to me.'

Although the Jewish girl remained in the next-door flat with her sister and mother until at least January 1945, this was the last time I saw her. I left my parents' flat early to allow time to travel to Lichterfelde to obtain the necessary letter of permission, which my commanding officer wrote without comment. Fortunately, I was able to travel to Oranienburg the following day to sign the release form for the body, a tiny scrap of solace among the multitude of tragedies striking families across war-shattered Europe. Since I never saw her again, I can only hope that girl somehow managed to get to Oranienburg in time to arrange her father's burial in the nearby Jewish graveyard.

Apart from the welcome news that our forces, which included the *Leibstandarte*, had managed to force an Allied retreat in the Ardennes, the arrival of 1945 brought no relief from the anxieties of war to Berliners. The frequent bombing raids had worn everyone down. Many had given up caring if they would survive the next onslaught. For those women with children, it was an unrelenting struggle to protect their offspring from the deprivations imposed by war. Their morale ravished by grief, thousands of them visited the graveyards of Berlin to bid farewell to sons and daughters whose bones had been crushed by falling masonry or the burning timbers of doomed buildings. Often they had no homes to return to, or husbands with whom they might share their grief. The relentless bombing had not only pounded their houses to dust – it had burnt out every emotion but despair and scorn for the phantasms of the fanatical cult that had led Germany into this situation.

On what proved to be my final visit to Strausberger Strasse, in the middle of January 1945, my father insisted on escorting me to the railway station when I was ready to leave. With a parent's instinct, he had foreseen the danger that confronted us on Grosse Frankfurter Strasse where a crowd seemed to form from nowhere. At first, they simply stared at me as if the calamity that had descended upon them was entirely my fault. Then a stone cracked against the wall a few metres in front of me, another stuck even closer, just missing my head. The situation threatened to boil over into an outright attack. As my father remonstrated with the attackers, I clasped my loaded pistol inside my uniform jacket, ready to fire into the air. To feel the wrath of my fellow citizens was an extraordinarily harrowing experience for me but it was not without good reason that they felt the need to vent their hatred of the Nazi regime. The British and American armies had broken our counter attack in the Ardennes and every day brought them closer to the Rhine. Disturbing accounts of rape and brutal mutilation recounted by refugees fleeing East Prussia were spreading like wildfire and Allied bombers flew over Berlin day in, day out. The Third *Reich* was on its knees. Bearing the name 'Adolf Hitler' on the cuff band of my tunic, they saw me as the personification of everything they detested. The days when people would go out of their way to curry favour with any member of the *Leibstandarte* had come to a bitter end.

On the bare twigs of a stand of young birch, a shower had left beads of water dangling precariously in the light breeze, each one a jewel shimmering with the colours of the rainbow in the crisp winter sunshine. It was Saturday morning, the first Saturday in February, mild for the time of year. Ingeborg had arranged for a babysitter to look after her daughter and I was looking forward to her visit as I led my platoon of recruits back towards Alt Hartmansdorf. They were in good spirits, singing soldiers songs – until a startled cry killed the melody and brought them to an abrupt halt. A recruit pointed in the direction of Berlin. '*Unterscharführer* – look.'

I shaded my eyes from the sun. A dark cloud hovered over our capital city.

'There must be a thousand of them,' groaned the recruit.

The silence of despair fell over my squad. As we approached Alt Hartmansdorf an hour later, the last of the American B-17 bombers had turned for home. Instead of rushing to the field kitchen near the slaughterhouse for their tasteless meal of boiled potatoes, the recruits turned their eyes towards the clouds of smoke billowing into the skies over Berlin.

Later that afternoon I cycled the five kilometres northwards to Fangschleusse, to meet Ingeborg at the rail station. I leaned my bicycle against the wall of the waiting room praying she had survived the bombing raid. At last the train from Berlin appeared, its wheels beating an unhurried clickety-clack as they crossed the joins in the rails. It drew to a leisurely halt alongside the platform. My eyes darted from one carriage door to the next as a trickle of visitors emptied onto the platform. Ingeborg appeared. She ran to me, pressed her body close against mine and sobbed. I held her close to quench her anguish.

'Oh Erwin it was terrible, terrible.'

'Tell me – was Strausberger Strasse hit?'

'Yes, but there's nothing to worry about. A bomb exploded at the rear of your parents' house but they had already left to stay with your uncle. A fire brigade officer said they would make it wind and rain proof with a tarpaulin.'

'I saw the planes when we were on a training exercise. It must have been terrifying in Berlin.'

'I was on my way to work when the sirens went. I was lucky. If I had arrived on time, it would have been the end of it for me. The building took a direct hit. It was completely destroyed.'

'Where did you go?'

'To the public shelter at Schlesischer Bahnhof,' she said amidst a fresh flood of tears. 'I met *Frau* Müller just before I left. She was beside herself with grief. The police had told her to go to the girls' school in Neuenburger Strasse to identify her daughter's body. The blast from the bombs stripped the girls naked, she said, more than a hundred of them. Some of them had been torn limb from limb and were unrecognisable.'

Saying goodbye to Ingeborg that evening was hard to bear. She lent from the open window of the carriage, waving until the curve of the track took her out of sight. I returned her wave and continued to watch as the train shrank into the distance.

On the afternoon of 14 February, my parents' wedding anniversary, and ironically Ash Wednesday, reports came over the radio that American and British bombers had burned Dresden. The masterpiece of baroque architecture, whose beauty was at least equal of that of Paris, lay in cinders. Refugees from East Prussia – mainly women and children desperate to escape the rape and murder perpetrated by the advancing Soviet soldiers – had crammed into Dresden unaware that many of them were doomed to be roasted alive as they hid in the cellars of buildings consumed by the hellish inferno.

On Monday 26 February, the American bombers turned their attention back to Berlin with merciless ferocity. With the centre of the city already a heap of rubble, it was inevitable that the bombers would extend their path of destruction farther to the east, towards the Friedrichshain district where my parents and Ingeborg lived. Two days after the bombing, black smoke still poured into the skies. Surely now there was nothing left to burn.

It was with a heart full of trepidation that I waited for Ingeborg's visit the following Saturday. Until then I threw myself with all possible vigour into training the recruits who had divided themselves into those whose fanaticism had been enflamed by the bombing and those who showed all the signs of despondency.

Winter returned with the beginning of March. An icy breeze swept the platform at the Fangschleusse halt. Exactly on time, the train from Berlin trundled into view. I stood on the edge of the platform peering into the slowing carriages for the first glimpse of Ingeborg. She gave a little wave of her hand. I ran alongside until the train came to a halt then opened the carriage door.

'Your parents are fine Erwin,' she said as she stepped from the carriage. 'Their flat was destroyed but they were already in an air raid shelter. They've returned to your father's uncle in the meantime. Memeler Strasse *Bahnhof* took a direct hit – hundreds were in there at the time. Bombs are still going off without warning.'

'Time delay fuses – they're designed to hamper rescue workers,' I explained.

'Oh Erwin,' Ingeborg sighed, 'I wish this was all over. I can't stand this anymore. What sort of life is this?'

I put my arms around her and held her near but could find no words of consolation as we walked the country lanes towards Alt Hartmannsdorf. She talked about her experience in the air-raid shelter; how the walls shook under the waves of detonations, how the electric lights failed leaving the terrified occupants in total darkness.

'Now,' Ingeborg said, as if relieved of a great trouble, 'let's just enjoy what's left of the day. I managed to find enough salami to make sandwiches.'

In the winter sunshine, we ate our picnic in the graveyard at Alt Hartmannsdorf, amongst the dead. She smiled once or twice, which was enough to lift my spirits. All too soon, it was time for her to return to Berlin. There was a hard lump in my throat as the train left the platform. Somehow, I knew I would never see Ingeborg and her daughter again.

The *Ausbildung und Ersatz Bataillon* was incorporated into *Regiment Falke*. A fresh batch of recruits arrived, all members of the *Hitlerjugend*. Oh, they knew it all – or at least thought they did. For them it was all, 'Hooray, we'll win the war for Hitler, *Sieg Heil*.' None of them showed the least desire to participate in the training exercises that might soon save their lives. Well, they came to the right place to have their arses kicked into shape. At two o'clock on a rain-soaked morning, I pulled them out of their beds for marching in full kit. As we made our way along a forest track, there were the usual complaints but one of the *Hitlerjungen* lads overstepped the mark.

'Nobody gets me out of bed for nothing. I tell you, he'll be the first to get it', said a boy at the front of the group without realizing I was within earshot.

I caught up with the cocky youngster, grabbed him by the shoulder and swung him round to face me. Before he could utter a word, I screwed the cloth of his camouflage jacket with my left hand, at his chest. The fist of my right hand, filled with live rifle ammunition, thrust at his chin. 'Here – take this', I growled as the rest of the squad looked on. 'Try it.'

In a faltering voice he said, 'I apologise *Unterscharführer*'.

I often spent the evenings at the *Drei Maedel Haus* in the company of my fellow instructors, chatting or playing cards. One evening as we drank our *Flieger Bier* – a low alcohol concoction and the only kind of beer available at the time – one of my companions told me the officers had decided to arrange a show to amuse the troops.

'They're looking for acts Erwin,' he said. 'Why don't you do that little sketch where you impersonate Hitler – the one where he tells women to shorten pregnancy for the sake of the *Reich*?'

The show went ahead – on the day before it was my duty to escort the recruits to witness the execution of deserters – and was a great success. A tango performed by an *Unterscharführer* and his partner had the crowd doubled up with laughter, a rare treat in these dire times. She was made of rags stuffed into a dress borrowed from a local girl and tied to the *Unterscharführer* at the ankles so that she matched his every step with perfect precision. But there was no impression of Hitler from me – openly making fun of the *Führer* would certainly have brought a visit from the *Gestapo*.

⚜·⚜

The execution of *Fahnenfluchtigen* (deserters) was a weekly routine that took place on Fridays, in front of a sandy hillock. To see at close range the atomised blood and guts blast out of the condemned soldier's back as bullets shot through his body must have shocked the recruits. Yet, even after witnessing this dreadful spectacle, a recruit from the platoon under my command went missing one night. In an act of mesmerising stupidity, he sent a postcard, stamped in Frankfurt, to his sister who lived there saying that he had deserted and wanted to meet her at the railway station.

The vigilance of the postman was the young man's downfall. As he was about to put the card through the sister's letterbox, he read the message and immediately alerted the police who arrested the sender as he waited on the platform. On his return to Spreenhagen, he received the inevitable, and inescapable, sentence of death from an *SS* court martial. The following Friday evening at 6 pm, he faced his executioners. 'God bless Germany,' he said stoically as awaited his fate. The bullets ripped through his body and he slumped to the ground, his tunic smoking at the exit wounds on his back. But a flicker of life still burned in the young heart. An officer stepped forward to aim his 08 at the young lad's head. He pulled the trigger – the tragic end of yet another life. Seventy years later, the horror of this shooting still visits my dreams.

26

The Last Redoubt

At 3 am on Monday 16 April 1945, the final act of the drama that would see the demise of Hitler's Third *Reich* opened with a massive Russian artillery attack on the heavily defended hills, the *Seelower Höhen*, overlooking the eastern approaches to Berlin. That evening, as I left the *Drei Mädel Haus*, I stopped to watch the clouds above the horizon pulse as if lit from within by violent lightning.

At around midday on 17 April, a convoy of trucks arrived from the Lichterfelde barracks. We hurriedly packed our machine guns, ammunition and personal belongings onto them and were soon speeding through the country lanes in warm sunshine. One of the youngest recruits – a boy with eyes as blue as flax flowers – wore a worried look on his face as he asked if we were heading for Berlin. 'I think it's the Oder front for us – a chance to put your training into practice,' I replied.

We joined the eastbound lane of the Berlin-Frankfurt *Autobahn* before heading south, through idyllic countryside, until we reached Beeskow where an *Oberscharführer* was awaiting our arrival in front of a school. He ordered us to stack our personal belongings in a corner of the hall. 'All documents are to be handed in – everything except your *Soldbuch*,' he announced. 'You must keep your *Soldbuch* with you at all times. If you are caught without it you will be taken for a deserter and shot.'

We left the school and travelled, this time to the north-east, through Müllrose and towards the Oder River. Their faces as grey as potter's clay, a deathly silence had fallen over the recruits – no more 'Hooray' and '*Heil* Hitler'. The thought of confronting the brutal Bolshevik – an image burned into their brains as they grew up – on their own doorsteps had chilled their blood. Now, I dared to think that defeat was not only possible but also inevitable.

By late afternoon, our twelve machine-gun crews were settling into prepared positions at the edge of a wood on top of a hill overlooking the Frankfurt–Müllrose road. Lichtenberg, a small village, lay a few kilometres to our rear. From the north, the ominous thunder of fierce artillery exchanges on the *Seelower Höhen* continued as we set our machine guns on their mounts. *Untersturmführer*

Schenk visited one machine-gun position after the other, telling the crews the settings for the range and sweep of their weapons. Having adjusted and checked these on the two machine guns under my command, I reported to him, '*Untersturmführer*, our positions are ready.'

'Good, good,' he answered with a slight tremble in his voice. 'Tell me – I believe you were with Army Group South until '43 – what do you think we should do now?'

'It might be wise to do a little research.'

'Meaning?'

'Send out an intelligence-gathering patrol to get early warning of an attack.'

'Who do you suggest should do this?'

As the only one present with first hand knowledge of fighting the Russians I volunteered, 'I'll take two recruits with me – it will be useful experience for them.'

Armed with machine pistols, we made our way to an industrial building that lay in the distance. Although it appeared completely deserted, we approached it with the utmost caution and made our way to a door at the side.

'Cover the entrance,' I whispered to my young *Kameraden*.

A sickly-sweet smell caught my nostrils as I pushed open the door. I listened to the silence from within for half a minute before stepping inside to see wooden barrels stacked against every wall: a *Schnapps* distillery.

One of the recruits banged the side of a barrel with a clenched fist. 'They're full,' he said, 'should we take some back for our *Kameraden?*'

'Just a little,' I replied. The last thing I wanted was for the youngsters under my command drink to themselves silly but a little treat might cheer them up. I kept a lookout while the two recruits found an empty pail of the sort used to store jam in these days. 'Fill it and then empty the barrels,' I ordered.

'*Unterscharführer* Bartmann, the *Schnapps* must be worth thousands of Marks – it seems a pity to throw it all away.'

'Don't argue with the *Uscha*,' scolded the other recruit. 'I've heard refugees from East Prussia tell how the Russian hordes behave when they overrun our towns and villages – they go wild on plundered alcohol. Do you want your mother and sisters raped and murdered by the drunken thugs?'

I moved along the rows of barrels opening the taps as I went. The two youngsters followed my example and soon the amber contents of every barrel was pissing onto the floor, forming expanding puddles whose advancing rims found their way to the drains.

We returned to our lines with the pail of *Schnapps*. I reported our findings to our youthful *Untersturmführer* who seemed relieved to know that there was no imminent Russian attack. Under my advice, he ordered the liquor in the pail to be diluted before offering a single mouthful to anyone who wished it. Most of the recruits, little more than boys, had never drunk strong spirits before and only a few of my squad took up this offer. As darkness approached, I poured the remainder of the *Schnapps* onto the ground.

Throughout that night, a heavy artillery bombardment shook the earth. Every young face bore the furrow-lines of fear. 'Don't worry,' I assured them, 'the detonations are too far away to do us any mischief. Ivan doesn't know we're here yet.'

'They're too close for comfort.' exclaimed one of the recruits whose shoulders yanked up tight at every whizz or bang.

'How do *you* know?' piped up the recruit who had complained on the overnight march. 'He's on old hare, he can tell.'

I felt my lips pull an involuntary smile. It was strange, but nevertheless gratifying, to hear myself referred to as an 'old hare' though I was not yet twenty-two years old. Yet it was easy to understand the recruit's anxiety – I had felt the same tension when crossing the Dnjepr under the protection of *Unterscharführer* Nowotnik.

'Settle down and get some sleep,' I said, feeling almost fatherly.

❦·❦

A depressingly grey dawn crept over the horizon, the signal for the start of a barrage of 15 centimetre Russian mortar shells that fell with frightening accuracy along our front line. No one could hear the screams of the wounded above the thud of continually exploding rounds; the land itself seemed to shake with fear. I popped my head above the line of the trench to make sure the Russian infantry had not crept up on us under the protection of the barrage. At that instant, a shell detonated close by, sending a gust of tiny slivers of steel blasting against my face. As I ducked back under cover, the recruits looked at me as if they had seen the devil himself. Only then did I notice the warm rivulets of blood trickling down my cheeks. Once again my guardian angel was at my side; none of the little steel needles had found my eyes and those that were imbedded in my skin were easily plucked out. As the bombardment waned, German steel helmets appeared above the lines of our trenches. Someone close by was shouting, swearing, as he pointed in the direction of the Frankfurt-Müllrose road.

A squadron of Russian T-34 tanks was heading south. I raised my binoculars.

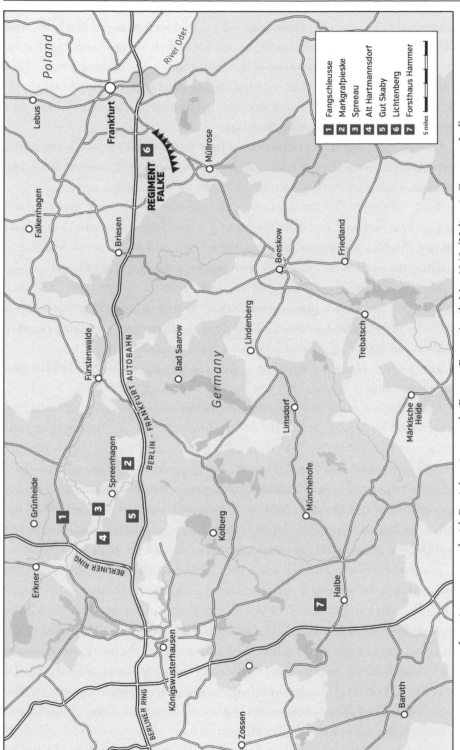

Locations connected with Erwin's actions on the Eastern Front, April–May 1945. (Helion & Company Ltd)

The image that loomed into focus sickened me to the pit of my stomach. Women and children were bound to the tanks' guns. Though they were too distant for me to hear their wails above the sound of the tank engines, the body language of the mothers told its own pitiful tale. Cold, silent, helpless rage filled my heart.

'What should we do?' yelled one my machine-gun crew, his boyish face contorted by an expression of confused agony.

One accidental pull on a trigger could have startled every one of our machine guns into unleashing a hail of bullets at the tanks, which were easily within range. 'Hold fire,' I said through gritted teeth. 'Let the officers decide.'

After a short but heated discussion, the officers let the tanks pass without firing a single shot but I dared not speculate the fate that might await the terrified hostages. We all knew of, and believed, the reports of Russian tanks deliberately squashing columns of refuges under their tracks as they fled East Prussia.

Russian fighter planes swooped on our trenches, raking the area with machine-gun fire. I made sure my recruits kept their heads down and we escaped the onslaught without a single casualty. By early afternoon, an enemy infantry battalion was gathering without hindrance just a kilometre away.

'Don't worry about the bayonets,' I told the youngsters of the machine-gun crew whose trench I shared, 'they won't get close enough to use them.'

Mutterings of anxiety continued to pass between the recruits as we waited for the inevitable onslaught. At last, the enemy infantry charged. Our machine guns unleashed a storm of bullets into their killing zone, scything through wave after wave of brown uniforms. The two crews directly under my command performed well and we managed to hold back the attack on our sector of the defence line. My experience on the *Ostfront* enabled me to keep our losses to just two men. One of these we buried in the *Friedhof* in Lichtenberg, the other, a handsome young chap, I buried with the help of two *Kameraden*, close to where he fell.

The next Russian attack was more determined. They had found a gap in our lines and *Untersturmführer* Gessner's infantry platoon left the cover of the woods to set off down the hill, ahead of our machine-gun positions, with the aim of throwing back the enemy attack. Unfortunately, he took his unit too close to the enemy for us to give effective machine-gun support. With the intention of fending off any assault on Gessner's squad, I led one of the crews down the hill to get a better firing position. Having covered about 500 metres, we came under intense small-arms fire and threw ourselves to the ground. When the firing stopped, I was horrified to see a Russian infantry platoon close on *Untersturmführer* Gessner. He was on his knees with a pistol at his temple. There was a puff of smoke and he slumped to the side. His courage had not failed him.

I pulled my machine-gun crew back to our lines at the edge of the woods only to find the other recruits exactly where I had left them. 'If you had followed us we could have saved *Untersturmführer* Gessner,' I roared angrily only to be confronted with an avalanche of excuses intended to justify their inaction.

The night passed without further event.

❄❄

Ingeborg? I could hear the whistle of thrushes in the trees behind our silent machine guns yet she came to me, smiling. A dream had taken me under its wing.

'One more time Erwin, I wanted to see you just one more time.'

A great happiness came over me. We were in Friedrichshain Park, sitting on a bench by the *Märchenbrunnen*, hand in hand in the sunshine. Ingeborg's daughter sat on the low wall by the pool, her hand splashing the water. A tantalizing fragrance, a scent of summer, seemed to promise contentment. A voice broke into my happy illusion. Ingeborg stood and took her child's hand. 'Goodbye Erwin, may your guardian angel always be with you.' I felt a hand grip my shoulder.

'*Unterscharführer* Bartmann.'

I opened my eyes. '*Untersturmführer* Schenk,' I mumbled groggily. The precious, illusory moments with Ingeborg melted into eternity. The feeling of happiness that had accompanied my dream gave way to a sickening melancholy.

'What do you think will happen next?'

I gathered my thoughts. 'They can't shift us with an infantry assault alone. They'll hit us with artillery or tanks as soon as they get organised – then their infantry will come at us again.'

As I swigged at my water bottle to freshen my dry mouth, the air whistled and the earth shuddered under the mighty thud of a large calibre artillery shell exploding in the woods just behind our lines. 'They're finding the range, keep your heads down.' I warned my young *Kameraden*.

Soon we were helpless under a hail of shells so intense the individual detonations merged into a continuous, deafening thunder. The air, reeking of burnt cordite, rasped at the back of my throat. Then silence, a moment of peace that was soon obliterated by the wild howling of Russian infantry, '*Urra, Urra*,' a chant from hell, sung by vengeful devils.

'God save us – there are thousands of them.' a recruit exclaimed.

Uttering a 'brr-bbr', like a gang of chainsaws working in a forest, our machine guns cut into the charging Russians but still they closed on our lines.

'*Uscha* the barrels are overheating.'

'Keep firing.'

Wave upon wave of enemy infantry threw themselves against the storm of bullets that at last broke their attack. Amongst the heaps of Russian bodies, there were isolated movements and cries for help. Despite intermittent fire from our lines, the Russians made every effort to retrieve their wounded and dead comrades.

At around 3 am the following morning – the *Führer's* birthday, and a cold start to a wet day – the Russians attacked with renewed vigour and on a wide front. Once more, we inflicted heavy losses and managed to repel the attack – it would have been murderous chaos if they had managed to get amongst us while it was still dark. A second attack followed at about 6 am. Three great swathes of brown uniforms, one behind the other, came at us as if in a scene from an old war film. The first row threw themselves to the ground, behind them the second row knelt and behind these stood the third row. The air around our attackers turned white with gun smoke as each row fired, one after the other. We replied with a tempest of machine-gun fire, the barrels of our weapons smoking as we emptied belt after belt of ammunition without pause. In the Russian ranks, men fell as if suddenly transfigured into rag dolls.

Shells from the dreaded '*Ratsch-bumms*' shrieked overhead, exploding close to our rear. With our machine guns now jamming with the heat of continuous firing, and the Russian infantry threatening to overrun our first line of defence, we spontaneously rose as one to scarper through the storm of shrapnel to our second line of defence, across ground that might erupt under our feet at any moment. At last, we reached the relative security of our trenches, which although shallower than those on the first line, were still intact.

During a lull in the shelling, a *Wehrmacht Feldwebel* piled into my trench. With grunts and spits thrown in, he had invented his own novel expletives, which might be translated by, 'The shitty bastards – the fucking fuckers have fucked off!'

'Who?' I asked.

'The officers.'

Overcome with fury I joined in the cursing. 'The shits – backboneless shits – I take recruits to witness the execution of deserters and now they do this – the fucking arseholes.'

'That's a bitter pill for them to swallow,' hissed the *Feldwebel*.

Now all that remained was a desperate band consisting of anyone able to handle a weapon – abandoned *Wehrmacht* personnel, old men pressed into service as *Volkssturm* combatants and boys of the *Hitlerjugend* determined to make a name for themselves. Words cannot describe that theatre of chaos.

In an attempt to restore some sense of order, the few remaining *Wehrmacht Feldwebels* and I took command of the ragged survivors. Suddenly, though only an *Unterscharführer*, I found myself acting as *Kompanie* leader with the fate of about eighty men and boys in my hands.

Throughout the night, the Russians pressed home an attack in heavy rain but despite our inferior numbers and heavy losses, we managed to hold our ground. Sleeping was utterly impossible because of the continual skirmishing and there was no food except for our meagre iron rations. Every one of us was close to the point of collapse. Then, as dawn broke, the bitterest news imaginable filtered through. A large concentration of Seydlitz troops – German soldiers who had deserted to the Russian side – was attacking our positions.

Under constant fire, we pulled back to the third and last set of defence trenches. At about only a metre deep they offered minimal cover but had foxholes positioned at intervals to offer extra protection. *Panzerfaust* anti-tank weapons were distributed as Russian dive-bombers joined the attack. Bombs whistled to the earth, striking with frightening accuracy. As I cowered in my foxhole the horrifying thought came to me that if a bomb struck nearby, I would be buried alive. Suddenly, I relearned the art of prayer.

At last, the bombers left the skies but this was no respite from the fighting. The grunts of approaching tanks filled the lull in the cacophony of combat. I ventured a glimpse over the crest of my trench. A stand of birch at about three hundred metres quivered as their silvery trunks groaned and splintered. A Josef Stalin burst into view. With 122mm guns these tanks, the heaviest in the Soviet armoury, could punch gaps in our defences through which their faster cousins, the T-34s, would rush. I grabbed my *Panzerfaust,* removed the safety pin from the trigger mechanism, and snapped the sighting lever into the upright firing position. Having only used this weapon twice in training, I was not at all confident that I would hit the approaching tank. Every beat of my heart sent blood hammering through my body. I lowered my head to align my eye with the sixty-metre range slot on the sighting lever. The steel leviathan was trundling straight towards me, the dry high-pitched metallic squeaks from its tracks piercing the deep snorting of its engine. My thumb tightened on the trigger lever. I took a deep breath to calm my nerves and waited for the tank to come into range.

A cloud of white smoke billowed from a foxhole about fifty metres to my left.

Scheisse! A recruit had lost his nerve and fired his *Panzerfaust* too soon. The rocket swished through the air but landed ten metres short. The steel monster came to a sudden halt. Its engine revved hard, the gearbox grating as the panicking driver fumbled to engage reverse gear. Minutes later, the tank commander, his confidence restored by the arrival of several T-34s, resumed his advance on our lines, this time further to my left and out of range of my *Panzerfaust*. They were heading for the recruit, machine guns spitting a hail of fire. Flame flashed from the muzzles of the tanks' guns. Shells exploded amidst our lines creating unrestrained panic. When the tanks reached our shallow trenches, they turned to run their tracks along their length. Howls of agony rose up from German soldiers as the tanks crushed their bones. We left our wounded behind as we fled in ignominious terror.

As I rushed through the woods, I came across the young *Leibstandarte* recruit with flax-blue eyes. He had pulled himself against a tree trunk with a leg – it could no longer be considered *his* leg – sticking out to the side at a horrifying angle. The top of the thighbone and part of the pelvis was missing. His face ghostly white and glistening with beads of sweat, he raised his hand.

'*Unterscharführer* Bartmann, is that you?' A faint smile of recognition passed over his bloodless lips.

I knelt beside him. '*Naja mein Junge*, it's *Uscha* Bartmann.'

'*Unterscharführer* Bartmann,' he repeated in a steady voice, 'I have a request.'

Even before the words left his lips, I knew what the young man would ask of me. My stomach churned.

Tears threatened to spill from the lower rims of his eyes as his young life ebbed away. 'Please ... shoot me.'

My shaking fingers undid the button on my pistol holster. Steeling my nerves, I wrapped my hand around the butt of the weapon but it was impossible to draw it free. Though it would have been an act of blessed mercy, I could not bring myself to kill the brave youngster. Around me, there was the rush of hunted men hurrying through the undergrowth – the last of our defence line was fleeing for their lives. I wiped the recruit's brow with a field dressing and left him leaning against the tree, praying he would die quietly from blood loss before the Russians came upon him.

27

The Tale of the Three Generals

A handful of survivors from *Regiment Falke* and a few *Wehrmacht Landsers* latched on to me, pinning their hopes of survival on my experience. I led them to Briesen, a town served by a branch of the main Berlin-Frankfurt rail line, with the hope of catching a train to Berlin. As we marched, there were no soldiers' songs to raise our spirits. In every heart, the last smouldering hope of victory had flickered and died. Most of the men and boys under my command were from Berlin or its suburbs, and in their faces I saw a yearning to return home before war's brutal climax overwhelmed our once beautiful city.

We arrived at the station to find the platform already packed with confused soldiers and refugees. It was a frightful scene. Mothers, their faces white with terror, held their daughters close, knowing they would see them raped before their helpless eyes should they fall into Russian hands. A *Wehrmacht* officer, freshly shaved and smelling of expensive soap, stood on the platform with two leather suitcases at his feet. Stuffed to bursting, they gave him something of the appearance of a rich holidaymaker.

'Are the trains still running?' I asked.

'I am told one is due any time now,' he replied looking down his long aristocratic nose.

I waited with my squad at the edge of the platform and stared down the track. Half an hour passed and still there was no sign of a train. The longer we waited, I thought, the more tenuous would be our grasp on life. I gathered my rag-tag troop together. 'It won't be long till the Russians are on our heels,' I said. 'Those who wish to can stay here – the rest of us will head west.' Not a single man in my squad chose to remain on the platform.

We had covered only a few kilometres when we came across another mixed unit under the command of a *Waffen SS Sturmbannführer*. Being of superior rank, he ordered my ramshackle unit back to the so-called front line but at least he had the courage to lead us there, which I had discovered, was more than could be said for most of the officers from the *Wehrmacht*.

Confronted once more with the ominous sight of brown uniforms, the *Sturmbannführer* ordered us to make a stand at a line of vacant trenches. By good fortune, or so I thought, I came across an abandoned MG42, a machine gun with an extremely high rate of fire. Beside it were stacked dozens of full ammunition boxes and an upturned helmet containing a signal pistol and several flares. Ahead, an open field offered little cover – an ideal situation for a machine gunner. It would be easy to halt the Russian infantry in their tracks. I yanked back the charging handle and squeezed the trigger. Nothing. I repositioned the ammunition belt but the weapon refused to loose off more than single shots or brief salvos of perhaps ten rounds.

As I cursed the stubbornness of the weapon, the sound of foreign voices approaching from behind grabbed my attention. I glanced back to see a troop of Hungarians – young men seventeen or eighteen years of age equipped with nothing more than bolt-action *Karabiner* 98s and a handful of ammunition each. They knelt beside me and fumbled with their rifles – they didn't have a clue how to re-load the magazines. I grabbed the nearest K98 and gave a rapid lesson in how to insert the bullet clips into the slot in front of the open bolt as the Russians closed on our position. The young Hungarians learned quickly and opened fire to good account but there were large gaps in our lines and a Russian platoon managed to work its way around our flank to where our *Sturmbannführer* and his men lay in shallow trenches. There was an exchange of grenades and fire from machine pistols but the *Sturmbannführer's* position was rapidly overwhelmed. Now, as *Unterscharführer*, I was again the most senior rank present.

Appreciating the threat of encirclement, I ordered the Hungarians to stem the Russian intrusion. They bravely drew their bayonets and threw themselves at the enemy, quickly succeeding in straightening our defensive line for a few vital minutes.

The exchange of fire continued but the Russians, growing in confidence, worked their way closer, crawling on their bellies with only their rucksacks visible through the long grass. After a few erratic bursts, my MG42 failed completely. With cold sweat trickling down my back, I grabbed the signal pistol from the upturned helmet and fired. A red flame hissed at the tip of an arc of smoke that ended on a Russian rucksack. Squealing in panic, the rucksack's owner sprang to his feet, arms flailing as he tried to beat out the flames that threatened to engulf him. A volley of shots from my Hungarian friends put a speedy end to his struggles.

Surprised by their setback, the Russians pulled back a few hundred metres and I decided to withdraw my men while I still had that option. My intention was to head for the Berlin-Frankfurt *Autobahn* in the hope that we would meet up with a viable fighting unit under competent leadership.

As we approached the *Autobahn,* I saw a small group of *Waffen SS* men ahead. Among them was an old *Kamerad, Rottenführer* Alfred Schneidereit. I quickened my pace when I saw the look of surprise on his face. As I drew closer, I noticed he now held the rank of *Untersturmführer* and, between the lapels of his tunic, hung the coveted Knight's Cross. Despite his higher rank, we shook hands warmly.

'Ah Erwin,' he sighed, 'what a mess we're in now – a real mix up. Nobody seems to know what the devil is going on. Not like the old days when we ran the Russians ragged all the way to Rostov. I see you've recovered well from that splinter you took at Prokhorovka.'

'And what's this – the Knight's Cross?' I remarked.

A wide smile lit up his battle-blackened face. 'Picked it up in December '43 for taking out a tank or two – the *Führer* himself presented it.'

We talked a while longer before I set off once more to the west with my little band. With hunger gnawing at our stomachs, we came across several *Wehrmacht* soldiers standing guard at an ornate wrought iron gate, the entrance to a rich country *Gut* (estate). I asked the *Feldwebel* in charge if he knew where we could get something to eat.

'I can't help you,' he replied. 'You'll have to get written permission from the General if you want food.'

'Where is he?'

'In the *Gutshaus* – at the end of the driveway.'

When I tried to pass through the gate, the bayonets on the guards' rifles barred my way.

'You can't go in there without a pass.'

It was a classic 'catch twenty-two' situation but after pleading with the *Feldwebel,* he eventually sent one of his men to obtain permission for me to enter the grounds of the estate. The guard returned after about fifteen minutes. 'You can see the general,' he said pointing a finger at me, 'but your men must stay here.'

I walked as fast as my weary legs allowed along a tree-lined driveway until I reached the *Gutshaus* where a pair of sentries guarding the door allowed me to enter without further questioning.

Countless antlers decorated the oak panelled walls of the *Gutshaus'* great hall where a party of high-ranking officers sat at a long table warming snifters of cognac in the palms of their hands. As I marched up to them, a middle-aged general waved a cloud of cigar smoke from his face.

'Yes, what is it?'

'*Herr General*, my men and I have been without food for sometime now. We urgently need provisions.'

'How many men do you have?'

'About twenty *Herr General*,' I replied.

'Ah, twenty, I don't think we could supply food for that many but I can offer *you* something. Why don't you join us – eat as much as you like,' said the general stretching an inviting arm over the food-laden table.

'No thank you *Herr General*,' I replied, 'as a *Waffen SS* man it would not be right for me to eat while my men went hungry.'

'But you must eat,' insisted the general, his index finger wagging as if scolding a naughty child. 'As leader you must keep your strength up. How else would you have the energy to keep your wits about you and command your men effectively?'

By this time I was becoming somewhat exasperated. 'What good would it be if I had a full stomach and my men were too weak to fight?' I cast a deliberately malicious stare in his direction and, without waiting for dismissal, spun on my heels muttering: *how could we ever win this war when we have leaders like that? I hope the Russians get hold of that bastard and he gets what he deserves.*

☙❧

Perhaps my thoughts had been too busily engaged in thinking of food to pay much attention to the landscape so I cannot say how far we walked in our state of abject hunger but, as we passed a bullet-shattered barn, I stopped to sniff the air. 'Roast pig.' The words slavered from my lips involuntarily. 'Wait in the barn,' I said to my men. 'I'll find out who's doing the cooking.'

A little farther on, I came across an army command post set up in a house a little way from the roadside. After negotiating my way past a myriad of sentries, I found myself in the makeshift office of a *Wehrmacht* general.

'Ah,' said the general, as if he didn't have a care in the world, 'what is it I can do for you?'

'*Herr General* – my men – they haven't eaten properly for several days.'

'Where are they?'

'In a nearby barn – I left them there to rest.'

'And are they in good spirits?'

I briefly described our last few days to the general.

'Hmm, I'll see what I can do.' He took a pad from his desk and wrote out a pass. 'Take this to the field kitchen – present it to the cook.'

Salivating freely I followed my nose to a large black contraption with four ovens and a central chimney, the field kitchen. The cook, like the general, was a jolly-looking man with a wonderfully round belly and cheeks as red as a ripe apple. He wiped his hands on his apron before taking the pass from my hand.

'Ha, you're in luck my friend,' said the cook snatching a dishtowel from his shoulder. He bent to open the door of an oven and pulled out a roasted piglet on a large metal tray, placing it on top of the oven before handing me the dishtowel to protect my hands.

Desperate to eat, I had already turned to carry my prize to the barn when he called me back.

'Hey, hang on a bit,' he said going to a second oven from which he conjured another tray, this time piled high with roast potatoes. I could hardly believe my famished eyes. With a large ladle, he transferred a generous heap of potatoes to the tray in my hands. 'Don't bother bringing back the tray,' he said. 'I don't think we'll need it.'

In the dim light of the barn, every eye sparkled when I arrived with the bountiful tray of food. Involuntary grunts of delight burst from every mouth. We ate until our stomachs bulged and packed the remaining food to take onwards, keeping to the cover of forests as far as possible. I'm sure it wasn't long before that wonderful field kitchen became Soviet property.

❧·❧

The wind breathed in sorry sighs. Cooing doves, calling to each other across the treetops, seemed to mock the folly of war. In the shelter of the forest, civilians and soldiers alike could escape the strafing by Russian planes that, apart from the occasional appearance of a few Messerschmitt 109s, were free to roam the skies of Germany at will.

A recruit walking by my side cupped a hand to his ear. '*Unterscharführer*, did you hear that?'

I brought my squad to a halt to listen to the sounds. A faint metallic tinkling percolated between the trunks of the stout spruce trees. 'Goat bells.'

'Voices too,' said the recruit, 'and gunfire in the distance.'

I listened harder. The blast from the Tiger's gun back in Kharkov still dulled my hearing. 'Shh. *Ja, ja* – women's voices.'

A track led to a clearing where a group of civilians had gathered with cows, sheep and goats they hoped to rescue. The women held onto each other as the sound of gunfire and the shouts of men crashing through the undergrowth drew closer. Suddenly, bullets smacked into the surrounding trees throwing up clouds of scented conifer resin – stray shots, but they sent the civilians scattering for cover. In the distance, figures in German uniforms dashed between the trees. They wore the white armbands that distinguished them as *Seydlitz* traitors. Soon the skirmish was over and, through the undergrowth, a group of high-ranking *Wehrmacht* officers and their entourage of dishevelled soldiers approached. Some of the soldiers, heavily laden with a large canvas bags in their hands and rucksacks on their backs – filled no doubt with all the things generals need to live a comfortable life – staggered under the weight. Others guarded a few crestfallen *Seydlitz* troops they somehow managed to capture. One of the guards wore a red Egyptian fez and danced around the prisoners cackling like a madman.

An officer called out, 'Hey you, you from the *SS*, you won't mind shooting this lot.'

'They're your prisoners', I called back scathingly. 'I don't do that sort of work – why don't you shoot them yourself?' Hardly able to believe that I had spoken to a senior officer in such an abrupt tone, and not wishing to have any more to do with this bunch, I led my men away.

When we were out of earshot of the *Wehrmacht* unit, one of the recruits, a smart lad, laughed, '*Unterscharführer*, it's lucky they didn't see your rank insignia – they might have had you shot for insubordination. But your soft cap does make you look like an officer.'

28

The Junghans-Hengstmann Mystery

I decided to lead the remaining men in my troop to our old training ground at Alt Hartmannsdorf, near Spreenhagen, where I hoped to find the remnants of *Regiment Falke*. When we were within a few kilometres of the village, an open-topped VW *Kübelwagen* at the head of a column of three trucks approached from behind. I brought my men to a halt at the side of the road to let them pass but the *Kübelwagen* skidded to a halt as it came alongside. In the back seat was a *Waffen SS* officer with four silver pips on his collar.

'I'm *Sturmbannführer* Junghans,' announced the officer. 'Which unit are you with?'

'*Regiment Falke, Sturmbannführer*,' I replied. 'We were at Lichtenberg when the Russians attacked.'

'Ah, *Falke* – my brother is in *Falke*. Look here, I'm in charge of a regiment of foreigners – Hungarians mostly. It would be good to have German voices around me again. You and your men could join my unit – act as my bodyguard.'

Despite his high rank, his words sounded more like an offer than an order. '*Ja*, of course,' I replied without a second thought.

My recruits crushed into a truck while I joined Junghans in the *Kübelwagen*.

'I've set up my command post in a cellar of a farmhouse close to Spreenhagen,' said Junghans in a friendly tone as we bumped along the country road. 'When we arrive I would like you to form your men into a guard detail then report to my office.'

My spirits lifted by the prospect of having an experienced officer to rely upon, I enthusiastically replied, '*Jawohl Sturmbannführer*.'

When I called into his office, Junghans handed me an envelope saying, 'Here, read the papers inside and sign them.'

I glanced through the papers briefly, noticing that Junghans sometimes went under the name of *Obersturmbannführer* Hengstmann. I thought it strange that a man should have two names, each with different ranks and dates of birth, but made no comment to him at the time. I signed at the bottom of each of the pages and returned them to my new commanding officer.

The following day, I travelled with Junghans in the back seat of his *Kübelwagen* on a tour of inspection of our defensive positions and, having got to know him a little better, felt I could speak freely to him. '*Sturmbannführer*, how did it happen that you have two names?'

'If you had read my papers more carefully you would understand,' he replied with a secretive smile. He reached inside his camouflage jacket. 'Here – have another look,' he said handing me the envelope. 'And by the way, if it looks like the Russians have a chance to grab me I want you to shoot me. From now on, these papers stay with you. If anything happens to me you must burn them so that not a trace remains.'

When the opportunity presented itself, I read the documents carefully and learned that, before the war, Junghans had been an espionage agent in Russia for seven years, and had lived in South America and spoke seven languages. There were other details of his life that after nearly seventy years, I cannot now remember.

A little farther on, we stopped at a command post set up in a house. I followed Junghans past the guards at the door and down a short flight of stairs to a cellar where we found *Obersturmbannführer* Rosenbusch sitting at a table with his head in his hands. In the background, lesser officers were artificially engrossed in shuffling papers around their desks.

Evidently, Rosenbusch no longer had the imagination to believe in our ultimate victory, nor the composure to mask his doubts. 'I can't go on,' he sobbed. 'This is the end. We are all going to die.'

Although apparently inferior in rank, Junghans grabbed collar of Rosenbusch's tunic with both hands, yanking him to his feet. His face contorted by contempt, he snarled, 'Look at you – you're a disgrace – snivelling like a stupid little girl – we all die – it's how we live that counts. Honour and loyalty – we live by these things. Why are you not with your men?'

Rosenbusch turned his face from the storm of saliva droplets spewing from Junghans' mouth. 'I came back here to co-ordinate our defence – everything is out of control. There's nothing I can do – we're finished.'

Junghans pulled Rosenbusch closer, until their foreheads pressed hard against each other. 'Get back to your men,' he snarled, 'show them respect – keep your fears to yourself and show them courage.' Suddenly, he flung the trembling *Obersturmbannführer* back into his chair. 'Bastard, I should shoot you right now.'

⚜ ⚜

Our route back to Junghans' command post took us through Markgrafpieske where white sheets hung from the windows of the scattered houses. There was the crackle of rifle fire and some shots kicked up the dirt close to our *Kübelwagen*.

'*Obersturmbannführer*, I know another way to Spreenhagen – through Spreeau,' I yelled above the revving engine. 'We should take the next turning.'

As the driver swung the *Kübelwagen* into a country lane, a few bullets pattered through the bodywork of our vehicle without, fortunately, damaging the fuel tank or tyres. Travelling the back roads, we came to the outskirts of Spreeau where a grey-haired man wearing a waistcoat waved at our approach.

Junghans tapped the driver on the shoulder. 'Pull up – let's hear what he has to say.'

There was a look of despair on the old man's face. 'The Bolsheviks are in some of the houses already,' he explained, 'I thought I would get out while I could. Watch out – don't go over there,' he said pointing to a house off to the side of the main road, 'the owner of that farm is luring our boys into his house. He's in cahoots with the Russians and they shoot them when they go in. They've already killed men from the *Waffen SS*.'

'Thanks for the warning,' said Junghans.

As we drove into the village square, the sight of dead Germans – civilians and *Waffen SS* men – confronted us. Having gathered sufficient intelligence on the extent of the Russian advance, we returned to Junghans' command post where two trucks waited in the yard, engines running.

'Check what he's got for us *Unterscharführer*,' ordered Junghans as the driver brought the *Kübelwagen* to a halt. 'You'll find me in my office when you've completed the inspection.'

As the *Kübelwagen* left the scene, I approached the driver of the first truck. 'Ammunition?'

'*Ja, ja*, ammunition,' repeated the driver curtly.

I looked under the cover on the back of the first truck. 'What idiot sent this? We need machine-gun ammunition, not 88mm shells. Wait right here.'

I went to the command post to report the delivery of the 88mm shells to Junghans, who instructed me to tell the truck drivers to take them back to where they came from. On returning to the farmyard, I found the trucks had already unloaded their cargo into the nearby barn, a building with a timber roof and open sides.

'Here,' said the driver thrusting an invoice at me. 'Just hurry up will you – sign this.'

The trucks left in suspicious haste. As I made my way to Junghans' office to report my concerns, the barn disintegrated in a searing flash. Shards of timber rained down, then a mist of fine dust. One thought ran through my mind – *Seydlitz* troops.

On 26 April, a column of Tigers and Panzer IVs belonging to *Obersturmbannführer* Kausch's *schwere Panzer Abteilung 202* appeared.

'Just what we need,' said Junghans with a wide smile lighting up his face. 'I've been waiting for a chance like this.' He strode over to the first tank, a Tiger, to greet the commander who perched proudly in the open turret.

'There's a little matter I would like to deal with,' said Junghans. 'The Russians are close by in Gut Skaby. I'll take a command of this tank to lead the attack.'

The tank commander protested. 'This is my tank – we are on our way to Berlin – you have no right to commandeer it.'

Junghans was having none of it. He climbed onto the Tiger and simply yanked out the commander and set off in the direction of Gut Skaby, with my men and me trotting along behind the tanks for protection. As Junghans' Tiger passed through the gate at the entrance of the Gut Skaby grounds, there was the metallic thump of steel against steel. Smoke belched from the open turret of Junghans' Tiger. I tried to get to the burning tank but was turned away by medics whose ambulance seemed to have appeared from thin air at precisely the right moment. Ignoring my demands to accompany my commanding officer, the medics loaded Junghans into the back of the ambulance and whisked him off to the first-aid post at our headquarters where he died soon after arriving. I still had the papers listing Junghans' exploits inside my tunic and, true to my word, I burned them then broke up the ashes until I was certain that even in these, not a word could be read.

29

Sardines, Murder and Rape

Following the death of Junghans, I received news that Rosenbusch had shot himself. Without a competent officer left to lead us, and with the enemy threatening to overwhelm our command post, I decided it was time to split from the remnants of Junghans' unit. And since it was now abundantly clear to me that Berlin was about to become a death trap, I decided to make for the forests to the south of our wrecked capital city. Without a map or compass, I took my bearings from the sun and set off with nothing more specific in mind than to avoid the Russian units that by now would be pushing towards Berlin.

With hunger again clawing at our bellies we found ourselves at the entrance of a deserted farmhouse in heavy rain. I put a sentry at the door – a youngster called Mühs – while the rest of us went inside. As my men rested at a large table in the hall, I explored the cellar where I came across a cardboard carton full of tin cans. Silently thanking the absent owner, who had wisely taken the trouble to accumulate a good supply of food, I carried the carton up to the hall and set it on the table.

'Sardines,' exclaimed one of the young men as he ripped the carton open. 'I love sardines.'

When I had eaten my fill of fish, I returned to the cellar to see what else I could find. Empty handed I trod up the stairs and saw, sitting at the table where my men had been only minutes before, a Russian soldier gobbling the leftovers from our sardine tins. It was his last meal. As he snatched for a handgun on the table, I pressed the trigger of my machine pistol and the Russian recoiled on his chair. This was no time to hang about – I ran to the front entrance of the building only to stagger to an abrupt halt when I saw a Russian tank, engine running, in the front yard. Fortunately, the crew had not heard the burst of fire that dispatched their comrade. What now? And where was the sentry I had posted? At that moment, the tank's engine fell silent. I slunk back inside the farmhouse to look for an escape route and found my recruits gathered in a room at the rear of the building where two dusty windows, too small for a man to climb through, looked out onto a walled garden. I tried the handle. The door was locked, and too heavy to break down without causing a commotion that might attract the attention of the enemy tank crew. With my recruits following like a flock of lost sheep, I led them to an adjacent room, a windowless store, and found another door that, judging from the layout of the house, also led to the garden. A single blow from the butt of a recruit's rifle smashed the lightly constructed lock. I yanked the door open, expecting my squad to make a hasty exit but they stood rooted to the spot.

'We'll never get over that.' whined a recruit.

The wall was a formidable height but the last thing we needed in this situation was a loss of determination. 'You were trained to get over walls,' I said hopefully. The recruits looked at each other, the blank expression of a person stupefied by his own lack of ability on every face. I quelled the rising sense of panic by appointing teams of two 'lifters' to stand at the base of the wall. They grabbed the legs of a 'climber', hoisting him so that he could get a finger hold on the top. The lifters then pushed hard on the feet of the climber. The manoeuvre went well and, as the last man on the wrong side, I grabbed the hands of two recruits already on top of the wall. The eyes of the waiting recruits on the other side looked up at me. 'Don't just stand there,' I scolded. 'Make for the woodland at the top of the slope.'

Like deer with hounds at their heels, my squad ran up the hill without waiting for me. Halfway to the safety of the trees, out of breath, heart thumping, I glanced back. At the other end of the wall from the point at which we had scaled it, was a shell hole at ground level. Missing the gap in the wall was a serious error that might have cost us dearly but once more, my guardian angel had watched over me – and the youngsters under my command. When I reached the edge of the woodland, the missing sentry was waiting.

'Hey Mühs. What the devil are you playing at?' I rasped. 'We could have been killed.'

'Oh,' he said, 'I had to take a piss – when I came back the Russians were already there.'

After marching at a brisk pace for several hours, a sinewy fifty-odd-year-old man sporting a flamboyant moustache and a *Volkssturm* armband joined our troop. It was then that I noticed that Mühs was missing again. We continued through woodland until we reached a clearing where there was a large stone house – the forest manager's house – set beyond a wall with an open gate carrying a carved sign with the inscription: *Forsthaus Hammer.* Three butterflies danced nearby, one above the other, white as angels in a brief burst of sunlight that somehow managed to perforate the thick cloud.

Taking cover amongst the dripping trees at the edge of the forest, I observed the house until certain there were no Russians in the vicinity. I selected three of my squad to help me inspect the building while the remainder covered the approaches.

The front door stood a little ajar giving the impression that someone was at home. Music played on a radio in a side room – the overture to *Der Freischütz* by Weber. I knocked on the door. '*Waffen SS.*' There was no reply. My finger hovered near the trigger of my machine pistol as my foot eased the door fully open. Strewn across the floor of the hallway were books from a toppled bookcase, among them family photographs, witnesses to happy times.

A call came from outside. '*Unterscharführer*, come quickly.'

On the wet grass by the side of the house sprawled a man's bare-footed body – it was a Russian habit to take the boots from their victims. Fresh blood outlined the stumps of his broken teeth. His face, nut brown from working in the open, wore a look of unutterable anguish. Spread out a few metres to the side were the bodies of a woman and three young children, all girls, all naked, each with private parts butchered by bullet or bayonet.

'I hope they killed him before he saw what happened to his girls,' said one of the recruits.'

'I doubt it,' I sighed, 'but this is no time to think about these matters.' I took a deep breath and swallowed the anger in my throat. 'The Russians must be close. Search the house for food before we head off.'

We left the *Forsthaus* with empty stomachs. At the gate, Mühs had reappeared. He sat on the wall complaining of a wound to his foot. I glanced at his boots but there was no sign of any tear in the leather. Too preoccupied with our precarious position behind the Russian front line to enquire further into Mühs' supposed injury, I decided to leave him behind without making any fuss about the matter.

We trudged through wood and field until we came across an abandoned ambulance by the side of a minor road. Like scavenging crows hoping to find some edible scraps in an open bin, we ransacked every compartment of the vehicle but found only a few bottles of what smelled like alcohol. I poured some of the clear fluid into a jug and diluted it with water before passing the mixture round my young *Kameraden*. It tasted dreadful but at least we were able to extract some energy from it, which made us feel a little better even though the 'alcohol' was in fact medicinal spirits intended for the sterilization of wounds.

The sound of cracking twigs sent us diving for cover in the ditch at the side of the road, beside the ambulance. From a dense hedge at the edge of a nearby field two women appeared, one middle-aged wearing a headscarf, the other youthful enough to be her daughter. They waved their arms wildly. 'Thank God,' the older woman gasped. 'We don't know where we are.' Her eyes filled with tears. 'Please, please, you must take us with you. I can't bear to think what the Russians will do to us if they catch us.'

Having witnessed the butchery at Forsthaus Hammer, I couldn't leave them to fend for themselves.

Towards evening a repeating pattern of detonations – thud, thud…thud, thud – grew louder as we moved south. Eventually, we broke into open ground at the edge of a wooded hillside to see a road wind its way between a pair of hills. Every thirty seconds or so, two almost simultaneous plumes of fire and earth erupted from the valley floor. Two heavy artillery pieces, one on each hill, worked together to deny passage through the valley.

'Listen *Unterscharführer*,' said the gaunt-faced *Volkssturm* man cupping his wrinkled hand to his ear. 'Can't you hear it?'

In the lull between the detonations on the road, the rumble of continuous artillery fire loomed up from the south. Of course, it had been present all the while but I had become immune to sounds that posed no immediate threat.

'The Russians are in Halbe,' said the old *Volkssturm* man. 'I was in the last war, I can tell the difference between a skirmish and a full-blooded battle. What now?'

'You know this area?' I asked. Having neither map nor compass, I reckoned the old man's knowledge might prove invaluable.

'I do, indeed I do,' said the old man. 'My daughter lives near Halbe.'

I looked into the faces of my little troop; the wide-eyed *Leibstandarte* recruits who, bound by their oath of loyalty to the *Führer*, were prepared to follow wherever I led, the old *Volkssturm* man itching to travel on to his daughter's home, the two women shaking in terror. Should we join the battle at Halbe? What would happen to the women? We were a small force, too small and too lightly armed to defend ourselves let alone influence the course of a major battle. I pointed to the valley. 'Where does that road lead?'

'Past the lakes – to Kummersdorf eventually,' replied the old *Volkssturm* man. 'But surely we must help our *Kameraden* in Halbe.'

'We're not going to Halbe – it would be a death trap.'

The old man's brow wrinkled. He sighed and shook his head. 'In that case, I request to be allowed to leave your troop.'

I made no effort to stop him as he turned to begin his quest.

In the valley, we crept as close as we dared to the exploding shells. A pattern emerged. The gun on the right fired then the gun on the left. The shells fell close to the road, striking almost simultaneously the same spot on every occasion. I timed the seconds between the detonations on the watch my mother had given to me as a Christmas present – never more than thirty, and never less than twenty. During this brief interval, I sent my men through two at a time. When all but the two women and I had run the gauntlet of fire without loss, I slung my machine pistol onto my shoulder and stretched out to grasp a hand of each of the women. Their cold grip squeezed hard on my fingers as we waited for the pause in the shellfire.

We had not quite made it through the valley when a shell exploded nearby with a deafening crack. A splinter cut through the ankle of my right boot. Warm, fresh blood soaked into my sock but I was able to keep on running. When we reached safety, I discovered I had suffered nothing more than a flesh wound that a couple of stitches could easily fix. I applied a field dressing to prevent dirt getting into the wound – the last thing I needed was an infection that would hinder my escape from the Russians. The two women hugged each other, then me.

The hellish rumble battle emanating from Halbe faded into the background as we continued our trek to the west. Soon, our little band became the focus of hope for every German that spotted us and I found myself in command of a column of consisting of *Hitlerjungen, Volkssturm* men, *Wehrmacht* soldiers who had been separated from their units, and women burdened with sacks of household goods and children clinging on to their coat tails. Strangely, though there are many lakes in that area of Germany, I cannot recall seeing a single one of them. At night, we paused for a few hours under the cover one of the many woods found in that area until the sound of approaching small-arms fire suggested it was time to continue our escape.

As we broke from the cover of a forest I was surprised to see the radio masts of Königs Wusterhausen in the distance, a familiar landmark that told me we were close to Zossen, a town lying to the south of Berlin. Unfortunately, a troop of *Feldgendarmerie* (military police) spotted us. Known as *Kettenhunde* (chained dogs) because of the decorative gorgets hanging on chains around their necks, they had been unleashed to hunt for soldiers fleeing the now non-existent front line. With the power to execute summarily anyone suspected of desertion or defeatism, these were brutes best avoided. A hard-faced officer with pitiless eyes approached, pistol in hand. 'Who's in charge?'

I stepped forward. The officer stared at me with icy eyes. 'We lost our way in the forest,' I lied. To admit fleeing the enemy would have brought instant execution.

His face frozen into a sneer of derision, he looked me up and down. Having faced death on countless occasions, I refused to let this blockhead intimidate me and without flinching, returned his cold stare.

At last, the officer stepped to the side. 'Women and children may continue,' he said beckoning them onwards before returning his attention to me. '*Unterscharführer*, the Russians are in the woods. It is a soldier's duty to repel the enemy.'

Struck dumb by despair, the older men under my command followed bravely as I led them back into the forest. The *Hitlerjungen,* boys too young to remember peace, still had heart enough to face the threat of a futile death. Before long, we found ourselves embroiled in a bloody close-quarter skirmish with an enemy who seemed to lurk behind every tree. Bullets ripped through the foliage, smacked into the bodies of my *Kameraden*. We were quickly outflanked. Leaving the wounded to their fate, I pulled my troop back to edge of the forest where there was now no sign of the *Kettenhunde* – they had already left to save their own skins. After the pointless sacrifice of another dozen lives, those of us who had survived were free to continue our escape.

On the point of collapse through lack of food and sleep, we chanced across a group of four *Leibstandarte* men. The senior officer present was a sallow-faced *Hauptsturmführer* with staring, brown eyes. Accompanying him were two other officers – an *Obersturmführer* and my *Kompanie* chief from Alt Hartmansdorf, *Untersturmführer* Schenk. The fourth was a fellow *Unterscharführer* who was seldom without a smile on his face. His name was, I think, Heinrich. I politely asked *Untersturmführer* Schenk how it was he came to be there but he deflected my questions and turned his back on me. Naturally, in such a situation, one's suspicions are aroused but there was no point trying to pursue the matter. Every one of us had one aim in mind – survival. Our little band joined forces with them to continue our trek westwards.

With the River Elbe now within a few days walking distance, the *Hauptsturmführer* decided to allow those that had stuck with me to try their own luck in getting to the other side of the river, or to return to their families. Every one of them grasped the offer with willing hands and said their farewells. As soon as our companions were out of sight, we too set out towards the Elbe, keeping to the cover of woodland whenever the opportunity arose.

After a few kilometres, we quickened our pace when we heard the swish of whipping foliage and the snap of twigs – the sound of men running through the forest. The three officers, who were a little way ahead of Heinrich and me, took cover in a clump of bushes.

'*Scheisse* – they've spotted us,' said Heinrich.

We pressed ourselves flat to the ground behind a fallen tree and prepared to make our last stand. 'Save a round for yourself,' I said to my new *Kamerad*.

'So this is what it has all come to,' he said, grinning. '*Sieg Heil.*'

I pointed my machine pistol at figures dashing towards us through the undergrowth.

'Hold fire,' said Heinrich, 'don't waste the bullets – they're *Seydlitz* traitors – taken to their heels to save their skins before the end comes – they don't trust their masters.'

Relying on experience and instinct, the five of us continued without pause or food until we reached Jerichow, a village close to the eastern bank of the Elbe. *Wehrmacht* soldiers were everywhere but as far as I could make out, we were the only *Waffen SS* men present at that time. The final victory, the *Endsieg*, was at hand, but it was not our victory, not the promised victory – that belonged to our bitter foes, the Bolsheviks. With gusto, they had begun the 'liberation' of the German civilians from the yolk of fascism with vile acts of rape, torture and murder and we could do nothing to stop them.

30

Sanctuary in Jerichow

We knocked on door after door only to find *Wehrmacht* personnel who made it clear that our companionship was unwelcome. Exhausted, almost to the point of insanity, we came across a house on the edge of the village, our last hope of comfortable accommodation.

Our *Hauptsturmführer* knocked on the door as I peered over his shoulder fully expecting the occupants to turn us away. The door opened a little and an attractive young woman wearing a red polka dot apron peered round the gap.

'We need shelter for the night,' said the *Hauptsturmführer*.

The young woman smiled, welcomed us inside and led us to the living room where we slung our weapons to the floor. The three officers collapsed onto a large sofa pushed against a wall while my fellow *Uscha* and I flopped into the two small, ragged armchairs at the sides of a venerable but beautiful *Kachelofen* with blue tiles depicting idyllic pastoral scenes. On a small table, next to the chair I occupied, perched a *Volksempfänger*, a small, rectangular, brown Bakelite radio receiver. These were mass-produced and acted as a means of keeping the German public bombarded with propaganda without allowing easy access to foreign radio stations. Somehow, it gave the impression of a watching face with its linear horizontal tuning scale – flanked on either side by impressed images of the ubiquitous eagle and swastika – forming a letterbox-like mouth.

'You look exhausted,' said the young woman. 'Ute, Ute,' she called into the hallway, 'We have some worn out boys to look after – *Waffen SS*, five of them.' She turned back from the hallway to ask if we were hungry. The look of hope on our faces was our unspoken answer. The woman called into the hallway once more, 'Ute, come downstairs and help me make sandwiches with that sausage we have left.' Before leaving the room, she turned to us, and with a polite smile added, 'Please gentlemen, make yourselves at home.'

Carrying a large tin tray laden with five glasses of water and some thickly cut sandwiches, the girl returned. 'Unfortunately this is all I can offer you,' she said.

Our *Hauptsturmführer* took the first glass. 'Are you the only ones in the house?'

'*Naja*,' she sighed, 'our parents left just before you arrived. They've gone to our grandparents to bring them back here before the Russians arrive.'

As the girl held the tray towards me, I looked into her eyes. 'And your name?'

'Liza,' she said with a sweet smile. 'And yours?'

'Erwin.'

Grunting like starving dogs, we devoured the sandwiches. The *Hauptsturmführer* passed round the last of his cigarettes and turned on the *Volksempfänger*. Amidst swirls of slowly rising cigarette smoke, we listened to the rousing music of Wagner.

Liza bounced back into the room looking pleased with herself. 'We've filled a bathtub in the back room. I'm sorry the water isn't very hot but you look so dirty, we thought you might like the chance to get cleaned up.'

We bathed in strictly rank order. After Heinrich, I was the last to soak in the soapy water, which by now was hardly warmer than room temperature. This was however an advantage, since there was no need for me to hurry to vacate the bath for the next in line. I lay there, knees bent, neck on the rolled metal rim of the tub, halfway between sleep and wakefulness. Liza was suddenly standing at the open door of the room with a metal pail in her hand.

'I'm sorry if I wakened you – I hope you don't mind – I've brought hot water,' she announced.

Before I was alert enough to cover myself, she was pouring steaming water into the bathtub. 'Don't worry – you have nothing that I haven't seen before,' she said with the hint of a smile on her lips.

I lay in the bathtub until the water lost its heat, soaking up every luxurious second before I dressed and returned to the living room where I found a girl, a year or two short of twenty, with straight golden hair that fell onto the shoulders of her blue summer dress. Her skin was pale and clear. In her slender hands, she held two white pillowcases close to her bosom. She smiled demurely.

'Ah, you must be Erwin – I'm Ute, Liza's sister. She's been telling me about you.'

I tried to speak but, astounded by the brilliance of her eyes, I managed to utter nothing more than some senseless mumble.

'Liza – my sister – she brought the sandwiches.'

Still half-dazed by her beauty, I nodded.

'I've been to town to see if there was any news about food supplies,' said Ute.

I praised her and her sister's generosity and apologised for helping to gobble up the last of their precious sausage meat. 'And is there any news, about supplies?'

'Oh yes, it looks hopeful,' she said. 'The postman told me there was a barge stuck close to the riverbank a few kilometres upstream.' She held up the pillowcases for me to see. 'I just came back to collect these to carry whatever's on offer.'

I took the pillowcases from her. 'No, I'll go. The news will draw everyone from miles around. Who knows what will happen if there's a crush at the river's edge.'

She lowered her eyelids coyly, in a way that brought to mind a butterfly resting on a sunflower in a Ukrainian field. 'You *will* come back?'

'Of course,' I replied. 'My *Kameraden* and I haven't slept properly for days – we need a bed for the night. I'll be back, I promise.' It was one of those moments, I thought, when a young man and woman see in each other a spark that in happier times might have flared into a wild love affair.

❧ ❦

Heinrich and I were making our way towards the river to find the barge where we hoped to scavenge food for our charming hostesses. 'Nice girls,' I remarked.

'Nice girls,' he repeated, 'and *very* beautiful.'

I found myself thinking of the harmony of Ute's movements, her calm voice, and the moment when our eyes met. I consoled myself with the thought that, by finding food, I had the opportunity to do something practical to help Ute and her sister before we continued our escape to the west. As we followed a path close to the riverbank, the grounded barge came into view. The crewmembers shouted at a crowd waiting impatiently on the riverbank.

'We're not throwing tins one at a time – we'd be here all day and night and you'd fall into the water fighting for them – fetch a few planks.'

Squabbling broke out. None of the onlookers seemed willing to leave their place on the riverbank for fear they would miss the opportunity presented by the heavily laden barge. 'Who knows when we'll get food again – the Russians are on our doorsteps,' someone called over the murmur of discontent.

We pushed our way to the front of the crowd. 'Quiet.' I shouted. Immediately there was silence. The presence of two armed *Waffen SS* men was sufficient to calm the mood of the refugees. We ordered a small group of the fittest-looking men to follow us to the nearest farm to get the required timber – from the roof of a building if necessary. Fortunately, we found some planks in a dusty pile stacked inside a barn and returned to quell the growing impatience of the crowd by setting up a wobbly gangway.

Heinrich was the first to cross to the barge. When it came to my turn, I looked down into the swirling brown water between the shore and the vessel.

My fear of water held back my first step onto the gangway. I took a deep breath and followed my companion, sighing with relief when I reached the deck of the vessel without mishap. On board, the crew were busy stacking cases onto the deck, cases filled with tins of chocolate and grape sugar – foods that would provide plenty of energy – as well as tinned meats and a few other household items. We filled the pillowcases Ute had given us. Now I faced the risky business of getting back on shore with the heavily laden sacks. The planks under my feet seemed even more insecure than before. They bent alarmingly, threatening to snap when I was halfway across. I shuffled along, sliding one foot after the other until at last I reached the riverbank where Heinrich was already supervising the fair distribution of the food. As we made our way back to Jerichow, we compared the contents of the pillowcases and were pleased to find that what was lacking in one was present in the other.

It was already early evening as we emptied the contents of the pillowcases onto the kitchen table in front of Ute and Liza. With gasps of delight, they picked up each article in turn, reading the label aloud as they stacked it in a cupboard. Ute placed the last jar on a shelf and said, 'Thank you for bringing us this food, we know you must have been exhausted even before you left to fetch it.'

'Don't mention it,' I replied. 'We are pleased to be able to do something to return your hospitality.'

'Liza and I have prepared beds for you and Heinrich – in the front bedroom upstairs. We've put on clean sheets for you. The officers are in the bedroom next door. They're already fast asleep judging by the snoring.'

Though it was several hours until nightfall, the sight of two beds with clean linen was too inviting to resist. We threw our holster belts and filthy uniforms to the floor between the beds and slumped simultaneously onto the welcoming mattresses. Immediately, I fell into a deep sleep.

The creaking hinges of the bedroom door wakened me. Heart pounding, I reached out to the floor to retrieve my pistol.

A girl's voice whispered, 'It's us, Liza and Ute.'

In the soft grey light of dawn, the two girls stood at the open door, each clad in a nightdress of pure, white cotton. Ute smiled, her teeth luminous in the half-light. On the other bed, Heinrich was sitting upright, his mouth wide open. Ute slowly undid the tie at the front of her nightdress, opening it just far enough to reveal the rise of her breasts. At that moment, she was the most beautiful girl

I had ever seen. Gracefully, she opened the garment wider so that the front of her body was fully exposed, her nipples erect in the chill dawn, her skin smooth and silvery. At the fork of her legs, wisps of fine pubic hair caught the light like threads of gold. 'We've come to sleep with you,' she said glancing at her sister who shyly nodded her head, 'if you are willing.' Her nightdress slid to the floor.

Liza, her breasts small and firm with large pink areole, followed her sister's example. Completely naked, they stood at the end of our beds – an enchanting sight for two soldiers who had endured nothing but fear and exhaustion for the last ten days.

'The Russians will be here soon and we will be raped many times if the stories the refugees told us are true,' said Ute as she took her sister by the hand to lead her between the beds. 'If we are to get pregnant we don't want the children to be Russian.'

Liza climbed into Heinrich's bed. Ute slid in beside me, her body fragrant with a scent I had once smelled in a café when stationed in France. As I lay on my back, she caressed my neck. Her cool fingers slid slowly over my chest, stopping every now and then to tease my skin with gentle touch of her fingertips. Slowly, her confident fingers worked their way onto my lower abdomen. Such bliss – how could this happen when such cruel bestialities were being perpetrated only a few kilometres to the east? I closed my eyes to concentrate on the moment, to expunge all thoughts of war, of hatred, of death. The tips of her fingernails now sent quivers of pleasure racing to my groin. This wasn't the love a young man should experience. Where was the period of infatuation, the thrill of the first hesitant kiss? But it didn't matter – I was gripped by desire and every second, every teasing motion of her fingertips, prepared me for the moment our bodies would join.

Ute's skilled touch soon achieved its aim. She straddled my body, oblivious to her sister – who now lay on the other bed under Heinrich – and began a slow rhythmic movement. She paused, took my hands, pressed them against her breasts and, leaning forward slightly, her tempo began anew, slow at first but gradually gaining momentum. I was lost in a whirlwind of pure physical delight, a pleasure that seemed to stem from somewhere deep inside my soul. I bit my lip hard hoping the pain would quell my rising rapture and prolong our pleasures but it had been a while since I had been with a girl. How much longer I lasted I cannot say – time was irrelevant, there was no past, no future, only the moment. She groaned and fell forward onto me where she remained for a silent moment before rolling to the side, her arm still resting on my chest.

'Why me? There are plenty of other soldiers to choose from in town.'

She kissed my cheek – just a little peck – and giggled. 'You were the only *Waffen SS* men available – you and your officers.'

Well, I thought, so much for blissful romance.

On the morning of Mayday 1945, exactly four years after had I surrendered my body to Hitler, the *Hauptsturmführer* decided we should remain in the house in Jerichow to rest and build up our strength on the rations we had acquired from the barge. Radio reports continued to tell of the heroic resistance of the German forces and contained nothing concrete upon which we could base our next move. Still exhausted by our trek of the previous week, we took to our beds at dusk with the intention of setting off early the following morning but the rattle of Ute's knuckles on the bedroom door soon interrupted my sleep. 'Come quickly,' she urged, 'there is to be an important announcement on the radio.'

Heinrich groaned disapprovingly. '*Scheisse* – I only just got to sleep.'

I glanced at my watch, 'Heinrich, you fell asleep two hours ago.'

Ute's footsteps rattled neatly down the bare wooden stair treads. We pulled on our trousers and staggered sleepily down to the living room to find Ute, Liza and our three officers listening to Wagner's *Tannhäuser* on the radio. Suddenly, the music faded and a solemn voice said, 'An important announcement will soon follow.' The music changed to the sombre *Twilight of the Gods*. A few minutes later, the strident voice of the radio announcer called out, '*Achtung, Achtung*! An important announcement to the German People will follow shortly.'

'It's the *Wunderwaffe*, we've won the war with a new wonder weapon,' exclaimed Liza jumping to her feet, her words echoing those of my father just a few months earlier.

'Sit down Liza,' said Ute with more than a hint of impatience. 'Just sit and listen.'

We waited expectantly in the unlit room until just before 10 pm when an announcement on the radio said that Bruckner's Seventh Symphony was to follow. I recalled that our teacher, *Herr* Werth, had described this music as 'monumental' before playing a recording of it to our class. Bruckner, he told us, had included tubas in the symphony's adagio to honour his friend, Wagner. It was not the sort of music to precede a declaration of victory.

I went to the window, pulled back the blackout curtain, and gazed numbly into the dark, deserted street. Drum rolls brought Bruckner's symphony abruptly to a close. In the blistering silence, I bit hard on my lower lip.

'It is reported,' said the announcer, 'that our *Führer*, Adolf Hitler, has fallen at his command post in the *Reichskanzlei* fighting Bolshevism to his last breath.'

I gasped at the air as if it were the very first breath of life. The predatory *Zeitgeist* that had perched on my shoulder whispering its seductive promises into my fervent, youthful ear had suddenly flown. The *Führer* was dead, finished, the burden of my oath to him annulled by the Will of Fate. Now, all that remained of the Third *Reich* was the *Kameradschaft* of the men with whom I shared the confines of that room in Jerichow.

Ute turned off the radio. Silence, as hard as ice, fell upon the darkened room. Then Ute began to sob, deeply, as if she had lost the whole world.

31

The Wrong Side of the Styx

I checked my watch – five minutes to five. Heinrich and the three officers were already waiting for me in the street. I closed the door quietly so as not to waken Ute and Liza.

'There's no point in sinking into the quagmire of despair,' announced the *Hauptsturmführer*. 'Our oath was to Hitler and in that respect we are different from other branches of the armed forces. Hitler is dead. I have thought the matter through. We are, so to speak, on the wrong side of the Styx – only death and torture await us here. It seems sensible to me that we should continue to act together to find some means of crossing to the other side of the Elbe.'

I had realized since our retreat from the Oder that the end of our epic attempt to save Europe from the evils of Bolshevism was at hand, so the *Hauptsturmführer*'s defeatist words – conveniently ignoring that our oath extended to 'superiors appointed' by Hitler – did not shock me at all. Surrendering to the Russians was a poor option. We had witnessed too often the cruel fate that awaited *Waffen SS* men who fell into their hands. In such precarious circumstances, the mind blocks out everything except the will to survive and the *Hauptsturmführer*'s decision to abandon the fight came as an immense relief to me.

In a sunless dawn, I cast all thoughts of home into the woods. The world in which I had grown up was, quite suddenly, at an end. The single sharp crack of a rifle shot echoed in the distance – perhaps someone had decided to end his or her own life. A few kilometres marching across open country brought us to the shores of the Elbe and past the now abandoned barge where we had collected food for our charming hosts. A little farther downstream, we spotted a boat halfway across the river. Using a cable linking opposite banks, the crew – American soldiers – pulled the vessel towards twenty or so *Wehrmacht* soldiers waiting at the cable's end, on our side.

The *Obersturmführer* cocked his MP40 machine pistol. 'Why don't they fire on the boat?' he said angrily. It was the first words he had spoken in my presence since I joined the group.

Our *Hauptsturmführer* shook his head. '*Naja,* there will be a whole army of Americans on the other side – they can't fight them all, nor can we.'

'If we surrendered now, it would be a chance to get across the river – to the American side,' said Heinrich.

Without warning of his intentions, the *Hauptsturmführer* took matters into his own hands and yelled, 'Hallo, hallo.'

'We won't fire on you,' replied an American voice in perfect German, 'not unless you fire first.'

'We will hold our fire,' replied our *Hauptsturmführer* through cupped hands.

'Come over, I want to talk with you when we reach the riverbank,' called the American.

With our weapons slung over our shoulders, we made for the boat. An American officer stood at the prow, chewing gum. He introduced himself with a Jewish name (I think it might have been Cohen). 'I have a little proposition for you gentlemen.'

'Is the war over?' asked young *Untersturmführer* Schenk impatiently.

'No, but I reckon it will be in a few days,' drawled the American.

'You spoke of a proposition,' said our *Hauptsturmführer*.

It was an absurd situation – the war was not yet over and here we were, in possession of loaded weapons and the enemy, only a few steps away, showed no sign of concern.

'I'll take you across. I know you guys won't want to fall into the hands of the Russians. There's just one catch – I'm collecting stuff, medals, watches, rings and the like, and pistols, especially Lügers.'

We looked at the *Hauptsturmführer* for guidance.

After a moment of thought, he shook his head. 'Unfortunately I cannot accept your offer but I will leave it up to my men to decide for themselves.'

Only Heinrich threw in the towel. 'Fuck it. I've had enough of this adventure,' he declared. 'I'm going over.'

The American officer held out a hand to steady his new passenger as he stepped on board the boat to join the *Wehrmacht* soldiers, whose faces wore curious expressions that managed somehow to combine dejection with relief.

'Good luck Heinrich,' I called as the boat left the riverbank.

'Who knows, we might meet again when all this is over,' said Heinrich through a wide smile.

'These Americans – what are they up to?' I asked no one in particular as we waved Heinrich a final farewell.

'The Captain was a Jew,' replied the *Obersturmführer*, 'always on the lookout to make money – a good businessman is *always* ready to grab an opportunity – it will be the world we must learn to live in – if we survive.'

Hope of finding a suitable vessel was fading when a motor boat came into view. It was in a still part of the river where a bed of tall reeds grew. We splashed through the shallow water and tried to pull the boat from the mud but it was stuck fast.

'Climb in,' said our *Hauptsturmführer*.

With the sudden prospect of escape to the west lifting our spirits, we scrambled into the boat and began to use our weight to waggle the vessel from side to side. The mud slurped and gurgled against the hull. His voice rich with optimism, the *Obersturmführer* called out, 'Harder – it's coming free.'

Plumes of water spurted around the boat. The stiff stems of reeds toppled as if mown down by an invisible blade. We jumped into the waist-deep murky water. Somehow, I managed to escape the hail of machine- gun bullets. My guardian angel had returned to my side in my time of need. Covered in mud, I came across the three officers a little farther downstream.

'The Amis must have a deal with the Russians to stop anyone getting across the river,' said Schenk. 'Our Jewish friend back there was probably working on his own initiative.'

We continued to follow the river downstream, until we emerged from a clump of willow skirting a meadow. I spotted an unlikely formation of bushes near the riverbank. The *Hauptsturmführer* sent me to investigate while he and the other two officers kept me covered from the shelter of the trees. Under a heap of foliage, I discovered a long narrow clinker-built boat, well varnished and equipped with a pair of oars. With the prospect of escaping across the river lifting my spirits, I made my way back to my waiting *Kameraden* to tell them the good news.

'Well done *Uscha* Bartmann,' said the *Hauptsturmführer*, 'but we can't risk a daylight crossing except in an emergency. We'll guard the boat from the shelter of the trees and wait for nightfall. In the meantime we'll split into two pairs – one to guard the boat, the other to return to Jerichow to keep an eye open for the Russians. If they're getting too close for comfort it would be good to get some sort of warning so they don't catch us in the middle of the river like sitting ducks.'

Schenk and I returned to Jerichow while the two higher-ranking officers remained hidden in the clump of willows to guard the boat. We intended to use the house where Liza and Ute lived as a base until it was time to return to river. Because we had left early that morning, I had not thanked Ute and Liza for their warm hospitality and looked forward to the chance of rectifying that omission.

Our route took us to the southern edge of Jerichow where we encountered a stream of refugees heading towards the village. 'Where are you heading,' I asked a young woman who, with a heavy suitcase tied to her back, struggled to keep up with the flow of humanity as she dragged two exhausted children by the hand.

'To the railway bridge at Tangermünde – it's lying in the river,' she said, 'but the word is they've managed to rig up some sort of crossing for civilians and I don't intend to hang around waiting for the Russians to knock on my door.'

Away from the main street, Jerichow was eerily quiet. With knuckles caked in dried mud, I knocked on the door of the girls' house. There was no reply. I turned the handle – the door was unlocked – and went inside. Whimpers came from within the kitchen.

'It's Erwin,' I called. I heard a stool fall as the girls rushed to the kitchen door.

'Oh Erwin,' sobbed Ute, 'we thought the Russians had arrived.'

'They could take a day or two to reach here but you should leave before it's too late,' I said. 'The Americans are already on the other side of the river, you'll be safe there.'

'How could we leave? Everything we have is here – and our parents have not yet returned. Perhaps the Russians are not as bad as they say,' said Ute putting her arm around her sister's trembling shoulders.

❧ ❧

With no Russian activity to report, Schenk and I set off for the riverbank as evening approached. We were relieved to find that 'our' boat had remained undiscovered. As we made ourselves comfortable, a cold breeze rustled in the freshly unfurled leaves of the old willows skirting the riverbank. Our *Hauptsturmführer* decided we should head for an *SS* surgery unit based in Königslutter, about a hundred kilometres west of the Elbe. No one questioned his decision and at least we had a goal to aim for. Moreover, because he had passed up the chance of crossing with the Americans, I began to suspect that he somehow harboured the hope of escaping captivity altogether. All we had to do now was to wait for nightfall.

There was movement in the bushes close to the riverbank, on the far side of the meadow. We slung our weapons from our shoulders and braced ourselves for a firefight. A group of around twenty figures in German uniform emerged from the undergrowth.

'They might be *Seydlitz* troops – we'll nail them if they are,' whispered the *Obersturmführer*. 'These bastards deserve what they get.'

'They're not wearing armbands – they're probably regular *Wehrmacht*,' I said. The leader of the troop, a *Feldwebel*, spotted our boat almost immediately and quickened his pace.

'Keep them covered,' ordered the *Hauptsturmführer* as he broke from the shelter of the copse. 'Don't fire,' he yelled. 'We're *Waffen SS* – that's our boat.'

Every weapon in the *Wehrmacht* patrol's possession pointed at our *Hauptsturmführer*.

'What unit?' called the *Feldwebel*.

'*Falke -Leibstandarte Adolf Hitler*,' replied our *Hauptsturmführer*.

'How many?'

'Three others – two officers and an *Unterscharführer*.'

'Show yourselves.'

Our *Hauptsturmführer* signalled for us to join him.

The *Feldwebel* turned to his men and ordered them to lower their weapons, an act that did little to lower the tension between the two groups. We stood our ground as the *Wehrmacht* patrol approached.

The *Feldwebel*'s eyes narrowed. 'You say it's your boat?'

'We found it earlier today. We intend to cross the Elbe at nightfall,' replied our *Hauptsturmführer* curtly.

The *Feldwebel* shook his head. 'So you say, but I'm commandeering the boat,' he announced, 'for our general.'

'It's *our* boat,' said our *Hauptsturmführer* firmly.

'I'm sorry – I have my orders,' insisted the *Feldwebel* as he started to make towards the boat.

Our *Hauptsturmführer*, a whole head taller, smartly stepped in front of the *Feldwebel* to block his progress. 'I said, it's *our* boat.'

Instinctively, I raised my machine pistol. Schenk and the *Obersturmführer* echoed my example in a desperate action to save the precious boat. The men of the *Wehrmacht* patrol, who outnumbered us by at least four to one, replied in kind. We were at the focal point of a semicircle of rifles. The slightest unexpected movement could easily have triggered a deadly close-range exchange of fire. It was a tense situation, a trial of willpower.

The *Feldwebel* stared angrily into eyes of our *Hauptsturmführer* who resolutely stood his ground. A grunt of irritation broke the *Feldwebel*'s silence. He ordered two of his men to fetch his general. Here we were at the end of the *Reich*, German confronting German, staring down the barrels of each other's weapons, waiting for something to loosen the stalemate.

Twenty interminable minutes later, a high-ranking *Wehrmacht* officer arrived with the two runners sent out by the *Feldwebel*.

'Lower your weapons,' he ordered his men and, turning to our *Hauptsturmführer* he bellowed, 'I am the superior officer here.'

Our *Hauptsturmführer* refused to flinch.

The general's face reddened. 'Now look here – I *insist* you allow my men to take that boat without further hindrance.'

'We will not hand it over,' replied our *Hauptsturmführer* in an unyielding tone.

The general grumbled but eventually gave ground. 'Very well,' he said shaking his head, 'but I'm sure we can come to some sort of agreement that would satisfy both of us.'

Our leader, showing no sign of retracting from his hard-line position, remained resolutely silent.

'Look, we all want to get to the other side,' said the general adopting a conciliatory tone. 'I'll leave two men with you – they'll take you to the other side and return with the boat – that way we all get across.'

�-�

When darkness at last embraced the river, we boarded the boat with the two strong-looking youngsters from the *Wehrmacht* unit acting as oarsmen. As we left the protection of the riverbank, an unexpectedly powerful current caught the boat. In the distance, I could now make out the wrecked railway bridge at Tangermünde,

'*Scheisse* – we'll be in Hamburg by morning,' cursed the *Hauptsturmführer*. 'Put your backs into it,' he urged our oarsmen.

By the time the boat's prow scraped on the gravel on the western side of the Elbe, at the foot of a steep embankment, we had travelled several kilometres downstream. We clambered ashore and pushed the boat away from the riverbank. Whether the two *Wehrmacht* lads made it back to their general, I cannot say but, as the current and darkness took the boat out of sight, it did not seem to me that the crew were making a determined effort to get back to the other side of the Elbe.

I scrambled to the top of the steep embankment and poked my head over rim. '*Verdammt.*'

'What is it?' whispered the *Hauptsturmführer*.

'Tents – hundreds of them – and heavy artillery pieces, American probably.'

'Guards?'

I peered into the darkness. 'No guards.'

We skirted the riverbank with the *Hauptsturmführer* leading the way until we reached the cover of woodland a little farther downstream, then continued along a forest track. In the emerging daylight, we found that the track ran parallel to a road only fifty metres or so to our left. The whole woodland thrilled to the music of birdsong, a chorus of joy.

'It's a beautiful country,' said the *Hauptsturmführer*.

Ignoring the grumbling of my empty stomach, I closed my weary eyes to listen to the sounds of spring, to nature's melodious miracle.

'*Volle Deckung*,' cried Schenk.

Instinctively I dived for cover amongst the wet undergrowth just as an American jeep passed close to the edge of the woods. A heavy machine gun on the rear of the vehicle opened fire. Bullets zipped through the foliage but the jeep continued towards the Elbe without slowing.

'That was close call,' said the *Hauptsturmführer* as he brushed the dew from his uniform. 'There's no point taking risks at this stage of the war. From now on we will travel only under the cloak of darkness.'

❀·❀

With the last of our food rations exhausted, we greeted the first light of a new day with empty stomachs and shivering bodies. A rickety cottage near the edge of a field seemed to offer the prospect of respite from the cold and perhaps, from hunger. As we approached, the door opened.

A thin man with hollow eyes appeared. His collar length black hair and bony face reminded me of a crow. 'Now, what do we have here?' scorned his croaky voice. 'Well I'll be damned – it's the *Waffen SS* come to save me from … '

'Cut the shit,' I interrupted. 'We need something to eat.'

The crow-faced man stepped to the side as we pushed past, then slammed the door to follow us inside.

'Broth – that's all I've got to offer,' said the man. 'Just look at you with your medals – what good are they now? The Americans have already met up with the Russians at Storkau on the Elbe – big celebrations – dancing in the streets over the graves of Germans and there's nothing you can do about it.' He went to the oven in the corner of the miserable little room and opened the lid of a pot. 'It's not exactly hot but there's nothing else.'

We ate the spicy broth with relish.

'How long are you staying?' enquired our resentful host.

'Till nightfall,' replied our *Hauptsturmführer* stifling a yawn. 'We'll get ourselves cleaned up then rest till it gets dark.'

The man shrugged his pointed shoulders. 'There's a washbasin on a stand in the bedroom but you'll have to fetch your own water,' he grumped. 'You'll find the pump at the back door. Oh, the jug on the washstand – don't break it.'

I flung my camouflage jacket onto the bed and, as I emptied the last of the water from the jug into the basin, caught sight of a face looking back at me from a mirror hanging on the wall behind the washstand. Four years had passed since I joined the *Leibstandarte* but it seemed like only four months. The mirror told a different story. Tiredness and red bristles had added ten years to my appearance. I slid my silver death's head ring from my finger, placing it beside a dirty glass in which a solitary toothbrush stood. As I bent forward to splash the water in my cupped hands onto my face, the crow-faced owner of the house battered on the door of the bedroom with his fists.

'The Russians are coming – your friends are waiting for you outside.'

It was only when we were clear of the house that we gathered our wits.

'The cunning old swine,' said the *Hauptsturmführer*, 'he probably made up that story about the Russians to get rid of us.'

Only then did I notice that I had left my ring behind in a moment of carelessness that still causes me great irritation.

❦··❦

Feverish with hunger, drinking from muddy streams, stumbling along forest tracks in the dead of night, we pressed onwards until we found ourselves in woodland at the northern outskirts of Königslutter, just as the sun cast its first bright rays through the leaves. The endless sheets of cloud had given way to silent blue skies, free from buzzing aircraft. The air had a summery feel.

'We should we remove all identification that links us with the *Leibstandarte* and *Waffen SS*,' announced our *Hauptstrumführer*.

In solemn silence, I picked the stitches from my cuff band with my knife and, for the last time, gazed at the name, 'Adolf Hitler', written in silver thread. I hung the cuff band on the twig of a tree, close to those of my *Kameraden*. Nearby, I buried my weapons and identity tag, and with it a youth wasted by war.

32

Captivity

The nights spent slinking past villages and trudging through woodland had left little meat on my bones, and it was with tremendous relief that I gazed at the entrance of the *SS* hospital overlooking Königslutter. Somehow, without map or compass, we had managed to find our goal. The *Hauptsturmführer* went inside while I waited at the door with Schenk and the enigmatic *Obersturmführer*.

The *Hauptsturmführer* reappeared. 'The war is lost,' he mumbled, the enormity of the catastrophe imprinted on his face. 'Germany has surrendered without condition.' Eyes lowered, he turned on his heels and we followed him into the hospital where I caught glimpses of patients as they moved about in a side ward. Some had suffered hideous loss of flesh from their faces while others wore grotesque masks of grafted skin. The hospital was a centre for reconstructive plastic surgery.

After a nurse cleaned and bound the flesh wound in my foot – picked up when running the gauntlet of shellfire near Halbe – she showed me to a room in the hospital basement where a mattress and a couple of blankets waited. My three travelling companions, all officers and completely unscathed, were directed to a private room on the first floor. At least I was given the same food rations as the patients, and for that, I was extremely grateful.

On the second morning, after two blissful nights of undisturbed sleep, a nurse visited to change the dressing on my wounds. As she finished tying the bandages she said, 'I believe you don't have a permit. Without a permit we really shouldn't be treating you at all, we stopped accepting new patients when the end came.'

Not wishing to cause any problems for the hospital authorities, I asked where I could obtain such a permit.

'From the town hall – it must be signed by the *Burgermeister*.'

I promised to rectify the matter and as soon as the nurse left, I dressed and made my way to the officers' room. My uniform was a disgrace – the trousers were filthy and worn through at the knees and the tunic ripped in several places. I felt sure young Schenk would respond favourably to my request as I knocked on the door of the officers' private quarters.

Dressed in pyjamas Schenk, the only one present in the room, invited me in. I noticed there were four beds. Evidently, they did not wish to share their space with a lowly *Unterscharführer*. Still, I was not annoyed with this situation – it was pleasant enough in the basement and it would have been unbearably awkward to share a room with three officers who now had very little authority over me.

'I agree you look a mess *Unterscharführer*,' said Schenk after I explained my predicament, 'but I must confess I am reluctant to lend you my trousers.'

'But it's only for a short time,' I pleaded.

'What happens if you get lost? Do you want me to be left here without trousers?'

Having paraded the streets dressed like a scarecrow while making my way to the *SS* hospital in Vienna, an experience I was determined not emulate, and sensing a weakening of Schenk's resolve, I promised, 'I'll come back, straight away.'

At last, Schenk's resistance collapsed. He went to his locker and brought his beautiful leather trousers to me. Handing them over he said sternly, 'Remember – as soon you get back.'

'As soon as I get the permit,' I assured the young officer. 'I shouldn't be gone for more than an hour. It's not far and it's early so I'll be the first in line at the *Burgermeister's* office.'

I left my belongings – my tattered uniform and the watch my mother had given to me as a Christmas present – in the basement and set off for town dressed in Schenk's leather trousers. My own brown *SS* shirt was barely visible under my pullover and therefore unlikely to draw hostile attention. I carried my identification, my *Soldbuch*, tucked into the leg of my boot.

It was an idyllic morning, filled all the little sounds that signify a peaceful summer's day. A light breeze rustled the leaves of the roadside trees as I turned from the hospital driveway onto the road that would take me to Königslutter. A swooping blackbird folded its wings to pass confidently between the vertical iron bars of a gate. At that instant, it was difficult to believe a vicious war that had ripped Europe asunder had just ended. I strolled downhill barely able to contain the elation surging through every nerve in my young body. I had survived.

The thump of a hand on my right shoulder brought me to a sudden halt. '*SS*?'

A cold shiver down my spine. '*Ja, Leibstandarte*.'

'You're coming with us.'

'I was on my...'

'I said you're coming with us.'

The hand tugged hard. I spun round to face three sturdy men. On the right arm of their jackets were armbands bearing the word *Hilfpolizei* (Police Auxiliary) and the official stamp of the American military authority.

'Where are you going?'

'I need a permit form the *Burgermeister's* office to stay in the *SS* hospital until my wounds heal,' I explained.

'You won't find anyone in *Burgermeister's* office,' chuckled my captor. 'The whole place is closed. Don't you know what day it is?'

I had stupidly overlooked the possibility that it was Sunday and had little option but to let them lead me to the prison in Königslutter. Around six o'clock that evening, my captors came to my cell. After a lengthy interrogation, they searched me and found my *Soldbuch*. One of my captors grunted in disgust as he opened it. He tore the picture of Hitler from inside the front cover and threw it on the ground before examining the document in minute detail. When he returned my *Soldbuch*, I stretched out to retrieve the picture of Hitler from the floor of the cell, an act that brought no censure. By the time my interrogation was complete I was almost fainting through lack of food and dehydration. 'Before you go,' I said to my captors, 'I have a question.'

'What is it?'

'Am I a prisoner of war?'

'*Ja.*'

'Then I must be treated as such. You offered me nothing to eat or drink since you arrested me. It's your duty to make sure I am properly fed.'

The three *Hilfpolizei* left the cell without comment. In the corridor, a conversation took place, but I was unable to follow what was said. A short time later, one of my captors returned to my cell and we conversed politely until his two comrades came an hour later carrying a tray laden with food. Astonished by both the quantity and quality of the food on offer – hot soup, fresh bread, the finest salami and creamy milk – I had to restrain the urge gorge it down as quickly as possible.

My captors remained in my cell for several hours chatting about the war and my life in Berlin. Naturally, I responded by asking questions about their own lives and soon found out that the trio had been prisoners in the Dachau concentration camp, near Munich. My inquisitors looked well fed and I asked, 'How come the three of you are so fat?'

'It's all water,' one of them said rubbing his belly. 'It causes such terrible pains, sometimes I can hardly bear it.'

To me, his words lacked conviction – it was hard to believe that water retention because of starvation could leave men looking so healthy.

The following morning, a new guard appeared at my cell door.

'I need to get a permit from the *Burgermeister* to stay in the hospital,' I complained. 'And my foot wound needs a fresh dressing. When will you let me return to the hospital?'

'You won't be going back there,' replied the guard.

The dressing on my foot grew filthier by the day and there was a serious risk of infection setting in. I called repeatedly through the bars of the cell door for attention but my protests went unanswered. 'Where are the three that brought me in?' I yelled, hoping they might prove more sympathetic to my plight.

'On the hunt for *SS* members,' laughed the new guard.

My days in solitary imprisonment passed slowly and, with no sign of a companion with whom I could at least have a conversation, the isolation was beginning to erode my morale. I spent most of my time dozing with thoughts of my parents and Ingeborg spinning around inside my head.

❦·❦

The cell door crashed open. I sprang from my mattress. Six burly American soldiers standing in the doorway came into focus, their machine pistols aimed at my chest. An officer pushed past the soldiers. '*Sprechen Sie Englisch?*'

'*Nein, leider nicht,*' I answered, careful not to make any sudden movements that might provoke a nervous twitch of an American finger. The sideways jerk of the officer's head told me I was leaving the cell.

In the street, three jeeps waited, engines running, one behind the other. A guard pushed me into the back of the rearmost vehicle while the officer sat with the driver. As we left the town, it soon became apparent that we were not heading for the *SS* hospital. I tried to make my disappointment clear by gestures and pleas in German but the officer steadfastly ignored them.

We travelled out of Königslutter and through wrecked villages – scenes of heavy fighting that must have taken place only days before. I could tell by the angle of the sun that we were travelling to the east and the thought crossed my mind that I was being taken to the Elbe to be handed over to the Russians. When we reached Helmstedt, about twenty-five kilometres to the east of Königslutter, the jeeps pulled up at the steps leading to the entrance of a substantial building. The officer jumped from the jeep and signalled for me to follow him up the steps leading to the entrance. Once inside, my guards pulled me to a halt at the start of a long corridor with a beautiful polished marble floor. As I waited, wondering what would happen next, a mighty kick in the rear sent me crashing headlong and I slid, face down, across the shiny floor. Even before my momentum was spent, strong hands twisted my shirt collar and pulled me roughly to my feet.

'In there you bastard,' sneered the guard as he pushed me into a side room where three American officers sat at a desk.

Around the walls, hefty soldiers kept watch as the guard flung me into a seat opposite the officers, all three of whom had a good command of German. They fired questions at me from every direction. After a while, a second team of inquisitors continued the interview by asking exactly the same questions. It was not at all clear what they wanted to find out from me but whenever I paused for thought, I earned a robust smack to the back of my head or a punch in the back. It gradually became clear to me that my interrogators were interested in my connection with the name *Falke*. It took considerable repetition to persuade them that *Regiment Falke* was simply a cobbled together *SS* regiment based around Spreenhagen. Of course, they never explained why the name *Falke* had so firmly captured their imagination but I surmise that an incident involving someone associated with that name had occurred and they were doing their level best to hunt him down.

Throughout the interrogation, I was made to stand, then to sit, an episode that brought to mind my performance in the *Maskenball* at Lichterfelde. The whole affair went on for hours and my foot wound, which had begun to fester, throbbed hotly. When I brought this to the attention of my inquisitors, they simply brushed the matter aside saying, 'Later, later.'

When the interrogation was over, my guards escorted me to Helmstedt's nearby *Rathaus* where, after further hours of questioning, they flung me unceremoniously into a small prison cell with a solitary bunk. Several hours later, my solitary confinement came to an end when the cell door slammed behind an officer in a *Wehrmacht* uniform. He carried a small case and wore an armband, both emblazoned with a red cross. 'Ah at last, a doctor,' I said swinging my legs over the edge of the bunk to roll up my trouser leg. 'A wound in my foot's been festering for a few days now.'

The officer shook his head, 'Oh no, I'm a dentist – a fellow prisoner – some chap in town denounced me as a Nazi.' A single step brought him to the bunk and he sat beside me. 'I was brought in to await trial and sentencing,' he explained.

As we exchanged stories, the door of the cell slammed behind a third prisoner, this time in civilian dress. The arrival of new prisoners went on until evening by which time I had eleven companions, mostly soldiers, in my cell. The opening and closing of adjacent cell doors told a similar story.

We waited expectantly for food and water but as time passed, it became clear that our wait was in vain. With so many men crammed into the tiny cell, which was without a toilet and evidently intended to hold just a single prisoner for only a short time, it was impossible to sleep – a further addition to our misery. By shouting from cell to cell, we established that there were over fifty prisoners crammed into neighbouring cells.

Shortly after dawn, the door opened. At gunpoint, we made our way to a small, enclosed yard to join the prisoners from the other cells, several of whom were high-ranking German officers. Although everyone was relieved to breathe fresh air, there were mumblings of discontent among my fellow prisoners. Many of them had been stripped of their military decorations and wound badges – all they had to show for years of combat and service to their country.

'You have fifteen minutes exercise time,' announced a guard.

With only three toilets available, it was an anxious time for those who had held on desperately until morning to relieve themselves. Somehow, everyone managed to do what was necessary before returning to his cell. Cramped together like sardines in a can, the hours passed slowly and still there was no sign of food and water. By the time we gathered in the yard the next morning, looks of dejection tainted the pasty faces.

After enduring three hot, uncomfortable nights of torture by cramped confinement, a *Hauptmann* in the adjacent cell had had enough. 'I demand to see the commanding officer.' he bellowed like a mad bull. 'This is inhumane treatment.' He banged on the door of his cell with his fists until the guards found it impossible to ignore the din.

An American Lieutenant appeared but was unable to placate the raging *Hauptmann*. Following a heated exchange of words, the Lieutenant agreed to summon his commanding officer who, when he saw the conditions in which we were held, immediately ordered his Lieutenant to organise transport to take us to a proper prison camp.

When two trucks arrived, we gathered at the main entrance of the *Rathaus*. Once more, our *Hauptmann* began to raise a commotion. 'We will not move another step until we have our decorations returned,' he roared to shouts of approval from his fellow German prisoners.

The guards swore and pushed against us in an attempt to force us down the stairs. We pushed back and refused to give way despite the threatening butts of rifles. Standing our ground, we replied with our own vehement curses. 'We have been robbed, we have been robbed,' we chanted.

A German-speaking American officer came to our rescue. After a brief conversation with our *Hauptmann*, he turned to a guard. 'Where are their medals?' He repeated his words in German so that we understood his intent.

'In the guardroom sir,' replied the soldier.

'Then go and get them, everything, medals watches, insignia – everything – I will not have thieving going on right under my nose.'

Ten minutes passed before the guards returned with upturned German steel helmets filled to the brim with items stolen from prisoners. The *Hauptmann* was the first to retrieve his decoration – a Knight's Cross. Now I could understand his determination to have his award returned – the Knight's Cross was awarded only to those who had given exceptional service to the *Reich*.

A journey of a few hours took us to a recently vacated displaced persons camp with a boundary marked only by a low fence consisting of two horizontal runs of smooth wire. The Polish guards, having got wind of our imminent arrival, welcomed us with a shower of stones thrown from the perimeter fence. With smirks and taunts, they issued each of us with a thin blanket and led us to huts they had made sure were without doors, windows or bunks. Glass wool insulation obtained from the nearby armaments production facility, the *Hermann Göring Werke*, covered the floor. At night, tiny needles of glass soon found their way into every crevice of my body causing an itch that I scratched until my skin turned red – a torment worse than any infestation by lice I suffered on the *Ostfront*. Thankfully, a British unit took over the running of the camp, protecting us from further mischievous acts by the Poles who continued to hang around in the hope of scrounging food.

I soon struck up a friendship with a fellow *Waffen SS* prisoner who happened to act as camp interpreter. As the camp filled with ever more German prisoners, we could only stand back in horror as a fever of denial fell upon our compatriots. None of them, they declared, had ever been members of the *NSDAP* (the Nazi Party). They professed their utter hatred of Hitler and those old enough vehemently denied ever voting for him. This refutation of their once unshakeable loyalty to the *Führer* – no doubt designed to convince their captors of their innocence of the terrible crimes that the liberation of the concentration camps unearthed – culminated in a vicious vendetta against fellow prisoners. A *Wehrmacht* officer soon gathered a gang of followers who made it their goal to track down any 'Nazis' in the camp. Those found to have the same surname as a high-ranking Party officials such as Frank or Heydrich, were hauled in front of a kangaroo court – God alone knows on what charge – and inevitably found guilty. The punishment was always death by hanging, a sentence carried out at night in the camp's boiler house.

Fortunately, I was dressed in the clothes I wore when arrested in Königslutter – Schenk's leather trousers, a shirt and a pullover. There was nothing to mark me out as a member of the *Waffen SS* Division *Leibstandarte Adolf Hitler* and I had kept my possession of my *Soldbuch*, and therefore my identity, a secret. Simply being a member of a regiment that carried the name 'Adolf Hitler' in its title would have been irrefutable proof of my guilt even though I was only eight when the election took place that brought Hitler to power and had never been a member of the *NSDAP*.

❦

As I lay in my bunk one afternoon, listening to the soothing patter of rain on the roof of the hut, a loud shriek grabbed my attention.

'Ah, now who is this?

Every eye in the hut focussed on my *Soldbuch,* held aloft by a victorious hand as if it were a trophy won in a competition. A shudder ran through my body; the cold fist of fear clenched hard on my heart. Somehow, my *Soldbuch* must have dropped from inside my trouser leg. I fought to quell any outward sign of the alarm coursing through every nerve in my body. There was a rush towards the man holding my *Soldbuch*. Amidst a clamour of bodies, hands feverishly grabbed at the damning 'evidence'. In desperation, I dived through the melee and somehow managed to snatch my *Soldbuch* from the finder's hand. Before anyone realised what had happened I managed to hide it inside my trouser pocket. There was a commotion as the pack hunted for it. Fortunately, the rich red beard that covered my face had masked my identity. Although the war had ended, my guardian angel had remained faithfully by my side. I am certain that if the vigilantes had known of my membership of the *Leibstandarte*, I would have been the next victim of the kangaroo court. Never before, had I felt myself to be in such imminent danger. From then on, I lived with the fear that my membership of the *Leibstandarte* would be uncovered.

The staged 'trials' continued even while the British authorities investigated the murders. As is usual in such circumstances, none of those questioned knew the slightest thing that would help identify those responsible.

One afternoon, as we hung about the prison yard in the sunshine, my interpreter friend called me over. 'Listen carefully Erwin,' he said. 'Tomorrow at about 11 am there will be an announcement over the camp loudspeaker. It will ask anyone who feels themselves to be in danger from the lynch mob to gather at the main gate.'

'What will happen to them?' I asked.

'They will be taken to another camp. For your own safety, you mustn't mention this conversation to anyone.'

Possessing only the clothes I stood in, there was no packing to be done the following morning, an activity that might have aroused the suspicions of the self-proclaimed Nazi hunters. After breakfast, I made certain I was never too far away from the entrance to the camp. Sure enough, a truck arrived at 11 am. It stood outside the compound with its engine running. A guard detail of British soldiers under the command of a captain gathered by the sentry box at the gate. Then the announcement came over the loudspeakers. I quickly made my way past the hostile eyes of my fellow Germans, into the protection of the British guard. Four others, all *Waffen SS*, also elected to take the opportunity to get out of that dangerous place.

A short journey took us through a landscape heavily pockmarked with craters left by Allied bombs to the concentration camp that had recently housed the forced labour serving the *Hermann Goering Werke*, not far from Braunschweig. Sleeping accommodation was provided by bunks piled six high. We soon discovered that because of their flimsy construction, the slightest movement of a person occupying a lower bunk made the topmost bunk sway like a tree in the wind so that any occupant was sure to suffer an attack of vertigo. Furthermore, the dormitories were located under a viaduct carrying the main road and with the continual movement of horses and carts, it was impossible to get a good night's sleep. Still, we were safe and, because we were the first occupants of the camp, able to select the best of these uncomfortable bunks.

Within a few days, another batch of *Waffen SS* men arrived at the camp. I was pleasantly surprised to see Heinrich among them. 'How did they treat you?' I asked after we exchanged greetings.

'Ha. Those Americans that took us over the Elbe – they had us standing chest deep in a stinking swamp for hours.' He slapped my shoulder saying, 'But we made it Erwin, we made it through to the end.'

After a few weeks, under the staring eyes of a guard of Poles, we helped gather the harvest from nearby fields. It was not exactly freedom but the outdoor activity was a relief from the oppressive confinement of the camp. It was sobering to think of the thousands of workers forced to endure years of incarceration there while they toiled for long days in the nearby armaments factories. As a reward for our efforts in the fields, the farmer prepared thin soup on top of which floated globules of melted lard. Unfortunately, our starvation-shrunk stomachs were unable to cope with such food and the concoction soon sent us running to the side of the fields with diarrhoea.

After harvest time, our duties were varied and pleasant enough. We tidied the officers' beds, blanco-ed their belts and polished their boots and four of us were allocated the task of cleaning up the officers' canteen. After carrying out this duty on several occasions, we left the canteen to find four plates of porridge and bread on a small table next to the entrance. One my comrades made to eat the porridge.

'Don't.' I warned. 'It's a trap. If they catch us stealing who knows what will happen to us.'

The following day, a British officer stood by the table, again with four plates of porridge. 'Go ahead, eat,' he said with a welcoming gesture. 'The food *was* meant for you chaps.'

During my time at the Braunschweig camp I was, with one exception, treated well by the men of the Northamptonshire Yeomanry. Unfortunately, an exceptionally tall Scots corporal took sadistic pleasure in humiliating me in front of the other guards and prisoners. Several times, after tending to my duties in the officers' barracks, he made a point of intercepting me as I made my way across the open ground of the camp yard. 'Right then my lad,' he would say laughing, 'bend o'er an' see whit ye think o' this.'

I felt the thrust of something hard in my rear end. Fortunately, it was only a pistol that stabbed into my arse.

❦

Just before Christmas 1945, a British guard detail counted us into wagons that, judging by the black dust covering their floors, had recently carried coal. Looking like chimney sweeps, we disembarked from the wagons and marched to a camp standing on a hill overlooking the pleasant Belgian countryside. Ironically, the guards were ex-members of the 28th *Waffen SS Grenadier Division Wallonien,* a division of Belgians that fought alongside Germans in our quest to destroy Bolshevism.

On arrival at the camp, we gathered in the assembly area where a British officer asked if there were any joiners amongst us. Well, nearly every hand went up – I suppose the men were desperate to try anything that would relieve the cold and the boredom of camp life. Next, the officer asked if there were tradesmen bakers present. Again there was a sea of hands but the officer, having learned from his previous mistake, soon weeded out the unskilled hopefuls and I was selected to join a small band of fellow bakers.

Working in teams of three on twelve-hour shifts, two men kneaded dough by hand while the *Wasserman* measured and added the water. My training at the Glaser bakery now stood me in good stead. I told the *Wasserman* to add just an extra pint of water to every two bags of flour – not enough for the British guards to notice but it allowed us to bake six extra loaves that we were able to keep for ourselves. Occasionally a piece of fish was added to the rations and this was cooked in the same ovens where we baked the bread.

On a dismal, drizzly, dark winter's morning in January 1946, trucks took us to the harbour in Antwerp where we boarded a trawler along with British soldiers returning home on leave. As might be expected, we were given the least comfortable accommodation – the hold at the prow of the boat, lit only by the porthole that led the anchor chain to the outside. When we left the shelter of the harbour, guards herded us onto the deck where we remained until arriving in Tilbury in total darkness, shivering and soaked to the skin. A short march took us to the rail station where, to our utter astonishment, we boarded a train of Pullman coaches equipped with tables and chairs.

After a long but luxurious rail journey, we arrived at a camp near Chepstow where, after a good night's sleep in comfortable accommodation, we assembled for morning roll call. A sergeant then escorted small groups of wounded prisoners to a hut for a medical examination. Those of us fit enough to exercise – the wound to my ankle had finally healed – remained in the yard.

'Gentlemen,' said a well-spoken officer as he and his sergeant moved among us, 'today we are going for a little run. Our route will take us through the town – give the locals a chance to see what a sorry looking bunch the Jerries really are.'

As he passed between our ranks, he stopped in front of me and looked me up and down. Our eyes met. 'My, my, you do look well fed,' He turned to his sergeant and laughed. 'Better fed than most of the bloody locals – I spotted another two of these chappies earlier on today. Where are they getting the damned food?'

From Chepstow we moved to Aldershot where we stayed for a few weeks before boarding a rickety passenger train that carried us northwards. Every now and then, the train stopped to drop off one or two coaches. At around mid-day, under towering, white summer clouds, the train arrived at the little station in Longniddry, Scotland, where we stepped onto the platform. This must have taken the old stationmaster by surprise because he ran around in a panic screaming, 'The Germans are here – the *SS* – they'll kill us all.'

With only a handful of British soldiers guarding us, we waited on the platform until around 6 pm before marching to Gosford camp near Aberlady, a handsome little village overlooking the wide waters of the Firth of Forth. Despite being overcrowded, life was comfortable enough there with a cinema providing entertainment and a football pitch offering the opportunity to take part in sporting activities.

After my release in 1948 – still wearing *Untersturmführer* Schenk's leather trousers from which I later fashioned a wallet – I settled in Edinburgh where fate eventually had its way and I took up my old trade, as a baker.

Epilogue

Life was hard on the *Ostfront*. Arrow sharp rain that persisted for days on end stung our skin and turned the soil into deep, black mud that found its way into our boots to rot our socks and feet. We ate food that was, by any civilized measure, inedible. We suffered the despair of endless exhaustion and the constant itching caused by lice. We endured cold so intense it could freeze the fuel in our vehicles and kill a man in an hour. We stepped into mortal danger when every instinct told our bodies to run. Only those who have suffered these hardships can understand the life of a soldier on the *Ostfront*. Yet, against every wall in my house where the geometry of the room allows, there stands a bookcase crammed with books or videotapes about the Second World War. On the uppermost shelf of the tall bookcase at the foot of the stairs sits a model of a Tiger tank and a clock from the cockpit of a Heinkel He 111. On the walls between the bookcases hang mementoes of my German origins – plaques and photographs. A large flat-screen television dominates my lounge. A satellite dish picks up stations in Polish, German and Russian, one of which is almost certain to broadcast a programme about the Second World War, or Hitler, at some point during the day. On the internet, I am a member of numerous forums that discuss every aspect of the Second World War. I cannot cast aside memories of my youth and the time I spent as a soldier of the *Leibstandarte*. I look back with pride to the comradeship I shared with my fellow soldiers whose memory will stay with me until I die, a comradeship beyond the imagination of the aimless youth of today. But I am no old Nazi, constantly mourning the fate of our *Führer* or the lost chances and stupid decisions that cost us the war. Of course, like any other loyal soldier, I hoped we would win the war but things turned out as they did and there is no point on dwelling on the 'what ifs' in life. At a personal level, our defeat cost me dearly, though less, much less, than the price paid by many others on both sides of the greatest conflict in history. Despite the myth that every *Waffen SS* man was a fanatical Nazi, I was never a member of the Nazi Party nor was there ever pressure put on me to join. Even high-ranking officers of the *Leibstandarte*, such as Joachim Peiper, declined to become Party members. I was a member of the *Lebensborn* movement but was never called upon to take part in their breeding programme for Aryans – in fact I had never heard of this during my years at the front or in Berlin and I remain unconvinced that it was ever used as such, a least on any meaningful scale. As far as I was aware, *Lebensborn* was an organisation dedicated to the welfare of members of the *SS* and their families and helped, for example, to place orphans of *SS* men who had died for *Volk und Führer* with suitable families.

I had just turned nine when Hitler came to power and had no clear concept of the ultimate aims of the *NSDAP*. Since most of the men with whom I shared the dangers of battle were also around ten years old when Hitler came to power, it is a fair bet that most of them were unaware of the insidious aims of the Nazis when they volunteered to enlist in the *Waffen SS*. We grew into our teenage years under Hitler at a time when he had restored Germany's pride. Amidst the national euphoria, who would hear the prophets of doom? History contrived to offer us the choice of either believing in the *Führer*, who promised order and progress, or in a Soviet style of Communism that merely substituted one form oppression for another. Many in Germany, including my parents, chose Hitler. Like blind fish, they took happily to the murky brown waters of National Socialism.

One cannot choose one's Fatherland – that is a matter of fate – but serving it loyally, at least for me, was a matter of duty. For us young soldiers of the *Leibstandarte*, war offered adventure and the chance to fight Bolshevism, the brutal cult that threatened the destruction of the civilized world, or so we believed. From all over Europe young men, from Spain to Estonia, from Scandinavia to Ukraine, threw their youth, their very lives, into the game. As volunteers, they joined the *Waffen SS*, gambling on the greatness of our leaders without realising the odds were always set heavily against their survival.

That Germany was not alone in its fear of Bolshevism was further demonstrated by the establishment of the 'Arms Race' that pitted the Western Powers against Soviet Union almost as soon as – if not before – Germany capitulated.

If I may permit myself a single 'what if' it is this: what if Hitler had not confronted the threat of communism, where would the boundaries of the Soviet Union have been drawn? In his book *Diplomacy*, Henry Kissinger quotes Stalin's response to an American diplomat who congratulates him on the conquest of Berlin. Stalin responds with a wry smile, 'Tsar Alexander reached Paris.'

Our leaders orchestrated monstrous crimes against humanity and, with hindsight, it is easy to say that the ordinary German citizen should have done more to resist the rise of Hitler. But even those who at first opposed Hitler were mesmerised by the turnaround in Germany's meteoric economic fortunes, even they became ardent supporters of the *NSDAP*. Every German living in or near a sizeable town must have known of the presence of concentration camps – how could they have failed to notice the gangs of forced labourers working in the fields or forests or repairing bomb damage? But the vast majority were, as was I, unaware of the existence of the death camps. The *Leibstandarte* was always in the front line, too busy confronting the enemy to be fully aware of what was going on behind our backs. Even if one knew what was happening to the Jews, it would have been impossible to contest this without risking one's own life and few individuals are blessed with such courage.

❀-❀

Association with the activities of other branches of the *SS*, particularly the *Sicherheitstdienst* and their *Einsatzgruppen*, tarnished the reputation of the *Waffen SS*. This matter still causes me great bitterness. Every branch of the *SS* became the scapegoat for those Germans who found it pragmatic to declare their innocence, perhaps in an attempt to assuage their personal sense of guilt. As victors, the Allies proclaimed the whole of the *SS* a criminal organization – a convenient means of warding off attention from their own acts of ethnic cleansing, mass murder and rape, particularly those of the Soviets.

Of course, I cannot vouch for the honourable conduct of the whole of the *Waffen SS*, nor even for the whole of the *Leibstandarte*. I can only avow that during my time with *4.Kompanie*, I witnessed the heroism of young men dedicated to their country, men who fought hard and treated the enemy with respect. Even to this day, I live my life by the maxim imprinted on our soldiers' belts: *Meine Ehre Heisst Treu* (Loyalty is my Honour).

❀-❀

War's wild cry still visits my dreams. Even after almost seventy years, I see in them the Russian soldier recoiling under a burst of fire from my machine pistol as he eats from a tin of sardines, or the recruit with a leg attached only by a few strands of muscle as he pleads for me to end his suffering. For any normal person, killing a fellow human at close range twists every nerve to breaking point and leaves an indelible imprint on the mind. But these same dreams also bring enchantment, fleeting illusions that restore moments from my childhood or bring to life the smiling face of a fallen *Kamerad*, images that the flood of time cannot dispel. And every now and then, I see the eagle, symbol of the *Zeitgeist* cultured by Hitler, perched on the parapet of the Lichterfelde barracks, wings arched, ready to launch into the heavens. I glance at the cuff band on my left arm to read the words 'Adolf Hitler' and feel pride swell in my chest. I watch, from the perspective of a lifetime passed, the young *Leibstandarte* soldier that I once was, offer his life to the *Führer* with the words *'gehorsam bis in den Tod'* (obedience unto death). I can never completely escape that *Zeitgeist*. It lands uninvited on my shoulder to whisper seductively in my ear like a rejected lover whose guile targets not the heart, but the innate biological responses of the body. And it took, not the worst, but the best of German youth for its perverted purpose.

⚜·⚜

Candles are lit at the site of Hitler's mountain retreat in Bavaria, the *Berghof,* on the 20 April each year, but do not imagine that those who commemorate the life of the *Führer* in this way are old veterans like me. On the contrary, people too young to remember the war or its hardships perform this act of homage. And it is not only Germans who indulge in such rituals. Today, even in Russia, Neo-Nazis raise their right arms. Hitler set the *Zeitgeist* free, nurtured it, stirred it from its slumbers but he did not create the beast. There is a darkness lurking within the soul of man that opens his heart to the eagle, to the swastika, a darkness that will haunt me until the day I join once more with my *Kameraden* from the *Leibstandarte*.

Now, at the age of eighty-eight years, I am ready to sum up my life, which if I could live over again would live exactly as I have done given the same circumstances of history. I regret none of my personal choices or actions. When my father lay on his deathbed, he said, 'I have never been untrue to myself.' I am able to say the same thing.

> Here's freedom to him who would speak,
> Here's freedom to him who would write,
> For there's none ever feared that the truth should be heard,
> Save him whom the truth would indict.

Robert Burns (1759–96)

Notes

Chapter 1

The achievements of the black American athlete J.C. (Jesse) Owens at the 1936 Olympics are legendary. Although I never witnessed any of the events in which he participated, Owens was the subject of great praise among my fellow pupils. A school friend, the son of a wealthy lawyer, attended the long jump medal award and told me that the whole stadium had chanted 'Jesse Owens...Jesse Owens'. On the podium the second placed athlete Luz Long, a German, embraced Owens in congratulation, a scene that certainly could not have taken place at that time in many parts of the USA without provoking riots. At the time, American and British newsreels reported that Hitler had snubbed the athlete but Owens himself recognised that Hitler did not congratulate any of the winners that day – and there were Germans amongst them. Despite winning four gold medals, Owens did not receive a congratulatory telegram from the US President, Franklin D. Roosevelt (FDR). In Jeremy Schaap's book *Triumph*, Jesse Owens is quoted as saying, 'Hitler didn't snub me – it was FDR who snubbed me.' We can see in this example how the media can manipulate and mould public opinion in any political system. Even today, the myth of Hitler snubbing Owens lives on.

Chapter 3

When the Russians took over Lichterfelde barracks, they cut off the heads of the Eternal Corporals and encased their bodies in concrete, so that they are now hidden inside the pillars at the main gate to the Lichterfelde barracks which now house Germany's Federal Archives. There is a saying among us few remaining veterans that fresh cracks appear in the concrete when the Eternal Corporals try to salute any *Leibstandarte Kamerad* who stops to reminisce in front of them.

Long after the end of the war, a fellow called Helmut Mader and I became long-standing pen friends without realising we had met before. When touring Scotland in 1991, he took the opportunity to drop into my home in Edinburgh. As we reminisced about our time in the *Leibstandarte*, my time as a recruit cropped up in conversation and, as I told him about the story about the dust, I saw the look on his face change. After nearly fifty years, I had not recognised him as the *UvD* with the white gloves, the Laughing Devil, nor had he recognised me as his victim. It was the first, and only, time I have seen an adult male blush so uncontrollably. We laughed together about the incident and of course remained good friends.

Chapter 5
Heinz Nowotnik, won the coveted Knight's Cross in May 1944. He survived the war and died in 1999.

Chapter 6
It is widely reported in books and on internet sites that Sepp Dietrich, our divisional commander, ordered that no Russian prisoners were to be taken during the three days following the discovery of the bodies in the well in Taganrog. However, as far as I am aware, I have to say that none of this is true. Although angered by the torture of our *Kameraden* – and we doubtlessly fought with extra vigour during the next few days – there were prisoners taken. During the entire time I spent in Russia with *4.Kompanie*, I was never told 'don't take prisoners'. Despite the cruel tortures inflicted by the Russians on German prisoners, our instructions were to treat captured Russian soldiers, as far as was practicable, in a way that we ourselves would wish to be treated. On several occasions I saw men of the *Leibstandarte* use their own field dressings to cover the wounds of enemy soldiers. Of course, one never hears indignation expressed about the torture of the men found in the well – their murder was evidently not a war crime since it was done in the defence of Mother Russia.

Nowadays there is no shortage of books written about the *Waffen SS* and their crimes. In my view, many of these texts (particularly those written in English) are by historians who have only second or third hand knowledge of the conditions on the *Ostfront* and have a financial interest in giving a biased and sensationalised version of the truth. This applies in particular to reports given by 'historians' that, after the fall of Taganrog, the *Leibstandarte* massacred wounded Russians in a hospital. Having given an interview to one such 'historian', he wrote a book in which he ignored my account of the events in Taganrog. When I challenged him on this matter, he simply waved his hand and said, 'it's not the sort of thing that will sell my books'. My *Kompanie* fought in that area and I can affirm that this episode simply did not happen.

Just after the capture of Taganrog, I had occasion to visit the hospital in question, to take a message to a wounded *Untersturmführer*. We had suffered many casualties and I can confirm that we took the hospital for our own use. Also, like many other men in the *Leibstandarte*, I contracted an intestinal infection – picked up because much of the food we ate had not been cooked – and spent a few days before our attack on Rostov in the same hospital. There were no bodies, no blood-spattered walls or floors. Believe me, when a person is shot by a military weapon within the confines of a room, it makes a mess. It is of course possible that the Russians evacuated the hospital; after all, they managed to evacuate whole factories shortly before our arrival in Taganrog.

If the reader considers the foregoing, coming from a *Waffen SS* veteran, implausible I would ask him to ponder just two examples of the Russians playing fast and loose with the truth. Firstly, in the forest near Katyn, the Russians murdered more than 20,000 Polish officers and intellectuals before retreating. When they finally retook the town, they immediately tore down a memorial to the Poles, erected during the German occupation, and began to plant 'evidence' incriminating the Germans. On 24 August 1943 Churchill, already fully aware of the truth of the matter, assured the Soviets: 'We (the British) shall certainly oppose vigorously any "investigation" by the International Red Cross or any other body in any territory under German authority' (quoted on p.20 of Steve Crawford's *The Eastern Front Day by Day, 1941–45: A Photographic Chronology*, Potomac Books, Dulles VA, 2006). Secondly, nowhere- except as far as I can ascertain in Solzhenitsyn's *Gulag Archipeligo* – is it mentioned that in Taganrog, German troops came across a train of burnt out freight wagons which had been systematically drenched in oil and set alight. Inside these wagons were hundreds of charred bodies in various hideous poses – prisoners of the Gulag system that the Bolsheviks had burned alive. And what was the purpose of this unspoken atrocity? Was it an act of mercy to prevent the prisoners falling into German hands? Or was it to silence the many mouths that would joyfully expose to the world the truth about the cruelties of Comrade Josef Stalin, staunch ally of the Americans and British? War is a dirty business and the Allies didn't always wear the clean white vest that 'history' would have us believe.

Chapter 9

Our retreat from Rostov had been contrary to Hitler's orders and the commander of Army Group South, the venerable Gerd von Rundstedt, was relieved of his command for his decision to withdraw from the city. It was his good judgement that saved us from annihilation. Clearly, at least some of the German High Command did not always blindly follow orders issued by Berlin.

Chapter 10

It might seem unlikely to the reader that a *Waffen SS* unit provided shelter for those civilians unable to find accommodation with friends or relatives in the hinterland but this is what I saw with my own eyes. In such harsh weather it was easy to empathise with the local inhabitants and, despite the many tales about the dishonourable behaviour of the *Leibstandarte*, I have to say that for the most part the local people in the Ukraine responded well to our presence among them. There was no talk of '*Untermenschen*' amongst the troops in our *Kompanie*. On the contrary, we had come to respect the stoic bravery of the Ukrainian civilians, and the tenacity of the Russian soldiers. At that stage of the war, the majority of the civilians in the areas we occupied still seemed genuinely pleased to be free from the oppression of Stalin's communist regime.

Chapter 13

Heuss' father had evidently used his contacts to get his son into the *Leibstandarte*. After all, being a member of such an elite unit – Hitler's own Division of the *Waffen SS* – was bound to enhance one's credentials in a victorious Germany. I wonder to this day if it was merely coincidence that first President of the *Bundesrepublik Deutschland* in 1949 was also called Professor Heuss.

During a trip to Germany in 1993, I visited the Freys but by that time Lotte was already quite ill, but I shall always remember her as a spirited young woman with a zest for life. In 2003, Albert Frey shot Lotte, who was by then very ill, then turned the gun on himself.

Chapter 19

The Russians always ignored the large red crosses on the flags at the front and rear of our ambulances. They had not signed the Third Geneva Convention and showed no sympathy for wounded Germans.

Chapter 20

I discovered some time after the end of the war that Saint Stephen's Cathedral, a monument to human creativity, had come perilously close to destruction on the orders of my own regimental commander, Sepp Dietrich. From a distance of around 10 kilometres, he had seen a white flag flying from one of the towers – placed there by anti-Nazi resistance members to welcome the incoming Russians – and ordered the *Wehrmacht Hauptmann* in charge of an 88mm *Flak* battery to reduce the cathedral to rubble. *Hauptmann* Klinklich refused to carry out the order, so saving the cathedral from a pounding by artillery shells. But, in the end, fate had its way and only a few weeks later, sparks from nearby burning houses set the roof of the cathedral on fire causing its total collapse. Fortunately, the most of the stonework was spared and the cathedral was rebuilt after the war. Gerhard Klinklich went on to raise funds to help pay for the restoration and maintenance of the cathedral.

Chapter 24

After the war, I became friends with Rochus Misch, a fellow *Leibstandarte* veteran and communications officer in the *Führerbunker* until the final days of the *Reich*. The topic of the special bombs came up in conversation. 'Three bombs,' he said, 'where did you hear that? There were nine.'

There has been much speculation about the possession of atomic weapons by Germany. Whether the bombs that my brother mentioned were conventional or atomic remains a matter of conjecture.

Chapter 25

There were, as far as I know, no substantial units of *Waffen SS* or *Wehrmacht* in Dresden at the time of the bombing. On the contrary, the city was crammed with refugees from East Prussia. There is no doubt in my mind that the bombing was designed to inflict terror on the German civilian population and demonstrate the might of the Allies' air superiority to the encroaching Russians.

Chapter 28

The puzzle of Junghans remains with me to this day. What was the secret of his two identities? When I first started to take an interest in the historical aspects of the Second World War, I discovered that Junghans' wife was still alive. I tried to get in contact with her but I got the impression that efforts were being made to prevent me from getting her address. In 2005, I was informed that Junghans' wife knew about the two names, Junghans and Hengstmann.

Related titles published by Helion & Company

Adventures in my Youth. A German Soldier on the Eastern Front 1941-45
Armin Scheiderbauer
ISBN 978-1-906033-77-4 (paperback)
ISBN 978-1-907677-49-6 (eBook)

Twilight of the Gods. A Swedish Waffen-SS Volunteer's Experiences with 11th SS-Panzergrenadier Division 'Nordland', Eastern Front, 1944-45
Thorolf Hillblad (ed.)
ISBN 978-1-874622-16-1 (hardback)
ISBN 978-1-907677-41-0 (eBook)

Panzer Gunner. From My Native Canada to the German Ostfront and back. In action with 25th Panzer Regiment, 7th Panzer Division 1944-45
Bruno Friesen
ISBN 978-1-906033-11-8 (hardback)
ISBN 978-1-907677-07-6 (eBook)

The Rzhev Slaughterhouse. The Red Army's Forgotten 15-month Campaign against Army Group Center, 1942-1943
Svetlana Gerasimova
Translated and edited by Stuart Britton
ISBN 978-1-908916-51-8 (hardback)

The Viaz'ma Catastrophe. The Red Army's Disastrous Stand Against Operation Typhoon
Lev Lopukhovsky
Translated and edited by Stuart Britton
ISBN 978-1-908916-50-1 (hardback)

Demolishing the Myth. The Tank Battle at Prokhorovka, Kursk, July 1943. An Operational Narrative
Valeriy Zamulin
Translated and edited by Stuart Britton
ISBN 978-1-906033-89-7 (hardback)

HELION & COMPANY
26 Willow Road, Solihull, West Midlands B91 1UE, England
Telephone 0121 705 3393   Fax 0121 711 4075
Website: http://www.helion.co.uk